SOLITUDES OF THE WORKPLACE

solitudes *of the* workplace

Women in Universities

Edited by
Elvi Whittaker

McGill-Queen's University Press
Montreal & Kingston · London · Chicago

© McGill-Queen's University Press 2015

ISBN 978-0-7735-4632-5 (cloth)
ISBN 978-0-7735-4633-2 (paper)
ISBN 978-0-7735-9808-9 (ePDF)
ISBN 978-0-7735-9809-6 (ePUB)

Legal deposit fourth quarter 2015
Bibliothèque nationale du Québec

Printed in Canada on acid-free paper that is 100% ancient forest free
(100% post-consumer recycled), processed chlorine free

This book has been published with the help of a grant from the Canadian
Federation for the Humanities and Social Sciences, through the Awards to
Scholarly Publications Program, using funds provided by the Social
Sciences and Humanities Research Council of Canada.

McGill-Queen's University Press acknowledges the support of the Canada
Council for the Arts for our publishing program. We also acknowledge the
financial support of the Government of Canada through the Canada Book
Fund for our publishing activities.

Library and Archives Canada Cataloguing in Publication

Solitudes of the workplace: women in universities/edited by Elvi Whittaker.

Includes bibliographical references and index.
Issued in print and electronic formats.
ISBN 978-0-7735-4632-5 (bound). – ISBN 978-0-7735-4633-2 (paperback). –
ISBN 978-0-7735-9808-9 (ePDF). – ISBN 978-0-7735-9809-6 (ePUB)

1. Women in higher education – Canada. 2. Feminism and higher education –
Canada. 3. Sex discrimination in higher education – Canada. 4. Universities
and colleges – Canada – Sociological aspects. 5. Women's studies – Canada.
I. Whittaker, Elvi W., editor

LB2332.34.C3S65 2015   378.00820971   C2015-905523-7
                                                     C2015-905524-5

This book was typeset by Interscript in 10.5/13 Sabon.

Contents

Preface and Acknowledgments

Books have origins and careers. Yet, despite many urgings, investigations of our own productions are rarely pursued, leaving a large gap in the knowledge industry. This Preface attempts a modest contribution to such missing connections. It recognizes the complexity and chaotic nature of an enterprise where pre-texts become crucial parts of any production of knowledge and offer not only clues to the origins of the work but also where it seeks to situate itself.

Over several years, I taught an early morning class, the preparation for which brought me to campus in the dark hours and allowed daily conversations with those still cleaning the offices of my building. I viewed their work as solitary, seemingly with no interaction with anyone but myself. Yet they extolled the virtues of the independence they enjoyed. These fortuitous encounters brought into sharp focus the recognition that the busy workplace that I shared with my colleagues was as foreign to the cleaners as the interpersonal and interconnected nature of our academic work that took over their domain barely an hour later. The solitude of their working experiences was a striking feature of their accounts and added to my as yet unrecognized accumulation of experiences, or data, on the university as workplace. After many decades, first as a student and then as a faculty member, I had essentially, and unintentionally, been doing fieldwork, participant observation, in what was to become "the field." I also realized that my accumulated knowledge was distorted by myth and prejudice, mostly from "the community of scholars" discourse, from the student and faculty bias, and from the need to steer my own way through the vagaries of the institution. I became aware of the unspoken interpretations and intentions always present, usually referred to as "hidden agendas," and their effect on identity claims and shifts. These in turn played a part in creating cultural enclaves. "Something ought to be done about it" proclamations continually caught my attention. It was, however, many years before I took a serious academic interest in these matters.

An offhand encounter with one of the authors in this collection, who in describing her workplace circumstances as one of "solitude," conjured up the two Canadian solitudes. Thus the metaphor framing the volume came into being. This choice seemed to honour an earlier metaphor, "the chilly climate," which has been a powerful part of the gendered discourse about institutions. While the acknowledgments of such background features can only ever be partial, the social situatedness of knowledge is more than a theoretical fad. Therefore, the intent here is to recognize the existence of the hidden texts that position the work.

Solitudes in universities seemed to extend beyond the familiar workplace experiences. They exist in the introduction of new paradigms and theories, in the loneliness of tenure candidacy, and in the not-so-subtle exclusionary rites afflicting low-status workers. Solitudes include disruptions in the workplace, sometimes routine, sometimes unexpected – uncertainty about work continuance, needs to establish and reinforce identities, problems created by age, gender, race, class, or disability, as well as by the powerful discourses of silence, disrespect, and stigma. Other solitudes are less accessible and outside the domains of responsibility recognized by universities. What of individuals with severe illnesses or with acute family problems? Institutions seem unable to deal with personal tragedies, "*tristesse et mélancolie*," as Paule Desy writes in her unpublished manuscript, *Sur les marches de l'Université, je me suis assise, et je n'ai pas pleuré*, with its nod to Elizabeth Smart's novel.

The authors in this collection approach their topics through qualitative methods – auto-ethnographic narratives, interviews with selected workers, focus group conversations, ethnographic descriptions resulting from fieldwork, and the analysis of documents and policies. Some combine several of these approaches. Occasional support from quantitative data enriches the arguments. The authors come from a range of disciplines, including education, engineering, history, psychology, nursing, sociology, administration, women's studies, and anthropology.

Every collection of essays expects questions about representativeness. In Canada this is often deemed to be a geographical accounting, with its political inferences. While this collection did not focus on this specifically, some geographical diversity was attained. Authors in the collection are either located in, or write about small, liberal arts, medium-sized, and large universities. They range through most niches of university life: students, support staff, contract workers, professors, and a university president. Some familiar work categories are missing from the collection – librarians, museum staff, editors of university presses, campus police, food service workers, and custodial staff among them. Questions of representation, however, were secondary considerations to the task of discovering ongoing research on workplace experiences – the central theme of the collection.

Earlier writings about Canadian women in the academy have set the stage for this volume. As befitted the time of their publication and the position of women at that time, one set of works considers the status of feminist thought and feminist advocacy at universities. Among these are the edited volumes by Himani Bannerji et al., *Unsettling Relations: The University as a Site of Feminist Struggles* (1991), Susan Brown et al., *Not Drowning But Waving: Women, Feminism and the Liberal Arts* (2011), Jessica Yee's *Feminism for Real: Deconstructing the Academic Industrial Complex of Feminism* (2011), and Meg Luxton and Mary Jane Mossman's *Reconsidering Knowledge: Feminism and the Academy* (2012). Other works provide accounts of the "chilly climate," such as the volumes edited by the Chilly Collective, *Breaking Anonymity: The Chilly Climate for Women Faculty* (1995), Jacqueline Stalker and Susan Prentice, *Illusion of Inclusion: Women in Post-Secondary Education* (1998), Elena Hannah, Linda Joan Paul, and Swani Vethamany-Globus, *Women in the Canadian Academic Tundra: Challenging the Chill* (2002), and Deborah Keahey and Deborah Schnitzer, who, through poetry, short stories, and other genres, take on the struggles of academic women in *Madwoman in the Academy: 43 Women Boldly Take on the Ivory Tower* (2003). Marilee Reimer's edited volume, *Inside Corporate U: Women in the Academy Speak Out* (2004), presents feminist writings on corporatization. Finally, the collection edited by Anne Wagner, Sandra Acker, and Kimine Mayuzumi, *Whose University Is It, Anyway?: Power and Privilege on Gendered Terrain* (2008), stakes out a different terrain – race, class, gender, disability, and violence – using gender as an organizational theme. These titles are a small sampling of a large body of work that has emerged since second-wave feminism.

With few exceptions, the history of universities has been written from the perspective of the culture of academic men. Women's writings provide a counter-history and counter-ethnography. Once considered irrelevant, writing by women is now recognized as important, authoritative knowledge production. The differences between the traditional versions written by those once privileged to have a stake in universities – namely, men of status – are note merely minor matters of opinion. Rather, they are direct reflections of the authors' positions and experiences within the institution, and thus reveal significant gaps in interpretation and perception of university histories, affairs, and policies. In short, the titles listed above provide new and alternate ethnographic views of universities.

The emphasis in many of these volumes, with some notable exceptions in individual chapters, is on faculty and students. In this collection, however, we adjust the focus to a wider range of work in universities and to the varying repertoires of knowledge in these complex workplaces. These knowledges created by women could be formal ones – such as the texts of women's studies and feminist analysis – or more informal, everyday knowledges, those shaped in discrete campus enclaves. Each contribution arises from the idea of "solitude," whether structured by the workplace, or by enduring biases about gender or age. Women in work categories such as administrative assistants, non-academic administrators, support staff, contract teachers, and contract researchers are included. A chapter about students is also included, despite the prevailing tendency to separate their activities as "study," not as "work." The term *work* is rich with inferences, and perhaps, most simplistically, refers to an income-producing activity. As students describe their own activities as "work," this volume does likewise.

An early attempt to address workplace issues came in 2010 when I organized sessions on women and universities to honour the twenty-fifth anniversary of the Women's Network of the Canadian Anthropology Society/Société canadienne d'anthropologie. For helping to make these sessions possible I am grateful to former presidents of the association – Paule Desy, Janice Graham, Ellen Judd, and Deirdre Meintel who chaired the sessions; to the plenary speakers – Regna Darnell, Harriet Lyons, and Lynne Phillips; and finally to those who delivered papers – Joan Anderson, Myrdene Anderson, Pauline Aucoin, Judith Brown, Jean Chapman, Peg Cruickshank, Salinda Hess, Ellen Judd, Patricia Kaufert, Lelia Kennedy, Winnie

Lem, and Jill Tories. Several of these papers later became the bases for chapters in this volume.

There are many debts to acknowledge. Finding people in Canada working on specific issues could not be accomplished without help from colleagues in many fields. Many suggestions and referrals were offered and I am thankful to Pauline Aucoin, Jeanette Auger, Judith Brown, Gillian Creese, Janice Graham, Kersti Krug, Carlos Kruytbosch, Susanne Luhmann, Siobhan Nelson, Sharon Roseman, Katherine Side, Sally Thorne, Julita Vassileva, Jo-Ann Wallace, and Jean Wilson. Other acknowledgments are due to Monique Layton, Joanne Richardson, and Neil Eaton who were indispensible in offering editing advice. One of the authors, Kersti Krug, lent her copyediting skills as each of the essays was distributed among the contributors for comment and suggestions. Sally Thorne provided challenging conversations about analytic and philosophical issues, and dropped words here and there that have found their way into these pages. A dialogue with Adele Clarke on anticipation and hopefulness deserves special mention for helping clarify some of my thoughts. The reviewers chosen by the press gave valuable advice about the organization of the writings, offered relevant references, shared important thoughts on the analysis, and pointed to the ways in which the manuscript could be improved. Kyla Madden has been an exceptional editor, dealing with troubled waters, dispensing reassurance and advice when needed, and always being only a few email hours away. Of importance to all of us has been the work of gifted wordsmith Joanne Muzak, for her careful copyediting. We also acknowledge the help of Ryan van Huijstee for steering us through the final stages. I owe more to those whose writings make up this book than I know how to acknowledge, not only for making this volume possible, but for what I have learned about the workings of universities. Special words of appreciation go to my family near and far for their patience with my distracted presence and general absentmindedness. My sons are to be thanked for affably doctoring to all of my computer woes. I dedicate my work on the volume to my granddaughter, Zoë Alexandra Whittaker and her future workplaces. We dedicate the whole volume to social justice, equity, future workplaces and, ultimately, to hope.

Subtexts and agendas crowd the writings and the topics chosen. A couple of participants have observed, always with ironic whimsy, that the volume could be seen as the product of a bunch of activists, or, as one suggested, tongue-in-cheek, of feminist ancient mariners. All acknowledge that writing is an important form of activism, so they write texts of resistance about what worries them, hopeful that somehow the future might promise a phoenix rising from universities.

The volume opens with a prologue of a conversation with Martha Piper, former president of the University of British Columbia. There are a few ways of being successful in the academy, and reaching the highest echelons of administration is one of them. Yet, as the first woman to hold that position at her university, Piper's story reveals a new perspective on women's positions in the workplace and intersects with the chapters that follow.

The introductions to Parts One and Two are my social science narratives, constructed to offer an interpretation of the narratives that make up the volume. These are narratives about the authors' narratives, which themselves are about the narratives of others. All texts of infinite regress. Together, the chapters are a rounded testimonial to what Paul Ricoeur has called "life in quest of narrative."

A View from the Pinnacle:
Conversations with Martha Piper

SALLY E. THORNE

Martha C. Piper, OC, OBC, served as the eleventh president and vice-chancellor of the University of British Columbia (UBC) for nine years, between 1997 and 2006. The first woman, and the first American-born person, to hold that position, she obtained a BSc in physical therapy from the University of Michigan in 1967, an MA in child development from the University of Connecticut in 1970, and a PHD in epidemiology and biostatistics from McGill University in 1979. She thereupon launched an academic career as director of McGill's School of Physical and Occupational Therapy before moving to the University of Alberta in 1985 to take up senior leadership positions, first as dean of the Faculty of Rehabilitation Medicine, and subsequently as vice-president for research in 1993, combined with vice-president for external affairs in 1995.

Although Martha Piper was not the first woman president of a major Canadian university, she was unquestionably the most prominent and influential of her era both inside and outside the university. Over a remarkable senior academic leadership career, Piper received numerous honorary degrees, and in 2002 was made an officer in the Order of Canada. In 2005, she was appointed a public governor of the board for the Canadian Academies of Science. That same year, the *Globe and Mail* recognized her as one of five Canadian "nation builders." She attracted considerable acclaim as a leading force influencing both the Chrétien and Martin governments toward a suite of key policies on behalf of Canadian universities, including unprecedented investments across the Tri-Council funding bodies as well as such game-changing innovations as Canada Research Chairs, Canada

Millennium Scholarships, the Canada Foundation for Innovation, and Genome Canada. As Heather Munroe-Blum, former university principal and vice-chancellor of McGill, once wrote, "there has never been a university president from west of Ontario who had a more dominant influence in Ottawa" (Littlemore 2006).

...

Five years into her retirement from the UBC presidency, Martha Piper reflects on that career, considering the opportunities and challenges that shaped it, and on the intersectional and experiential dimensions that characterized the life of a high-profile female university president within the top echelons of academic influence for an extraordinary decade in the evolution of Canadian universities. Still fully engaged these days in the world of policy and decision making through her roles on various private and public sector corporate boards and advisory committees, she agreed to slow down long enough to contemplate the role of women in universities at this time in our collective history. Intrigued by the challenge of thoughtful commentary on how being a woman may have shaped her own academic leadership career, Piper graciously shared a wide range of observations and reflections on how gender relations, gendered leadership styles, and gender politics had played out for her and for other female academic leaders around her. Theorizing on the complex dialectic between that which is clearly changing, and that which seems to remain the same, her reflections offer a rare glimpse into the evolving world of women in academia when viewed from the very top.

BECOMING

How does such a career begin? What inspires and shapes the myriad of decisions and actions that set an aspiring young academic on the kind of career trajectory that might eventually lead to high office? Martha explains, "I didn't grow up knowing I wanted to be a university president. And quite frankly, right up until the time I decided to put my hat in the ring, it was not an ambition of mine. And I think that's fairly common, for women particularly, and perhaps even for men." Martha believes that a burning ambition for that kind of role would be a mixed blessing. "You are damned if you do and damned if you don't. If you don't have a real passion for the role, that's a problem. But on the other hand if you seek it too actively, sometimes it's seen as inappropriate." In her case, "I didn't have that kind of aspiration, it just kind of unfolded. The opportunities present themselves. The hard part isn't seeking or crafting the opportunity, the hard part is responding to it, and knowing what the right response is."

Martha explains that there are always individuals whose timely and wise advice helps turn the corner of decision making in those transitional opportunities within a career. In terms of her decision to seek the presidency of one of Canada's leading universities, "the person who was critical – aside from my husband and family – was [former federal cabinet minister] Don Mazankowski. I was at the University of Alberta, vice-president of Research, and really enjoying my position. And I was thinking that when this ends I'm going to go back into the ranks and be a researcher and scholar. It wasn't the first call I had had for a presidency, and I never took them too seriously. But when UBC called, I remember it clearly. Don and I were out in the parking lot after a board of governors' meeting, and it was freezing cold in Edmonton, and he was trying to help me get my car scraped. I didn't know who to confide in at that time, so I just said to him, 'Don, I'm in this dilemma and not sure what to do.' His advice was pivotal. He reminded me that 'Lots of things come your way if you are on a trajectory, and most of the time you know it is not the right time, not the right position, not quite what I want to do right now. But if you are extremely lucky, maybe once, and maybe even twice, but rarely in your life, an opportunity does come along that you really have to pay attention to. If you want to be president – not just of any university but of the University of British Columbia – then this is it. This opportunity won't come around again.' And it was like 'bang.' Had I not had that conversation with him, I'm not sure I would have agreed to stand as a candidate."

Martha's early career had also been strongly encouraged by other mentors who helped her seriously consider possibilities that she might otherwise have let slip. "Right after I finished my PHD, I was approached to consider the position of director of the School of Physical and Occupational Therapy at McGill. Now I had never held an academic position at that point. All I wanted to do was do research. I had a freshly minted PHD in epidemiology and I was ready to go. And my PHD supervisor, Barry Pless, took me aside and said, 'If you want to really have an impact on how physical therapy is practised, and how research becomes embedded in it and it becomes a knowledge-based profession, you as a researcher will have some impact, but if you could lead a school and change it that way, it's going to have a huge impact.'" As she reflects on these decision points, Martha concludes, "Every single one of my opportunities I was ambivalent about. But individuals who I trusted and respected really did affect my decisions. And I think they were all men."

Although she felt at the time that "the question of gender never came into it," Martha also recalls wanting "to be absolutely certain that I'm not being considered just because I'm a woman." She recalls that at the time of her appointment there had been considerable public pressure on major universities to expand beyond the traditionally male model of president. Within that context, and in an era of increasing sensitivity to a broader range of employment equity issues, the public posting for the position had included an explicit line encouraging applications from women and members of non-dominant groups. While such language has now become familiar in job postings across the university system, its novelty within that context attracted debate within the university community, with some critics suggesting that the equity statement was inappropriate as it might actually disadvantage white male candidates. The controversy within the university drew national attention, which increased the expectation that a woman would be selected. As a result, following Martha's appointment, a journalist for a major national newspaper expressed surprise in a highly sarcastic opinion piece that a woman had emerged as the successful candidate. However, for the most part, overt attention to the gendered aspect of her appointment soon shifted. "At first there was enormous emphasis on the fact that I was a woman, and I always downplayed that. Initially it was a big deal to other people. It wasn't to me and I never really thought that that was the case. I never thought that I had been selected *because* I was a woman."

As she reflects on that initial period, however, she does acknowledge "that's the only time I felt a little compromised with regard to gender." She remembers in particular a conversation with a woman who held a senior academic administrative position at another major Canadian university. "This woman picked up the phone and called me, and it was kind of like a backhanded complement. 'It is great that they picked a woman,' and then she said, 'But don't mess up. A lot is riding on you, because all the women will be watching.' And I was just flabbergasted, and I just thought, 'Well, we tend to eat our own. What I intend to be judged on is my performance as president, not my gender.'"

HOLDING A POSITION OF INFLUENCE

Although by virtue of having been a university vice-president she had felt somewhat familiar with the "perspective you have when you become part of that top inner circle" as well as the "daily grind" of a presidential role within a university, she also acknowledges, "You never know it until you are really in it." She describes a perspectival shift that necessarily occurs when "you no longer think of the university solely through the lens of your academic unit. You are exposed to all the legalities, the fiduciary issues, the labour issues, the government issues, the student, alumni and donor issues." Martha recalls, "I had a fairly good idea of the complexity of the issues I was going to face. What I didn't really understand was all the wonderful things that come with that."

Martha views the position of president of one of the world's leading universities as one of unparalleled opportunity. "It's the most privileged position, I think, almost in society. You have access to the most brilliant minds, the most influential people, the most interesting ideas, and probably the most challenging issues of the day." She recalls "the experience, the learning, the friendships, the associations, the people I got to know. And those things never leave you." She feels that she gained from the role more than she gave. "And I don't think I had any idea of that privilege when I took on the job."

BEARING A SINGULAR RESPONSIBILITY

An intrinsic complement to that rare privilege is the extraordinary level of responsibility that the role entails. Martha reflects, "With that privilege comes an enormous responsibility. It is huge and it weighs on you all the time. There's no escaping it."

Although all levels of academic leadership within a university involve high responsibility, the role of the president is somewhat unique among them in terms of the nature and scope of the pressures. As Martha explains, "You have many constituencies that are almost always in conflict. And you are a convener of ideas and trying to find resolutions to very difficult problems that have been around for centuries." She believes that "the scope of universities has changed dramatically in the last decade or two, to where it is not only a collegium of academics and ideas, and scholars and students, but it is also a big business. You wear these two hats that are often in conflict. You worry about the sustainability of the institution, the integrity of the institution, while at the same time honouring its underlying principles and its academic mission. And that's what keeps you awake at night."

In attempting to describe the experiential scope of assuming a role at this level of responsibility, Martha compares it embarking on new parenthood. "You can be well prepared for the physical side, have a checklist with the babysitter lined up, the diaper bag checked off, all of that. But you have no idea of the emotional vulnerability that comes with parenting until you get into it. And I think that's a good metaphor for it. I had no idea of the incredible emotional piece of it. The fact that you are part of something much bigger than you ever imagined."

When asked about whether it was lonely at the top, Martha replied, "I was too busy to be lonely!" Reflecting on the question, she explained further, "Lonely isn't the right word, but you were *it*. With all the advisors and all the people around you, and all the support that you garner, no one can do the job but you. And that puts enormous demand on you. You can consult all you like but at some point you have to make the decision and you have to bear the responsibility of that decision. You are the persona of the institution. You don't spread the responsibility. When the people are upset about whatever, it is you they are upset with."

Even with the best team and the best family providing ongoing support, "there are many times when you cannot depend upon others or discuss with other people what you are struggling with." In this regard she emphasizes the fundamental importance of the role of chancellor. She sees the chancellor's position in Canadian and British universities as being the wise and non-judgmental person who is accessible to the president on complex matters. The two chancellors she served with were leading industrialist Bill Sauder and former chief justice Allan McEachern. "I could always go to them. Both would give absolutely the best advice, and without any expectation that I would take it." She describes both chancellors as being "so incredibly generous with me" and concludes, "You couldn't pay for that wisdom." From her perspective, the appointment of exceptional individuals who can fulfill the role of chancellor as intended in the governance structure of a university is a critically important decision. "And by golly we got the right people!"

INTERPRETING THE NUANCES OF GENDER

Invited to share her perspectives for the purposes of this scholarly collection, Martha took the opportunity to reflect on the ways in which gender had shaped her experience as president and to consider the extent to which her gender may have privileged or disadvantaged her capacity to fulfill that role. As she recalls, the element of her being a woman in the role was an unavoidably and excessively prominent feature of her early presidential days. "The first six months there was enormous attention on that, and then it just went away." She feels that focusing her own attention on the gendered element would have been a serious strategic error. "If you perform, it becomes totally insignificant." Nevertheless, Martha also acknowledges gender as an intriguing subtext throughout her term. "I do believe it was an advantage in some ways because I think people are fascinated by a woman doing this job, and they want to know everything about you. That can be a problem and also an asset." She notes, for example, that "when you go in a room and you are the only woman, you will be remembered. Some people think that's a terrible thing, but I always think that's somewhat of an advantage. That when you spoke, people will remember what you say. So you can have an impact."

Martha recalls wondering, even during her selection process, whether gender might pose barriers to some elements of the role. UBC has strong linkages across Asia, and she knew that there had been very few women university presidents in Asia at that time. As she noted, "You do feel that there's a culture that goes around this, whether it be drinking or playing golf, or any of these things, and you ask yourself, 'How is this going to work?'" She recalls with great delight one particularly memorable encounter in Taiwan with a person of considerable influence who later admitted being quite taken aback when her physical appearance failed to meet his expectations. He told her, "With the name 'Martha' I was expecting someone more like Madeleine Albright!" However, as she engaged with the role over time, she became fully confident that any potential disadvantage could be effectively managed. "Maybe I was blind to it, but I never felt that UBC was compromised, or that my voice was not heard, or that I didn't garner the respect that I needed to have from my colleagues around the world." As she concluded, "I honestly don't think it's gender; I think it's performance."

Interestingly, as Martha reflects on the positionality of person within a presidency, she surfaces multiple layers of intersecting perceptual bias. "I think more difficult for me than gender, and maybe there was a convergence of these two things, was my discipline. People just cannot believe that a physical therapist is running a university!" She reminds us, "If you sit around the table of the top fifty universities in the world, the large majority are male, and they are either in the hard sciences – physicists or chemists or molecular biologists – or they are lawyers. Occasionally they are physicians, but not very many. But they are all in the legitimate, respected disciplines of science or letters." She remembers with amusement, "You could see people around the table. They were like, 'What? And she's a woman too?'" And she wonders if perhaps, in her case, debate around the impact of her discipline might have distracted the selection committee from being overly concerned about the impact of gender.

Martha most certainly recognizes that being a woman positioned her quite differently in the public eye, shaping her experience in ways that were different from that of male university presidents. She recalled, "The things people will say to you that I don't think they would say to a male colleague are quite remarkable. Everything from commenting on your hair or your nails or what you're wearing or how tired you look or what are your children doing, and 'Don't you miss being at home?'" She describes this aspect as a constant throughout her presidency. "You just kind of get immune to that. And that to me is just kind of background noise."

In Martha's experience, the role of family in a position such as president does play out quite differently between men and women. "It's probably less now, but being married and having a family and having a husband who was engaged in his own career, people couldn't figure it out. It's not like a full time spouse to be part and parcel of the role." She recalls explaining to the selection committee, "I can't guarantee that my husband will be at every event and working the crowd. He hasn't signed on for that. So if you want the traditional couple, then you've not got the right person." Martha does believe that stage of family life may be a more critical influence on the career decisions of women than men. In her case, at the time she considered putting her hat in the ring for the position, her children were already launched. "I have often said I'm pretty sure I couldn't have done it with my kids being younger." And for a married woman, a supportive husband would be essential. "My husband of course was extremely supportive. He's always said, 'The decision is yours. I will support you in the decision, and we'll make it work.' I personally could not have done it without that."

During her term in office, the matter of family was clearly an important point of discussion among university presidents in general. Martha recalls, "At that time, there was considerable discussion about a president of a major Canadian university whose wife got a salary from the university to be the hostess. A lot of debate around that. And I can remember going to a G10 meeting* where all the colleagues were men. And I can remember during the cocktail hour before dinner one night it was the talk of the town. All of these nine men saying, 'Good on you! Being wife of the president is an important role. Let's get our wives on the payroll.' They were all talking about how much time all their wives put in. And I had to hold my tongue, which I don't do well. But eventually I said, 'Excuse me. We have, and I'm sure all of you have, a full-time events coordinator who is a professional who looks after all this, who we can hire and fire if they don't perform well. What is this all about?' In reality, it is more common in the United States, and I think it was a way of increasing the president's salary. If that is the case, then it disadvantages women. Can you imagine, if the public feels entitled to information about you, what they'd do with a husband getting a salary for being a hostess? But at the time I was amazed at how many of my male colleagues were fascinated by it."

Martha feels strongly that the heightened scrutiny in the public domain extended to a woman president over her male counterpart plays a significant part in the experience of the role. "It is just a different way of seeing women, and what's okay, and what's not. We've seen men for centuries in those roles, so obviously we have to expect a different level of interest and intrigue, but it is different. Anyone

* Formed in the early 1990s, the G10 was an organization in which executive heads of Canada's ten most research-intensive universities would gather twice a year to collaborate in areas of common purpose, advocacy, and data exchange.

who says it is not, is being unrealistic." She particularly recalls the heightened attention to her around graduation season. "It was almost like clockwork, during graduation in the spring, our office would get a variety of calls asking things like, 'Where does she get her hair done?' Can you imagine? Now I can't imagine anyone calling and asking where Professor Toope [UBC president, 2006–14] does his. But did it bother me? Did it affect the way I handled things? Did it change the way that I viewed the position? If it did, I'm not aware of it. It was not an irritant. It was not something that I spent any time thinking about. Honestly, I was just so overwhelmed by the job and the things that had to be done that it was nothing to me."

EXPLORING THE CAPACITY TO SHAPE DIRECTION

Despite her determination not to make it the main story, gender was not irrelevant to how Martha used the role to effect a meaningful impact on both her own university and the role of universities within Canadian society. From the outset of her presidency, she sent out strong and clear signals that she intended to enact the role with a difference. In planning for the installation event during which she would formally assume office, Martha recalls a conversation with the university official in charge of ceremonial planning. "When I said, 'I'm thinking about baseball caps. I'm doing this thing around thinking, and I think it would be kind of fun to have thinking caps everybody put on as they left the auditorium with the slogan *Think About It* on the front and *UBC* on the back,' I thought he was going to choke!" She recalls that risky decision as one that "received great reviews from the external community and was damned by the internal community. I think there were a number of people in the community who felt that I was compromising the university by watering it down and commercializing or marketing it, or cheerleading for it. There were detractors, there's no question. But it was remembered."

In a similar vein, Martha took seriously the capacity for impact occasioned by the graduation addresses she delivered at multiple ceremonies each year. "I'm a great believer in storytelling. And especially when you only have five or six minutes, stories are incredible vehicles to get big generic messages across. People remember stories." At the time, the common wisdom was a more generic presidential speech. As one of her staff explained it, "These are just protocol." But Martha recalls, "Part of my strategy at the time was to get people to feel something about the moment of this graduation and the responsibility that comes with being an educated citizen" and so she spent a great deal of time thinking about and writing those speeches. "I never let anybody write those. Those were mine. I thought to myself, 'When do I have an active audience of thirty thousand people?' And I do know that they were controversial. There were detractors who felt they were not academic enough. That's the cross I bore. There's no question that I was not seen by some as not scholarly enough. I used to reflect on that and think, 'Who am I speaking to? The graduates and especially the families, but not the academics.'" She recalls her persistence with her own style of graduation speech as something of a risk. But she knows they were memorable. "People still come up to me, like in airports all over the world, saying, 'I remember those speeches.'"

Controversy aside, Martha maintained throughout her presidency an abiding commitment to capitalize on the privilege of the role to articulate and develop what she termed a "civil society," defining it as "a vigorous citizenry engaged in the culture and politics of a free society." As she explained to the university community at the time of her 2002 Killam Lecture, "If we are to achieve this goal, the building of a civil society, I would like to suggest that we need to build our understanding along three lines of inquiry in the human sciences: first, we must encourage knowledge and scholarship that will enable individuals to better understand themselves, their values, and the roles they play as citizens; second, we must pursue knowledge and scholarship that will assist us to define our Canadian identity and our role as global citizens; and third, we must advance knowledge and scholarship in those areas that bear on legislation, public policy and social programming" (Piper 2002, 8). This commitment underscored a profound recognition that universities exist within society for a purpose much greater than their own success, and this perspective fuelled her enthusiasm for pushing boundaries within the role.

Martha ponders whether being a woman in the role may have allowed her to feel freedom not to conform to traditional expectations. "I don't know what drove it. It wasn't so much strategic, it is just what felt right. Most of what I did, that's just who I am." She genuinely believes that authenticity is a key to success in the role of president. "If you try to be something you aren't, then it creates a lot of problems. One of the strengths I was reinforced for by the community was being real. I don't think I ever reined myself in, to be someone else. I remember someone saying to me, 'You need to be more presidential.' I think that's the last thing that would have worked for me."

Martha explains how being true to her own style rather than conforming to expectations made her effective in her role. "I think what captured people's fascination was that I didn't give up. I spent a lot of time in front of people in central Canada, promoting not UBC, which would have been expected, but promoting universities in general. And that model wasn't typical. A lot of people would go to Ottawa and just promote their university." She remembers that approach attracted a lot of constructive attention. "Now we had a university president who was advocating for universities across the country. And that may have caused people to look at university presidents a little differently."

Martha recognizes that her gender advantaged her capacity for effectiveness at the federal level. "There have been women before obviously, and there were women at the time, but I do think being a woman allowed me to have a recognition." Significantly, she capitalized on that edge by representing a novel message. "My insisting that a university like UBC in the west was being acknowledged in central Canada – by just being there, by being relentless, going after it – was new." Recognizing that the traditional competitive model of university presidents had made them a very fractious group, she said, "Let's make peace. Let's change the culture. Let's go arm and arm to government and talk about funding for universities as a whole. That was a big step, and a big change." Martha also recalls working hard at trying to recognize the uniqueness of small institutions and their role in Canadian society. "I'm a great believer that we all benefit from the strength of the university system overall." At the same time, she concedes that, "Underlying it, of course, I knew that if you increase funding as a whole, UBC will do well. I knew that it was in UBC's interests to get the pie bigger." But she does believe that the unprecedented advances in educational and research funding afforded to Canadian universities during her time were a result of this new approach.

Another novel approach that served Martha well was "being very public about thanking the government." As she recalls, "I took a lot of heat for that from my colleagues. But I do think that was a different way of relating to the government." She remembers wise advice from a senior colleague to always remember that governments represent more than themselves. And if they don't like something it is probably because the public doesn't like it. And that was such an important lesson for me."

Martha does recognize that these effective features of her leadership style in the role of president are informed by her gendered style. "Women lead differently. We are more consensus building. We reinforce outstanding performance. Of course, men do that too, but I think it is more natural for us." In contrast, women's more characteristic approach to leadership may come at some cost. Martha recalls frequently believing, "If I just do it differently and I do it well, it will work." However, she acknowledged, "When it doesn't, you tend to take it personally. What did I do wrong? We always take it on ourselves."

Aware that she consciously tried to ignore the implications of gender throughout her presidency, she also acknowledges that it was not unimportant to her. "We were having this discussion around gender and I was kind of downplaying it. And my friend said, 'Women who have for whatever reason been given the opportunity for recognition, they play a very strong role for women who are coming up.' I had never really thought about it. I'm the last to think that a young woman out there would look at me and say maybe I could do that. But it is for that reason that I'm taking more seriously some of these kinds of issues." Martha reflects on the kinds of role models that are available to her own daughters and granddaughter. "I don't want to use the word *mentor*, but I realize that I didn't have anybody. I've had to look historically to find women, and how much nicer would it have been had there been someone that I could have watched. So I do think we all have that role to play."

TRANSITIONING BEYOND

After five years away from the role, Martha feels that an element of being an effective university president that may not attract the attention it deserves is knowing how and when to leave office. "I think there should be a book written about knowing when to leave. I'm a great believer in renewal and I tend to believe that certain people stay too long. You need to leave when you are too comfortable in the position. When you start thinking you are doing it pretty well, it's time to go." Among the historical figures that influenced her own career path, Eleanor Roosevelt served as an enduring inspiration.

Martha claims that she frequently reflected on Eleanor's oft-quoted encouragement to "do one thing everyday that scares you" (original source unknown). She believes that, "If you don't challenge yourself to take on and learn something different, it is not so interesting." Martha believes that we are all fallible, and there comes a point at which one is no longer fully effective. She also believes that "Those who stay in a role too long actually close the door on the future." In her case, that has meant sustaining relationships with world figures and issues about which she continues to feel a great deal of passion.

Martha's departure from the UBC presidency was very thoroughly thought out. "We worked at trying to find the right time. Lots of things that would not have been fair to leave to a new person." However, she also found that there was an astounding level of curiosity among colleagues and even among the general public as to what might be prompting her leaving. From her perspective, "I had given a lot of thought to what I was and wasn't going to do. I knew that I didn't want people reporting to me. I certainly didn't want to be president of another university, CEO of a major corporation, or run for political office. Any of those avenues were possibilities." Instead, she left the position to spend a year living in Oxford where her husband had taken advantage of an opportunity, and simply took "time off." She found herself surprised and somewhat defensive in response to media insinuations that she was not being truthful as to her future plans. "People must have seen me as more ambitious than I am. 'How could I be happy if I wasn't running things or on top of the heap?'" She recalls, "I found it difficult not to be defensive, because that's not who I am. I'm very happy doing some things I haven't done before – learning and being involved in things that are not university-driven." But to this day, people still ask her, "But what are you really going to do?" She finds that curious. "Is it wrong not to want to be the head of something?"

On reflection, Martha explains that the social prominence that accompanied the presidency was among the more difficult challenges of the role. "People would see us in the supermarket and couldn't believe that I would be cooking. I don't know what they thought. I do have to eat, you know." As she recalls, "That was a part of the position that made me uncomfortable, and I'm happy that I don't have that any more. I didn't like being out somewhere and having people notice what I wear. Some people yearn for that visibility but I really didn't like it. When I look back after five years, the thing that gives me enormous peace is that I don't have that any-more. I can do what I want to do most of the time." She recalls visit-ing with the Queen during the royal jubilee and being in awe of her graciousness within a life that has been led in its entirety in the pub-lic domain. Although she does not yet feel fully invisible in a crowd, the luxury of personal privacy is increasing over time. Her time as UBC's president has given her "a whole different perspective on peo-ple who are in the public eye, and what their lives must be like."

LOOKING TO THE FUTURE FOR WOMEN IN SENIOR ACADEMIC LEADERSHIP POSITIONS

Martha is convinced that it remains important to build toward a future in which an increasing proportion of senior academic leader-ship positions are held by women. "We now have more women pres-idents, but the real test will be whether we have more women second-generation presidents. By that I mean, when there's been a woman, whether the next person is a woman." As time passes, more experiential evidence will be accumulated to determine how those ongoing decisions play out. In this regard, Martha also asserts that it will be especially telling to observe the experience of the current cadre of women university presidents. "They are presidents at a time when it is so difficult to be president. They will be unfairly judged because of the economic climate being so difficult. And I think it is unfair to charge them on the basis of their gender."

Martha is concerned that "there are not as many women stepping up for positions as we would hope or expect, whether it be deans or heads or directors or associate vice presidents." From her perspec-tive, "I still think there's work to be done. There are many, many extraordinarily qualified women, but I think they are choosing not to take on these roles. I think there are more self-imposed barriers that women have than men. They want to do more things, they want to spend more time with their children, and so the timing may be more critical for women than it is for men."

Although Martha's account may have revealed some ambivalence in coming to terms with her contribution as a role model for other women coming up the ranks in the modern academy, it is evident that her mentorship has been effective in supporting the next generation. Indira Samarasekera, who served as vice-president of research under Martha Piper and went on to become the president of the University of Alberta in 2005, described her former mentor as "the best university president that Canada has had in a long time." Acknowledging the tremendous role that Martha's mentorship played in her own career progress, she wrote, "I would not be the president of U of A today without her" (Littlemore 2006). While it is well recognized that Canadian women still face a significant "glass ceiling" in university administration (Birchard 2005; Dehaas 2010) and that the majority of advances among women holding the top administrative positions have been in the community college and undergraduate university sector (June 2007), the path forward is not simply a matter of undoing obvious gender biases but also one of recognizing and supporting gendered career trends. According to Josh Dehaas, who showcased the perspectives of Martha Piper and several other women in leadership positions at Canadian universities for a 2010 special edition of *Maclean's*, the encouragement and support that prospective presidents require is highly dependent upon their career and family stage. Aligning professional opportunities with the stages during which women feel most comfortable accepting them seems a key to strategic and effective mentorship. Martha recalls that being a mother did influence some of her early advancement choices and potentially delayed her entry into increasingly senior levels of service. As universities learn to become more creative in providing family support across the spectrum of life, it is likely that some of the current barriers to women taking on leadership roles will begin to fade.

Of note, Martha's effectiveness has not only been enthusiastically acknowledged by the women who see her as a mentor and role model, but also by members of what one might consider the "old boys' network." David Strangway, a former UBC president, was quoted as saying, "It's difficult for the old guy to say, 'She really took UBC to great places,' but she did" (Littlemore 2006). Robert Birgenau, who later became chancellor of the University of California at Berkeley, recalled, "When I took the position of President at the University of Toronto in 1999, Martha was one of the first people to call and congratulate me. And when I took my first trip to Ottawa, I discovered that she was the single most prominent university president in Canada. She set the standard for how to do federal relations properly" (Littlemore 2006). Tellingly, their endorsements omit any reference to her gender, which would have been universally emphasized in accounts written in the earlier years of her term. Clearly, her influence was as an astoundingly effective university president, and the compulsion to characterize her by gender dissolved.

A visionary well ahead of her time, Martha Piper put university presidents on the map in Canada as a force to be reckoned with. She showed the academic world that women could thrive as presidents of world-class research universities, and that universities could benefit from the kinds of leadership that women academics bring to the role. She forcefully championed the role of universities – communities of people and ideas – within the public domain. She demonstrated that, with tenacity, clarity of commitment, and talent, the barriers that remain for women in senior academic positions can and will be overcome. And as Martha concludes, "I don't have any regrets."

PART ONE

Solitudes and Formal Knowledge

Narratives of Solitude

ELVI WHITTAKER

"A solitude is a stretch of experience disengaged from other people in perception, thought, emotions and action" (Koch 1994, 57). Solitude is often deemed as belonging to the domain of literature and myth, the assumption being that these are the proper genres for exploring the existential qualities of self-reflection and suffering. The familiar protagonists of solitude include figures such as Thoreau, Robert Stroud, Hester Prynne, Florence Nightingale, and Odysseus. They secure a place in our imagination as self-elected advocates of aloneness or as the stigmatized victims of exclusion. Also included among their ranks are prisoners, monks, the afflicted, the excommunicated, strangers in alien places, seekers of religious conversion, those ousted from a location or a status, and those undergoing that quintessential self-exploration called "finding oneself."

The question has been raised whether there are gender differences in solitude, whether freedom and inhibition are allotted in equal measure to male and female solitudes. Cultural depictions of men in solitude, whether sought (Thoreau) or imposed (Stroud), display achievement, initiative, contemplation, adventure, and high spirits. These gifts are reflected, with unmistakable dynamism, in the 1818 romantic painting by Caspar David Friedrich – *Wanderer Looking over the Sea of Fog*. A lone male figure stands at its centre, seemingly at the top of the world, gazing over a vast unknown landscape towards a distant heavenly light. His stance is masterful, unafraid, almost leisurely. The suggestion is that he could easily conquer the massive forces of nature situated before him. It would be hard to envision a woman in the same landscape, with the same calm self-assurance, unless she were of another world, an angel or deity.

Women's solitude is murkier. Women in solitude are often situated away from the light, in enclosed spaces. In literature, women's solitude has often been an enforced exile, a form of punishment, with implications of shame, evil, and madness (Koch 1994, 249). The figure of Charlotte Brontë's Mrs Rochester, imprisoned in the attic, is a compelling example (Gilbert and Gubar 1979). Edward Hopper has women looking out from minimalist, enclosed spaces, away from the sunlight, eating at cafe tables, clearly alone. Rarely is it ennobling.

Solitude for men, as Leslie Miller suggests, can be an honourable estate, linked to power, a solitary communion with nature, a form of "symbolic capital." For women there is a "slimmer tradition fraught with suicides, agoraphobia" (Miller 1992–93). Occasionally a "symbolic capital" emerges for women as in that greatest of proverbial gifts – a room of one's own.

Solitude allows a unique kind of freedom, intensified by self-knowledge, and thus a building block in shaping identity. Yet it can also perform the opposite – inhibit, eliminate opportunities, and corrode self-esteem. This dichotomy reflects the domains into which this volume is caste. The discourse of solitude frames the chapters that follow. The authors write about daily troubles, of feeling isolated as if by caste, or by fences inhibiting their potential and abilities. Some attribute their workplace insecurities and injustices to familiar social differences – gender, race, ethnicity, age, and class. Others try to introduce new knowledge and are spurned for it. Structural solitudes are inevitably imposed on faculty members fighting for tenure and on university presidents facing diverse responsibilities.

Clearly, solitude in the workplace is not confined to one gender. While the accounts of women make up this volume, men are also subject to solitudes and exclusions, even in the same work niches, and undoubtedly undergo some of the same marginalization. The focus on women in this collection acknowledges the belief that still, at this time in history, a prejudicial gender gap lingers in workplaces despite equity policies and continual adjustments. We are told daily of such inequities: that many workplaces continue to separate by gender; that women's salaries in most venues, and even in similar jobs, remain substantially lower than men's; that women tend to be in public sector workplaces with more prescribed limitations on advancement; that the number of women presidents of large companies or members of corporate boards is miniscule; that violence against women worldwide continues unabated. In universities, women students tend to be located in "soft" disciplines, such as the humanities, arts, and social sciences, as against the "hard" ones of science and engineering. While concerted efforts are made to invite women to the "hard" disciplines, few efforts encourage men to contemplate the "soft" ones. These adjectives are themselves synonymous with gender. The "chilly climate" lingers. In universities in English-speaking countries, women receive nearly half of the doctorates awarded, yet they are still disproportionately concentrated into lower-level faculty positions. Further, men claim 80 per cent of appointments considered prestigious (Baker 2012). There has been little change in the statistics about parenting among university workers. Fifty per cent of women are major caregivers compared to about 4 per cent of men (Currie & Thiele 2001). Added to this is the now famous unresolved equity dilemma in the appointment of Canada Research Chairs (Forsyth 2011). The continued existence of these matters invites, if not concentrated action, then at least sustained attention.

This volume is about women's experiences of the university as a workplace. The functioning of the workplace depends on separation by categories, divisions between groups and perspectives. It depends on these inevitable solitudes. The essays collected here resonate with these experiences, register frustration, often despair, but also the birth of resolve, and a growing solidarity with the like-minded. How are such solitudes actually created, imposed, and silently enshrined? How does this affect performance? How are solitudes manifested in everyday experience and what role do they play in the emergence of individual and group identity? What kind of imagined futures do they encourage? Various themes emerge in the chapters that follow – the presence of "power," the weight of tradition, the cultures of administration, the considerations of gender. Two themes stand out as linked essentials: identity and categories. This interplay between workplace activities and products, and the creation of self and behaviour, underlies each account.

The authors write from specific niches in the university, but their texts represent those in other niches within university and in workplaces elsewhere. The rest of this Introduction, therefore, concerns itself with the issues that connect the writings as a whole.

One distinguishing feature of the writings is their knowledge base of qualitative, narrative, and ethnographic knowledge. Some chapters involve the investigation of texts, academic productions, and university policies, organized herein as formal and documentary knowledge. Other chapters involve field research in the form of participant observation, interviewing, focus group discussions, narratives, and auto-ethnography. This is organized as everyday knowledge. The two contrasting sets of chapters therefore readily become Part One and Part Two of the volume. Through both sections, whether the documentary analysis of Part One or the reporting of daily interactions of Part Two, the authors consider the boundaries of their identities and their worlds, the categories and documents that direct their thoughts and actions, their former aspirations and their new ones, and an imagined future that beckons them. These dual themes describe every person's existence in the university and resonate throughout the collection.

Another powerful theme is tacitly raised by each essay and underlies both documentary and everyday knowledge. It is the awareness and adjudication of unvoiced moral beliefs and the resulting loudly claimed entitlements. It is the intriguing question of why these essays become possible at all, or why they do so at this point in time. In one sense it is the most important question. What would one have to believe or know to make them possible? Would they have been possible a generation ago, or a century ago?

THE STORY OF MORAL ENTITLEMENT

The moral question remains elusive. How is it that authors claim the right to write as critically as they do, to raise the problems and doubts that they do? How do those in the workplace claim this right? Clearly, they feel entitled to produce discourses of censure, to write critical texts, and to complain about their workplace experiences. They feel entitled when in earlier times the same matters would not be problematic, or may have been accepted as a simple given, "the way things are." When those reported on in these writings are queried about entitlement, they are surprised by the question. Their answers are innocuous, offered in the form of folk ideologies such as "things have to change," "it's not right," or about "our rights." There is a strong unvoiced and unexamined moral subtext here.

All writing is informed by silent moral precepts – the unexamined subtexts, the meanings below the surface, behind the seen and the expressed. They create the strong sense of right so visible in the chapters. Moral universalisms, as well as moral specificities, occupy an underground in all workplaces, allowing a status quo. At the same time, they clearly also support a critical stance and inspire troublesome questions. Perhaps surprisingly, these moral premises, the sense of "rights," are widely taken-for-granted, not openly acknowledged. Hidden in plain sight as it were. Thus hidden, the moral foundations of discourses, as of this very discourse itself, remain unvoiced. These unexamined texts play an important part in directing ongoing discourses. Knowledge of and acknowledgment of these conceptual principles might facilitate interpretation and might broker easier solutions to discordant issues.

Interestingly, social science has a generous literature on the ethics of research, in other words the agreed-upon objectified codes of practice. These codes are themselves based on underlying moral stances. It also has a corpus of studies on the morals of various groups, the sociocultural principles of right and wrong, derived from higher authority, by which individuals live. It has codes of ethics, yet it has no ethnography of the morals that inform its own productions, or of the moral culture or moral history within which it embeds itself. Such morals have not been made visible or considered a "legitimate object of study" (Fassin 2008, 333; Fassin 2012; Hitlin and Vaisey 2013). There is a current surge of interest in the topic. Ethnographic and theoretical efforts, as those in this volume, should help bring a growing awareness to this part of social science and make moral stances more visible.

Lacking intensive ethnographic efforts, however, all that can be offered at this stage are broad glosses of moral cultures and traditions. From these all too hazy positions, principled stands are vehemently assumed, idealistic worlds imagined. For decades, and even centuries, human rights, social justice, equity, ethics, pluralism, diversity, humanitarianism, liberalism, generosity, notions of a good life, everyday rights and freedoms, *e pluribus unum*, the public good, and "doing the right thing" have been widely recognized and extolled sentiments. Life is lived according to moral myths such as these. The contributors to this volume move to just such moral drummers – unvoiced, hidden yet passionately activated in their writing. These unspoken epistemes of the moral order fashion entitlements and provide the backdrop for ideology and action. They work towards change and a hopeful future, despite what some might see as vacuous political theatre frequently carried out in their name.

The issues raised in this collection rise from such abstract moral basics. In everyday life, we assume a shared moral grammar, even if a silent one, instead of the culturally diverse and relativistic one that rears its head from time to time. This unexamined assumption can easily create discontent and the sense of being a victim, unknowingly enmeshed in a different moral order. Being aware of these taken-for-granted issues, working to understand them, becomes what Fassin has called "an epistemological necessity" (2012, 5). The writings in this volume come from different solitudes in a complicated setting like the university, from differences in the "everyday moral intuition" necessary for interaction and practice (Habermas 1990, 55). In short, we all live in unspoken moral cultures. These moral cultures, transcendent discourses, are revealed in the narratives, and they provide a rich array of entitlements as well as loud proclamations in their name. Therein are the building blocks for future ethnographies of varying and divergent morals.

WOMAN'S JOURNEY IN THE WORKPLACE

This book opens with a success story in the form of a conversation about the career and achievements of Martha Piper, president of the University of British Columbia from 1997 to 2006. Her story is a direct answer to one of the proclaimed problems of the workplace – namely, gender equity. The book ends with a chapter that describes a different and more familiar side of the equity story. It shows women faculty facing equity issues that originally inspired the metaphor of the chilly climate. The intervening writings occupy various positions on woman's journey in this workplace. Together they serve as testimonials to a changing landscape. The view from the "pinnacle," the Martha Piper story, could be cast as one of merit and hard work, or as a culmination of the decades of women's writing and activism. It is thus a fitting prologue to a volume about the experiences of women in university workplaces. When followed by the other narratives, however, it highlights questions about what has been gained, what has yet to be gained, and about the uncertainties and ambiguities that persist.

Until a few decades ago it would have been difficult to envision the appointment of a woman as president of a large university. When it actually happened in Canada in 1974, it attracted considerable public attention. In some quarters such appointments of women to high academic office were seen as the recognition of individual merit, in others as the final outcome of years of advocacy by women, in others as the result of the liberating education offered by women's studies and feminist theory, and in yet still others as a way for the university to save itself from charges of gender discrimination.

A contrast to the Martha Piper story is Pauline Jewett's appointment as president of Simon Fraser University in 1974. There was in this earlier case a display of administrative inexperience, now unthinkable, that accompanied her ascension to the position. It began with a gauntlet of powerful objections and symbolic reminders of what was deemed to be appropriate for a woman. One such act, reported by the candidate herself, was having a member of the search committee turn his back on her in an interview (Crawford 2013). More benignly, but just as full of gender symbolism, was that at her installation she was given a corsage, an act heavy with meaning as part of a woman's rite of passage at debutant events, prom nights, and important first dates. At that time, a mere 15.3 per cent of faculties in Canada were female and the chilly climate flourished everywhere.

Although Martha Piper was spared this awkwardness, her early tenure in the position was not without persistent reminders that she was "the first woman" president of the university, an obvious achievement for the university. She had "woman" thrust upon her like a compulsory validation, almost as if it must be the true explanation of her success. As she relates, however, she wanted to be assured that gender was not the determining factor in her appointment. Yet this externally imposed gender-awareness reoccurred whenever she encountered questions about her children or where her hair was styled. As time passed, these allusions to her status as a woman, or similar nullifying and condescending distractions, abated. That such questions could be put to any male president is unimaginable.

Merit and Gender

The first issue worthy of rethinking is the conundrum of merit. Is merit to continue to be filtered through the distorted mirror of gender? University committees on appointments, tenure, and promotion debate merit on a daily basis. The merit of dissertations is argued, as are the introduction of new policies or the modification of old ones, and the appointment of new people to a position at any level. The inherent subjectivity and wide breadth of interpretation is apparent as the qualities called "merit" and "potential" are debated. The politics of merit become apparent, as individualized and readily recognizable undercurrents make their appearance. Factors such as age, class, ethnicity, education, place of graduation, and personality are also silently active, making it difficult to know just how committees ultimately make their decisions about merit or potential. The matter has been called "the mirage of merit," and the "ideal academic" has been deemed a "fictional construct shaped by power" (Thornton 2013, 140). The question of gender compounds the problem by exerting another silent variable into the equation of decision making. Merit and gender are the subtext to a number of the narratives in this collection, sometimes patently obvious, other times elusive.

Recognizing a Canon

Another key theme among the chapters is the awareness of an emerging canon in feminist writings. Some aspects of feminist theory belong to an earlier age, reflecting the pressing social concerns and the theoretical preferences that inspired them. George Marcus points to the complexities of canons, of creating "authoritative knowledge" and asks about its relevance to current conditions, whether a specific canon is actually "in the interest of some not as well conceptualized, but certainly more open and pluralist, conditions" (1991, 385). This idea could be applied to contemporary feminist writings. Earlier textual authority, while it sharpened imaginations some decades ago, does not always acknowledge current situations or processual changes and thus may speak to empty theoretical spaces. After forty years of feminist theorizing, it is not too early to recognize the existence of a canon, and honour the work of an earlier generation for their many contributions to the analytic generation of their times and to the discipline. Canons often live on, sometimes nostalgically, from formative years and can assume the canonical status, without regret, and remind us of the social times that inspired it, the moral community that created it. In thinking of canons, we might concentrate on concepts that were once central to feminist analysis but now require qualification.

Such decentring occurs in some of the following chapters. Annalee Lepp's chapter deals with the diversification, pluralism, and post-canonical landscape in contemporary women's studies where important theoretical advances incorporate contemporary social thought.

Winnie Lem performs another decentring, this time in the introduction of feminist writings to existing academic knowledge, where the canons of pre-existing thought are revealed.

The Binary Convention

Third, a part of the canonical domain is the allure of the binary conventions that have plagued social analysis, including feminist analysis, for some time. The chapters in this volume, and the feminist community at large, problematize the binary analysis of gender. This rarely questioned given in social analysis, from Greek thought to the present, has relied on oppositional entities such as analogy and polarity (Lloyd 1966), binary theorizing in the professions (Thorne et al. 2004), and also in everyday epistemology. It is often pointed out, as if it were unproblematic, that such thinking reflects the authoritative binary structure of the human body. This begs the question of how long social epistemologies will continue to unhesitatingly depend on the geography of the human body. But, of course, opposing polarities promise immediate satisfaction, uphold tradition, provide a tried analysis of current problems, and thus continue unabated. Yet, inspired by multiplicity of gender now widely recognized, they become impoverished as parts of contemporary epistemologies. Binary analysis is assuming canonical status in many fields, even if it seems to provide a quick, comfortable, and acceptable analysis. The move is from "binary" to "contrastive" and the new openness to diversity that the latter offers.

Related to the emergence of canons is the traditional descriptor "woman." It is well known that the category of "woman" and its attempted broad inclusiveness has been criticized since the beginning of the feminist movement. This liberally constructed oneness was an affront to women from the developing world, from non-academic positions, from gendered differences, from differing political persuasions, and from women of colour. They all question the academic, white, privileged fiction of oneness. It has become recognized as a canonical idealization. Further evidence of approaching official changes in binary and gender labels is occurring in identification documentation systems such as birth certificates and passports. Official identities already omit categories once considered crucial – race, class as in occupation, or parental occupation. Presently, the suggestion from some human rights groups is that "sex" be eliminated. This category, however, remains unadulterated in university affairs. "Woman" is still an unpolished generalization fueled by past traditions, if not by present administrative sentiments. It is clearly evident in the attempts for correction as in the new titles of academic departments and institutions that rely on "gender." Katie Aubrecht and Isabel Mackenzie Lay explore this issue in their chapter where "woman" is clearly not a preferred description or category.

Positionality

Several authors draw attention to the reality of "positioning" in niches and categories and how that affects one's very existence. Positionality appears in the juxtaposition that creates a universe of "we" and "they," at once alienated from each other, while retaining a relational tension. When no "we" exists, it is sought – as in the loneliness of the tenure struggle described by Pat Palulis. It is also sometimes imposed, strategically, as when a woman university president is informed that "all the women are watching you" – an immediate community with serious underlying expectations.

Depending on the text, the constructed "they" assumes various possible positions – oppressor, power broker, silencer, bureaucratic bully, rule enforcer. Sometimes this dominating Other is known simply as "the university," "male privilege," "the boss." Thus, in their solitudes, the "we" is forced, or allowed, to see themselves as victims or sufferers, a necessary component of most solitudes. Especially troubling in such binary distinctions is the wide gap in moral entitlements claimed by the opposing sides.

The result is that positionality makes it difficult to appreciate the worldviews and experiences of others (Rose 1997; Takacs 2003). The writings in this volume infer that positionality is entrenched, and yet is often believed to be open to negotiation. Complicating the issues, "power," the everyday explanation and immediate clarifier for all problems, is evoked from each niche. "Power," the gloss, becomes an instant, if superficial, analysis for the existence of divisions and the persistence of solitudes. Narratives about power are created positionally, and, ironically, they also work to keep people within their niches. Power awaits the tests of ethnography to put detailed meanings onto a skeletal explanation. Each narrative essentially contributes an ethnography about the operation of power.

Workplace discourses, whatever their positionality, are rife with ritualistic "troubles talk," the casting of troubles once private into a public forum. What is considered proper to relate? Which absent power is addressed or accused in each narrative? Who is seen as ultimately responsible for creating solutions? Troubles talk and its partner, the accused, become part of a binary universe in which the narratives tell as much about the accuser as about the dominating Other being addressed. Surprisingly, this dominant presence it is often woven into narratives and appears gender-neutral, and is positioned somewhere in the structure and machinery of the university. Too readily, however, the underlying belief and immediate interpretation is that this machinery is of the male gender.

KNOWLEDGE AS ORGANIZATIONAL TEMPLATE

The volume is structured using socially organized knowledge as the *lingua franca*, the bridge that connects all of the narratives. The chosen bipartite division recognizes the differences in the topics addressed, as well as the practices of research and analysis by which the knowledge has been produced. Two categories of knowledge reflect the differences in the chapters. The chapters in Part One involve the investigation of texts, academic writings, and university policies – formal and documentary knowledge. The chapters in Part Two involve qualitative field research – readily described as informal or everyday knowledge. The two parts reflect the organizational configuration of the university itself, when it divides seemingly effortlessly into formal categories of work, disciplines, departments, and multiple other workplaces, and thus into repositories of knowledge that underlie each unit. Yet these knowledge packages tell only part of the story. The other kind of knowledge lies in the everyday interactions and interpretations, the daily manifestations of a living culture, heretofore only sparingly documented. All of the narratives in the volume are located within these knowledge cultures.

Formal and documentary knowledge may be thought of as the "intellectual" knowledge characteristic of universities, the textual knowledge created and dispersed by them and grounded in their daily routines. It is considered their basic business. Disciplines and departments are the most obvious repositories of such formal knowledge. Indeed, disciplines may be thought of as solitudes unto themselves, heightened by the value they place on solitary creativeness, on "intellectual independence, academic freedom and individual heroism" (Ylijoki 2000, 344). If universities are knowledge factories, then formal academic knowledge is their intellectual capital. To make this possible, to preserve and develop it, universities are labour-intensive, with links spread throughout the institution in a great chain of inter-connectedness. Given the importance conferred on academic knowledge and the preferential treatment it receives, it is not surprising to find the category of "support staff," from clerks to teaching and research assistants, as part of this great web of interdependence. Moreover, these disciplinary and departmental units operate like tribes, with marked territories, codes of behaviour, and specified identities (Becher and Trowler 2001; Whittaker and Ames 2006).

Another type of formal knowledge is the knowledge embedded in documents. These are texts through which the ongoing life of universities is constituted, regulated, recorded, certified, and made "real." These include the familiar texts of university constitutions and policies, evaluation reports, promotions and tenure assessments, financial accounts, student grades, research protocols, minutes of meetings, mission statements, salary data, research ethics board reports, and all archival materials – in short, files of all kinds. In view of the arguments in this volume, they include the specifications for categories of work, job descriptions, data on each employee, personal and personnel records, and accounts of performance. It is not surprising that "complex inter-linkages between documents [documentary realities] create their own versions of hierarchy and legitimate authority" (Atkinson and Coffey 2004, 69). They solemnize the organization of the university. Reports on workers in various locations, the tenure and promotion reports on faculty, letters in support of appointments, and other matters are deemed inappropriate for general release. While some content in these texts is fully "restricted," their accessibility carefully guarded, their legal status is unclear and usually untested. Yet all those at the university are captured in such webs, making problematic the relationship of worker to the documentary knowledge that controls them.

The three chapters that comprise Part One describe the introduction of new academic knowledge to the university, and new documentary knowledge in the form of policies to university workers. Women's studies as a formal academic field is explored in the opening chapter by Annalee Lepp. The early history, politicization, changes in name, epistemologies and the current problematizing of earlier theoretical stances is documented. Lepp considers the deconstruction of "woman," the many complexities of gender, and the melding of feminist knowledge with current theoretical movements.

Winnie Lem addresses the question of whether political boundaries affect the contours of formal knowledge. Using Canadian anthropology as the example, she presents the processes that smoothed the way for feminism as new knowledge to be introduced into the existing orthodoxy. Citing early feminist writings in the discipline, the introduction of feminism is considered in light of the shaping of the national discipline itself. She asks, is there a Canadian feminist anthropology?

Prerogatives of equity for disadvantaged groups, as proposed by the Federal Contractors Program, are adopted as guidelines by some universities. Joan Anderson reports how such documentary knowledge has led to the eliminating and blurring of "identity," "race," "ethnicity," and "visible minority." Now invisible in policy, these identities remain very visible parts of everyday knowledge. The bureaucratic homogeneity hides identity distinctions thereby assuming a similarity of experiences. Fundamental issues are intersectionality and the nature of categories, their history and viability in institutions. Moreover, Anderson shows how universities often do not recognize everyday knowledges and practices and thus could be challenged about their omissions and effectiveness. She questions how equity is to be achieved. These early chapters constitute a formal gateway to the volume. Lepp and Lem present the perspective of women's studies and feminist social science, providing the theoretical stance and the formal background that inform the writing throughout. Anderson raises the central question of categories. Categorization is an integral concern, overtly or inadvertently, in every chapter and has a monitoring influence on identity as well as on the inevitable solitudes.

The second part of the volume is constructed around everyday, unofficial common-sense knowledge that determines daily interpretation. Centrally at issue in the chapters is the concern about identity. There is an everyday identity by which one comes to be known in the workplace, which is reinforced daily. Often problematically, there is also a formal identity, the one compelled by the workplace. Working in tandem with these is an imaginary identity – the hoped-for self.

There has been ample theorizing about everyday common-sense knowledge – by Alfred Schutz, who uses the term "stock of knowledge at hand"; by Clifford Geertz, who writes of "common sense as a cultural system"; and by Greek and other ancient philosophers, who refer to *doxa*. Most frequently, however, it is referred to as "everyday knowledge" (Gardiner 2006). Behind everyday interactions are unwritten scripts, persuasive cultural texts, and powerful moral positions. These are tailored to the place and the time, ready to shape common-sense philosophies and rationales. Just as often, as the chapters reveal, they are at variance with policy and formal expectations.

Everyday knowledge, often word of mouth, assumes a powerful authority of its own, and is passed on through generations as local history and cautionary tales. This oral tradition, actively afoot, is laced with a repertoire of long-standing folklore. It chronicles experiences in the workplace, is peppered with large doses of troubles talk, liberally laced with "if onlys," and is the undocumented background script in all workplaces. Contrary to claims that this is unimportant knowledge, it is very serious indeed, not only for its perpetrators but also as having severe consequences on a wider stage (Miller and Silverman 1995). It is rich with reminders about the moral entitlements of the workplace. It is the known culture, the said and the unsaid.

1

Building and Redefining Women's Studies in Canada

ANNALEE LEPP

Over its almost forty-year history, the interdisciplinary/disciplinary field of women's studies in Canada, as elsewhere, has undergone a number of significant changes. In the late 1980s, data collected by researchers affiliated with the Canadian Women's Studies Project (CWSP) indicated that of the 59 universities and colleges surveyed, 20 institutions offered a minor, combined major, or diploma in women's studies or had established a "special institute" (Eichler and Tite 1990, 8; Tite and Malone 1990, 29–33). In addition, 5 federally funded regional chairs in women's studies (at Mount Saint Vincent, Laval, Ottawa-Carleton, Winnipeg-Manitoba, and Simon Fraser) had been established in 1983. By 2012, the number of semi- or fully independent women's studies undergraduate and graduate programs had grown considerably. In addition to at least 20 colleges that offered first- and/or second-year women's studies courses or diplomas in the field, 48 universities had established honours/major (19), major (19), or minor (8) programs; there were also 18 MA and 6 PhD programs (WGSRF 2012).[1]

Besides significant expansion, in the last decade, many women's studies programs have undergone name changes. By early 2015, of the 48 programs housed in universities, 9 had retained Women's Studies; 27 were called Women's and Gender Studies (or vice versa); 4 referred to themselves as Gender Studies; and other variations included Gender, Sexuality, and Women's Studies; Gender, Race, Sexuality, and Social Justice; Gender Equality and Social Justice; Women's Studies and Feminist Research; and Gender, Sexuality, and Feminist Studies. At its 2012 annual general meeting, the Canadian

Women's Studies Association/L'association canadienne des études sur les femmes (CWSA/ACÉF), established in 1982, was renamed Women's and Gender Studies et Recherches Féministes (WGSRF). Also in 2012, *Atlantis: A Women's Studies Journal*, established in 1975 and a key Canadian scholarly journal in the field, was reconstituted as *Atlantis: Critical Studies in Gender, Culture and Social Justice.*

What the above cursory overview indicates is that the number of women's studies undergraduate and graduate programs, of varying sizes, administrative structures, and access to institutional supports and budgetary resources, have certainly grown in Canada since the first courses were taught in the early 1970s. Furthermore, many programs have, through name changes and revised mission statements, begun to redefine themselves in keeping with ongoing critical interrogation and rethinking in the field. With this broad context in mind, this chapter offers a general examination of the building of women's studies as an interdisciplinary/disciplinary academic field in Canada. While by no means comprehensive, the chapter draws on Canadian and selected US literature, and touches on some of the main debates, ongoing tensions, and recurring challenges that have shaped and reshaped, destabilized, and created new possibilities for women's studies during its almost forty-year history.

HISTORIES

In a collection of first-person memoirs titled *Minds of Our Own: Inventing Feminist Scholarship and Women's Studies in Canada and Québec, 1966–76* (2008), forty-six academics and scholars recount how and why they became active in the development of feminist scholarship in Canadian and Quebec universities, and, in some cases, in the establishment of women's studies courses and programs in the late 1960s and, especially, the early 1970s.[2] Many identified their own personal experiences of gender discrimination inside and outside academia as well as the formative texts, political activism, grassroots organizing, and consciousness-raising groups of the "second wave" women's movement of the late 1960s and 1970s as important sources of politicization about women's issues. Some also mentioned other social movements of the period as influential, such as the civil rights, anti–Vietnam War, student protest, gay and lesbian rights, Quebec nationalist, and Indigenous rights movements (Robbins et al. 2008, 326; Eichler and Luxton 2006, 79–80). Still others pointed to their involvement in "feminist anti-imperialist, anti-capitalist, anti-colonialist, anti-imperialist, and anti-oppression" struggles, and to personal experiences of racism and engagement in anti-racist work in Canada (Mojab 2006, 88; Dhruvarajan in Robbins et al. 2008, 148–54).

Within this radicalizing context and given the absence of scholarship and courses "on women," these academics and scholars, based mainly in the humanities and social sciences, sought to create spaces on university campuses where the androcentric biases and "conceptual ordering" (Smith in Robbins et al. 2008, 69) of dominant knowledge systems and the unacknowledged values and unexamined assumptions of "theoretical, scientific, and social models" (Robbins et al. 2008, 28) could be critiqued and challenged; new research methodologies could be devised; feminist knowledges, theories, and empirical studies could be produced, exchanged, and disseminated (through newsletters, academic journals, book publishers, scholarly networks, and research institutes); and a women-centred interdisciplinary curriculum, often demanded or in demand by students and activists, could be developed and taught using innovative, experimental, and critical pedagogical approaches. Integral to the discourse of feminist/women's studies' uniqueness, radicalism, and transformative potential in academia and beyond in this period was the commitment to centring and validating "women's" histories, voices, and experiential knowledges in all areas of endeavour: methodologies, theories, curricula, pedagogies, praxis, and strategies for social change.

Some women's studies scholars have noted that first-person memoirs of the heady days of the late 1960s and 1970s provide overly nostalgic portrayals of the historical origins of the field (Braithwaite 2004). Indeed, many of the narratives included in *Minds of Our Own* are replete with stories about women faculty members battling obstructive colleagues and administrators (some, however, were supportive), and about the exhilaration of developing collaborative research projects, building scholarly networks, inventing and sometimes co-teaching new undergraduate interdisciplinary courses, and experimenting with various pedagogical methods. With the exception of one racialized faculty member who recounted experiences of racism and a deep sense of unbelonging (Dhruvarajan in Robbins et al. 2008, 148–54) and a few muted references to "power struggles in many another women studies program" (Gillett in Robbins et al. 2008, 93–4) or debates over questions such as, "Is it permissible to make money on the women's movement?" (Eichler in Robbins et al. 2008, 200), this collective landscape as presented appeared to be largely devoid of ideological conflicts, theoretical tensions, or internal debates about women's studies, or of power dynamics along multiple axes of difference. That said, what were some of the main challenges and key debates that unfolded in the field?

ERASURES: DECONSTRUCTING
THE CATEGORY "WOMAN/WOMEN"

Beginning in the late 1970s, many of women's studies' (and feminisms') cherished foundations were profoundly destabilized when critical questions were asked as to "which women" and "whose experiences" were at the centre of scholarly inquiry, teaching, and praxis. These queries were accompanied by charges that the women's studies practitioners were producing and perpetuating an understanding of "woman/women" as an undifferentiated universal category with white (middle-class) women's "history, social, political and economic reality" positioned as normative and "all other women" rendered invisible or constructed as "deviations" (Carty 1991, 12; see also Bannerji 1987, 12). As one of two racialized women included in *Minds of Their Own*, Vanaja Dhruvarajan recounts her experiences of "everyday racism" not only as a graduate student but also as a sociology professor and a participant in the successful "struggles first to establish a women's studies program and then to win a federally funded chair in women's studies" at the University of Winnipeg (in Robbins et al. 2008, 151):

A chilly climate in universities prevails for women of colour, not only because of their gender, but also because of their "race," religion, and culture ... Racism was and still is part of academic common practice in North America; the inferiority of non-White people, our culture, and our ways of life are taken for granted in the curriculum and pedagogy ... My immigration to North America meant that I had to struggle against racism, imperialism, and colonialism, in addition to sexism ... The successful efforts of feminists during this period resulted in the eventual establishment of women's studies programs and departments, thereby providing contexts for the generation and dissemination of knowledge from feminist perspectives. But feminists who criticized men for using men's experiences to generalize to all human experiences, thereby ignoring the differences of gender, went ahead to commit a similar error by ignoring differences among women. There is a growing awareness of this tendency because of the challenges of scholars from marginalized groups. In spite of these efforts, the experiences of marginalized groups are not yet fully integrated into the mainstream of women's studies. (149, 152–3; see also Dhruvarajan 1997)

Writing in 1987, Himani Bannerji also asserted that she had

rarely, while doing work in Women's Studies proper, come across a framework or methodology which addresses or legitimizes the existence and concerns of women like us, or helps give our voices strength and authenticity … The great bulk of Canadian literature on women and what passes for Women's Studies curriculum leaves the reader with the impression that women from the Third World and southern Europe are a very negligible part of the living and laboring population in Canada … And this happens in a country with the history of a settler colonial state and economy, where "reserves" exist in large numbers for the indigenous peoples, where a working class is still being created through racist immigration policies and segmentation of the labour market, and where a U.S. dependent capitalism has long ago entered an imperialist phase? (1987, 10)

In light of such erasures and what Shahrzad Mojab has described as the necessary adoption of a "critical position vis-à-vis" and resistance to "White-middle-class Eurocentric, racist feminism" (2006, 89), anti-racist and Indigenous scholars and writers challenged the field's practitioners to engage in a fundamental reconceptualization of women's studies as an intellectual and political project (e.g., hooks 1981; Moraga and Anzaldúa 1981). This would entail rethinking dominant historical frameworks and periodizations with full attention paid to the intersections of gender, race, and class, as well as the histories of colonialism, slavery, systemic racism, and the complex struggles of the oppressed and marginalized in Canada (e.g., Dua and Robertson 1999; Bristow et al. 1994; Maracle 1996; Brant 1994).

It also necessitated revisiting feminist epistemologies, theoretical paradigms, research methodologies, social analyses, and empirical scholarship; rebuilding women's studies curriculum and course content; transforming hiring practices in women's studies programs; and attending to hierarchies of power and privilege in the classroom and in the field's praxis (e.g., Dhruvarajan 1997; Mukherjee 1992; Bannerji 1987; Murray 2008). As Linda Carty argued in 1991, this reframing at the program level would need to go beyond simply adding "women of colour" topics to or including previously invisible and marginalized histories, voices, and experiences in existing curriculum:

> After some twenty years in the academy, Women's Studies in Canada remains a very white discipline. Its exclusionary theory and politics focus on the reproduction of whiteness while maintaining pretensions of being inclusive ... Inclusion ... that stops at the level of adding some women of Colour and their texts is wholly inadequate. This has to be supported by the politics of inclusion ... Any serious exercise in this regard has to engage the politics of institutional racism. It must also engage questions of feminist epistemology – surely, how we come to know what we know has everything to do with our material location in the world – and definitions of history. Only then can we genuinely talk about anti-racist feminist pedagogy. (1991, 12, 17)

Cumulatively, these critiques of women's studies produced what Arun Mukherjee termed a "crisis of legitimation" (1992, 165).

Beginning in the 1980s, transnational feminist scholars similarly challenged prevailing ideas about a "women's global community" or "sisterhood," and critiqued "Western feminism" for its universalizing construction of the monolithic "Third World woman" as the foreign and subjugated Other. This representation was premised on, to quote Chandra Talpade Mohanty, "her feminine gender (read: sexually constrained) and being 'third world' (read: ignorant, poor, uneducated, tradition bound, domestic, family-oriented, victimized, etc.)," and was implicitly juxtaposed to Western women as "secular, liberated, and having control over their lives" (1984, 337, 353; see also Dhruvarajan 1997; Carty 1991). In effect, through this binary construction, Western feminist scholars glossed over the class, religious, cultural, racial, and ethnic differences among "Third World" women, ignored the diversities rooted in the specificities of history, geography, and local context, and overlooked the complexities of women's lives and *agencies* under globalization (Mohanty 1984; Dua and Trotz 2002; Carty 1991). Adopting a transnational feminist approach in women's studies, as Mohanty further argued, also meant going beyond additive methods – the "'feminist as tourist' model" ("where women's studies courses 'add women from other countries' into existing frameworks") or the "feminist as explorer" model (where courses about "Third World" women are incorporated into the existing curriculum without decentring the national focus on the United States or Canada or addressing the historical and contemporary realities of neo-colonialism, globalization, Eurocentrism, and racism). What was required, she maintained, was the adoption of "a feminist solidarity model," which would involve "teaching comparatively, especially about how the local and the global are simultaneously present in all contexts. This necessitates radically revisioning how the entire curriculum works and how the courses relate to each other. It means that the US or Canada is no longer the centre of the curriculum where everybody else gets added on" (Dua and Trotz 2002, 76–7).

In addition to the aforementioned critiques, scholars working in such areas as gender, disability, lesbian, queer, and trans studies made similar claims, arguing that women's studies with its dominant and unitary conceptualization of "woman/women" in its scholarship, theories, teaching, and praxis had ignored and failed to integrate other axes of difference and identities (e.g., Andreae and Coffey 1997), and had not "radically troubled" the "conceptual ground of gender" (Noble 2012, 281–2; see also Noble 2004; Salamon 2008). In the latter case, in mapping how the field has been resistant to incorporation of trans bodies (despite having long feminist histories) as well as trans feminist theories and scholarship, Bobby Noble has argued that

the existence of transmen and other feminist sons *qua* feminists, as well as trans scholarship more broadly, marks not "feminism and Women's and Gender Studies (wGS) under siege from the enemy within," but feminism's victories in producing (albeit in directions neither fully owned nor celebrated and often aggressively refused) choice about bodies and about politicized, critical masculinity as *feminism* ... While a rhetoric of openness, inclusivity and interdisciplinarity appear to be saturating Women's

and Gender Studies at an institutional level, the opposite is true
at an administrative and collegial level, where some of the
discipline's scholars and practitioners remain trans-illiterate –
passionately ignorant and deeply intransigent of what real integration of such entities will necessitate. "Integration" of trans
bodies necessitates structural and conceptual disintegration and
reconstruction of the sexed and gendered ground of the WGS
project. (2012, 277, 281)

By the turn of the twentieth-first century, some scholars, in reflecting on the field, characterized women's studies as a flawed or failed
identity-based project whose historically constituted object of inquiry
(the now deconstructed and destabilized foundational category
"woman/women") had been exposed as exclusionary and constraining (Brown 2005). For others, however, these ongoing intellectual
and theoretical challenges, in as much as they were and have been
taken up in individual women's studies programs, opened up possibilities for ongoing critical self-assessment in what was deemed to be
a dynamic and open-ended field, one always potentially in the process of "becoming" (Wiegman 2005, 57). While there may be little
consensus on future directions, there has been a growing commitment to integrative intersectional analyses, as well as anti-colonial
and transnational feminist perspectives, which "at its best, account
for multiply constituted subjects" (based on gender, indigeneity, race,
ethnicity, religion, class background, ability, sexuality, etc., that
intersect to shape one's social location) and "interacting systems of
power and inequality, globally and locally" (May 2012, 170–1;
Morris and Bunjun 2007). There have also been critical (yet clearly
limited and contested) spaces created within women's studies for the
incorporation of gender, masculinity, queer, and trans studies. Finally
and not surprisingly, this wholesale questioning of the "women" in
women's studies also precipitated the field's "naming debates" and
the proliferation of varied program name changes over the last
decade, on the understanding that no one name could capture the
complexities and expansiveness of the field.

INSTITUTIONALIZATION: ACADEMIA/ACTIVISM

Of the twelve contributors to *Minds of Our Own* who commented
on recent scholarly directions in women's studies, half of them

characterized developments in the field in very positive terms; the "increased emphasis on diversity" (Kimball in Robbins et al. 2008, 247) and the work of transnational feminist scholars (McFarland in Robbins et al. 2008, 260) were specifically mentioned. In the other narratives, however, there is a tone of lament. The collection's editors expressed concern about "the depoliticization of many women's studies courses," with "much of the highly specialized language ... more suited to a conversation among academics than a conversation with society at large" (Robbins et al. 2008, 336). One contributor referred to the loss of "clarity of its foundational assumptions" (Christiansen-Ruffman in Robbins et al. 2008, 194), and another indicated that she was "impressed" by the "intellectual acumen" of her younger colleagues but worried "about their being co-opted by the academy and socialized by the raw ambition and competitiveness it takes to succeed in that environment" (Nemiroff in Robbins et al. 2008, 140). Two contributors emphasized the various ways in which women's studies had become more inward looking. "It worries me," wrote Margrit Eichler, "that too little attention seems to be oriented towards what is still a mainstream scholarship that has been only peripherally touched by a feminist vision, and that too much of our efforts seem inward directed rather than oriented toward changing, not just scholarship, but the social world around us" (in Robbins et al. 2008, 202). Linda Briskin stated that, "I remember the early discussions about how women's studies would be the education arm of the women's movement. Alas, this too was naïve. Such a perspective did not take account of the institutional pressures on emergent programs in women's studies, and the difficulties finding the resources and the political will to maintain active links with community-based women's movements. Nevertheless, I continue to believe that women's studies can offer a vehicle to promote not only consciousness, but also activism" (in Robbins et al. 2008, 302).

There were indeed concerns expressed in the early 1980s that the establishment of women's studies programs in universities "might be the road to elitism: writing and thinking time for the privileged few, this time for white middle-class women" (Bowles and Klein 1983, 13). Some worried that women's studies could potentially become "'academic' in the sense of 'useless' and a 'discipline' in the sense of a department committed to a secret sign system" (Bowles 1983, 38). It was hoped, however, that "the links between the feminists

inside academe and the women's community outside will be strong
enough to prevent this from happening, as they point our research
and teaching in the needed direction" (Bowles and Klein 1983, 13),
and would "help keep women's studies from becoming just another
academic discipline, removed from the daily worlds of all of us"
(Bowles 1983, 42).

Despite such aspirations, critical discussions about the "dimin-
ished link between activism and scholarship" (Eichler and Luxton
2006, 83) or between "the women's movement" and "academic feminism" in North America also emerged in the 1980s. As a number of
scholars have noted, what counted as "activism," in what context,
around what issues, and according to whom were questions not
often complexified in these discussions (Side 2001, 75; Orr 2012).
Similarly, what was meant by "the women's movement" (Lenton
1990, 60–1) and whose perspectives, interests, and agendas were
represented and prioritized when the term was invoked remained ill
defined. That said, critics inside and outside academia basically
argued that, with the institutionalization (or cooptation) of women's
studies, its practitioners had become less engaged in or committed to
political activism and had become increasingly focused on building
their professional careers; the result was the tendency to produce
abstract theories (with the incursion of poststructuralism often identified as the most problematic) and inaccessible scholarship devoid
of radical political critique and practical relevance (Lenton 1990,
57–60; Luhmann 2005, 31). For example, in commenting on the
"great distance" between "women in the women's movement" and
"academic feminism" in the late 1980s, Lorraine Greaves pointed to
the "inaccessibility" of the latter's work in the use of language, concepts, and "forms of communication." She further questioned the
relevance of academic feminist ideas to activist feminists if they were
not grounded in "ordinary" women's lives: "The battles that we
engage in from these positions of privilege, whether with each other
or with institutions, can become less and less relevant to the ordinary woman. We must constantly ask the ordinary woman, particularly the ordinary activist woman what we should be doing. Failing
to do this not only renders us irrelevant, but more important, incomplete. Only by staying in touch with less privileged women's lives,
dreams, and ideas will we be enabled to use our access to the academic and the movement effectively and responsibility and for the
benefit of women" (1992, 155).

In light of such criticisms, the Canadian Women's Studies Project examined the level of political activism of different cohorts of 892 professors (780 women and 112 men with gender being the only identity variable) who, as of 1988, had taught "at least one credit course in women's studies or from a feminist perspective at a Canadian university or college that offers at least a bachelor degree" (Eichler and Tite 1990, 8–11). Among the women respondents, the data indicated that those who had started teaching such courses in the early 1970s were more politically motivated and involved in political and/or grassroots activism than those who began teaching in the late 1980s; the latter group had stronger "ties in academia" (Lenton 1990, 63). From this, Rhonda Lenton concluded that, while it appeared that women's/feminist studies had "become institutionalized in the university system," this process signalled "a change in how political activism is expressed":

> Later generations of feminists scholars continue overwhelmingly to be strongly committed to the feminist movement; they just define the movement somewhat differently than do members of older generations ... Many respondents outlined the work that still needs to be done to secure women's/feminist studies in the university, the problems associated with intellectual ghettoization, the conflicting pressures of administrative and intellectual labour, and other issues whose solutions were seen to require political activism. There was a popular sentiment that they viewed their work in women's/feminist studies as one component of the feminist movement and they were concentrating their efforts on that component. (Lenton 1990, 67)

Thelma McCormack seemed to capture this sentiment in 1985 when she stated that "feminist scholarship and feminist politics are marching to different drums. We will be criticized for being too ivory-tower, and that is a distinct possibility. Wherever possible, we should keep the lines of communication open, to collaborate, but I think we should have no illusions about the different demands made upon us" (1985, 8). At the same time, the CWSP's interviews with one hundred women's studies/feminist academics on this question further suggested that, despite citing such factors as limitations of time and energy, there was a sense that "if academic feminists are not involved in politics, they should be" (Eichler 1992, 127). The implication of this external and internalized expectation was that, as Judith Allen pointed out, "women's studies work *inside* the academy is either not political or not political enough" (1997, 371).

These tensions – institutionalization and its implications for women's studies and the academic/activist credentials of its practitioners (with some adopting the identity of "activist scholar" and others not and still others oscillating between the two) – remain unresolved. Martha McCaughey, however, has argued that perhaps the time has come to let go of what she terms the "simplistic notion" of women's studies "exceptionalism" – "as if we were the only field born of political incentives, the only field that encourages students to engage in service-learning and internships" and the only field in which "individual scholars" engage in "purpose-driven research," an increasingly valued commodity within universities (2012, 147–8). She further asserts that "in order to embrace the many forms of diversity that exist in WGS, and make room for competing perspectives that will fuel our field's success, we will have to give up the idea that we agree on political issues, teaching styles, or professional goals" (147).

DISCIPLINARITY/INTERDISCIPLINARITY

At the institutional level, the main strategic debate that surfaced in North America beginning in the late 1970s focused on whether pursuing a disciplinary or a mainstreaming approach would be the most effective means to radically challenge the prevailing orthodoxies of all established academic disciplines and transform post-secondary education. Growing out of discussions at the first National Women's Studies Association conference in 1979, Gloria Bowles and Renate Duelli Klein asked, "Is Women's Studies a discipline of its own, that place in the university where radical, women-centred scholarship grows, develops and expands? Or shall feminist scholarship, according to the integrationist model, be incorporated into the disciplines so that eventually Women's Studies as a separate entity will become obsolete?" (1983, 1–2; see also Nemiroff 1978, 60–8).

The CWSP's interviews with one hundred women and eighty-three male professors in the late 1980s indicated that there was little consensus on this question in the Canadian context. When researchers asked whether interviewees "would personally prefer to teach in a department of women's studies, or whether they would prefer another type of administrative structure," 15 per cent of respondents supported the creation of a "separate self-contained department for women's studies"; however, their reasons for choosing this option were not analyzed in detail (Tite and Malone 1990, 37). Other literature from the 1980s indicates that some proponents of the autonomous model were skeptical about the effectiveness of "transformation from within" the disciplines approach, suggesting that this strategy usually amounted to adding a course "on women" or projects that would attempt to reduce "sex bias in higher education curriculum" (Bowles and Klein 1983, 3–4). Rather, they argued that "the structure of knowledge can be changed only by radical, innovative feminist scholarship that is given a chance to grow in a setting where there is vibrant exchange and debate among autonomous feminist scholars who have control over their knowledgemaking" (2). Furthermore, Bowles asserted that "Women's Studies is concerned with that area of knowledge – women – that crosses all the disciplines" and hence "does not conceive of knowledge in a compartmentalized way" (1983, 39). In this sense, women's studies was envisioned as an interdisciplinary yet disciplinary site from which such scholarship and teaching would be promoted in, expanded to, and eventually mainstreamed in all areas of academia through, for example, mutual support and collaboration between feminist and autonomous women's studies scholars and via the eventual transformation of dominant knowledge systems (Bowles and Klein 1983; Kolodny in Robbins et al. 2008, 173).

Women's studies practitioners also highlighted more practical considerations, arguing that an independent disciplinary structure would enhance the field's capacity to achieve intellectual legitimacy and institutional stability. This would be accomplished by establishing permanent faculty tenure lines, directly participating in decision-making bodies in relevant faculties and in the university, forging stronger professional and research investments in women's studies among academics, fostering greater student engagement (rather than "dabbling") through the granting of undergraduate and graduate degrees, and independent planning and management of curriculum, thereby facilitating less reliance on instructors and (sometimes vaguely relevant) courses taught in disparate departments (Coyner 1983, 52–8; Nemiroff 1985, 48). As Andrea Lebowitz recalled with reference to the women's studies program at Simon Fraser University, "We were convinced right from the get-go that if we didn't have a room of our own, a program with an organized set of courses, the power to appoint faculty into the program, and control over it, we would not be intellectually coherent" (in Robbins et al. 2008, 180). It was also suggested that such an autonomous and embedded structure might more readily survive periods of fiscal constraint and budget cuts within academic institutions.

Other faculty members interviewed for the CWSP in the late 1980s, however, favoured various alternatives in equal proportion. These alternatives included the integration of "a feminist perspective" in all disciplines, the concern being that otherwise women's/feminist studies, research, and teaching would "become isolated" (Tite and Malone 1990, 37). As Nadia Fahmy-Eid recounted with reference to the Université du Québec à Montréal, the anglophone women's studies model was perceived as "too risky" and potentially "ghettoizing." "We believed," she recalled, "that the knowledge we were constructing should be integrated as quickly as possible into all fields if we wanted to succeed in complementing, correcting, and thereby revolutionizing all the fields of human knowledge from within" (in Robbins et al. 2008, 159; see also Caron in Robbins et al. 2008, 74–7). The literature also suggests that some women's studies practitioners feared that disciplinarity could potentially translate into intellectual rigidity (Coyner 1983, 65) and result in institutionalization within the very academic structures the field sought to fundamentally critique and challenge. Referring to the process of "cooptation," Deborah Gorham further argued that "Too often, the establishment of undergraduate [women's studies] degree programmes has drained energy away from teaching, research, and learning and squandered it in the sisyphian labour of administering units which are always underfunded and understaffed. It has meant taking energy away from transforming the disciplines and the university as a whole" (1996, 66). Finally, the rest of the CWSP interviewees either argued for the need to pursue both an integrationist and autonomous strategy with each buttressing and strengthening the other, or to take into account the specific institutional context and differing material realities when developing an appropriate strategy (Tite and Malone 1990, 37–8).

Besides concerns about women's studies becoming a marginalized and potentially static and rigid intellectual enclave within academic institutions, the somewhat ambivalent response to the idea that women's studies constituted or should "constitute a discipline" may have been due to the fact that out of a total of 892 professors surveyed

by the C W S P in the late 1980s, only 35 (4.3 per cent) "defined wom-
en's studies by itself (25) or women's studies and some other discipline (10) as their field of work" (Eichler and Tite 1990, 19). As
Sandra Coyner suggested in the US context in 1983, the issue of
disciplinarity was related to the question of intellectual identity, in
that "virtually all of us have been educated within a program or
department named something else" (1983, 46). In presenting extensive arguments for conceiving of and building women's studies as
a discipline, intellectually, methodologically, and administratively,
with the understanding that disciplines are not "single," fixed, and
"unified structures" immune to "change over time" (48, 51), she
pointed out the limitations of and possible dangers associated with
the structure of loose, non-standardized interdisciplinary women's
studies programs that were built on, for example, the coordination
of instructors and courses from various departments: "So long as
our participating faculty are connected to Women's Studies primarily by their teaching, and remain 'in the department' for their
research, and for evaluations of their research, we perpetuate the
notion that Women's Studies is a teaching program only, perhaps
with service added, and has no real place in the important research
mission of the university. So long as research is prepared for disciplinary publication according to methods and models of disciplines,
we delay and undervalue research *in Women's Studies* ... We must
do research 'in Women's Studies' so that Women's Studies becomes a
credible field for research achievement" (58; see also Allen 1997,
367–8; Braithwaite 2012, 209–24). In a similar vein, Greta Hofmann
Nemiroff argued in 1985 that, "notwithstanding the existence of
Women's Studies programs in many Canadian post-secondary institutions" (not to mention the establishment of the C W S A/A C É F and
several Canadian women's studies/feminist journals), "it is not considered a 'real' discipline, or accorded the respect of one. 'Real
Disciplines,' it would seem, are those in which we got graduate
degrees ... Of course, this attitude reinforces the marginality of
Women's Studies" (48).

Without taking a position on the integration versus autonomy
debate, Margrit Eichler and Rosonna Tite concluded that the C W S P
research findings with respect to disciplinary allegiances of faculty
members teaching feminist/women's studies courses "is relevant to
our understanding of how we conceptualize women's studies: as a
field of study or as a perspective that cross-cuts disciplines. For the

moment, it appears that the vast majority of people active in the area see themselves as working with a feminist perspective in a variety of other disciplines, rather than in a new discipline" (1990, 19). In practice, francophone Quebec universities opted for the integration-ist approach, whereas other Quebec universities, such as Concordia University and McGill University, and most Canadian universities pursued a two-pronged approach – mainstreaming feminist perspec-tives in existing disciplines and establishing women's studies under-graduate programs and, in some cases, freestanding departments and graduate programs (Robbins et al. 2008, 29–30).

It is difficult to make generalizations about Canadian women's studies programs as they have their own histories that over time produced different even fluctuating levels of institutional recogni-tion and visibility, budgetary investment, and student demand, as well as varying faculty configurations, and governance and curricu-lar structures. In 1994, however, Peta Tancred noted that, while there had been significant growth in the number of "solidly rooted" under-graduate women's studies programs in the 1980s and early 1990s, "the structure is fragile." The vast majority of programs, she empha-sized, consisted of "a coordinating unit that draws on existing departments for course offerings and which is reduced, at worst, to coordinating what it pleases the departments to offer, or at best, to bargaining with departments in determining the courses that are offered" (1994, 17; see also Webber 2005). Judith Allen character-ized such arrangements as "adding together disciplinary courses 'about women' (in an imaginary cocktail shaker)" (1997, 364). Seven years later, Katherine Side reported that, with the exception of seven programs that had achieved departmental status, each with varying numbers of dedicated faculty members, this interdisciplinary program model continued to be the most common one in Canadian universities. She maintained that it "has permitted faculty doing feminist research to be involved in teaching and in shaping women's studies curricula, no matter where their appointment is in the uni-versity," and "is credited with exposing many undergraduate stu-dents to women's studies." Side further noted, however, that the model had not necessarily resulted in the anticipated "integration of feminist perspectives and scholarship into existing curriculum" (2001, 72–3). Michelle Webber's interviews in one university con-text, for example, suggested that regular faculty, sessional instruc-tors, and teaching assistants, who taught "social science courses cross-listed with women's studies" comprised of a minority of women's studies and a majority of non-women's studies students, encountered significant student resistance to women's studies–specific or feminist course content; in response, some "try for a hidden pedagogy, others try to appease their student critics by not mentioning feminism/s, and many of the faculty fear the consequences of negative or poor student evaluations. In the end these survival practices undermine efforts to position feminist knowledges as legitimate" (Webber 2005, 181, 192). Furthermore, in an era of steadily decreasing government funding of post-secondary institutions, fiscal restraint, and more recently, the implementation of neoliberal and market-driven policies in universities that seem to disproportionately affect the liberal arts (Reimer 2004), Side questioned whether the interdisciplinary program model, albeit comparatively inexpensive to run, produced sufficiently stable institutional units. This is not to say that women's studies departments have remained immune to various institutional pressures (for example, with value measured by student enrollments and/or the number of majors) or have automatically been more committed to disciplinary coherence, but the argument has been that the more embedded the field is institutionally, "the more solid its foundation and the more protected it may be, although never entirely" (Side 2001, 72) from the risks of being phased out (Tancred 1994, 18).

The question of women's studies' interdisciplinary/disciplinary attachments and desired program structures, however, seemed to emerge most forcefully with the establishment of women's studies graduate, and in particular doctoral, programs in Canada and elsewhere (Side 2001; Brown 2005). Upon the creation of a freestanding MA and PhD program at York University in 1992, for example, Ann B. Shteir wrote that "urgent questions emerged," including ones pertaining to "field definition and discipline formation in Women Studies": "Is Women's Studies a lens, a perspective upon scholarship? Or, is Women's Studies a discipline unto itself, with its own methods and holy books? Some of our group take the position that all feminist approaches to scholarship belong in a Women's Studies graduate programme. Others hold the view that all Women's Studies is feminist scholarship, but not all feminist approaches to scholarship are 'Women's Studies'" (1996, 6). These issues, she noted, potentially shaped admissions criteria, the acceptance of dissertation topics, the content of women's studies core graduate courses, and the reading

lists for PhD comprehensive exams with concerns about "fragmentation" operating in tension with "charges of canonicity" (7–8).

Discussions among women's studies practitioners about discipli-
narity/interdisciplinarity and their implications for the field are certainly ongoing. Examining the issue of women's studies' historical
and current attachments to the interdisciplinarity as potentially
more anti-institutional and transgressive, Diane Lichtenstein asks,
"Can knowledge be simultaneously disciplinary and interdisciplinary? Does conceptualizing wGS as an interdiscipline get us any
closer to methodological, pedagogical, and knowledge-producing
synthesis? What would synthesis provide? And will crossing a disciplinary boundary result in the type of interdisciplinary knowledge
wGS seeks?" (2012, 48). Ann Braithwaite further posits that wom-
en's studies "is usually positioned as being composed of and equivalent to academic feminism in (all) other disciplines – as effectively,
the sum of these parts" (2012, 210). This is a symptom, she suggests,
of "a larger refusal to think about the question of the field's iden-
tity/ies in a more systematic way that could explore its similarities
to *and* its differences from those other academic feminisms" (211)
– or, for that matter, from other interdisciplinary programs, such as
cultural, sexuality, or critical race studies (Allen 1997, 359). In other
words, Braithwaite maintains that "the disavowal of this term
[*discipline*] has also often been the refusal to be accountable for (or
at least self-reflexive about) how the field is constructed or what its
structuring assumptions are, and has left it ill-equipped to articulate
an intellectual, institutional, and pedagogical project that isn't simply that sum of all scholarly feminist work" (2012, 215).

CONCLUSION

As this overview indicates, women's studies in Canada, as elsewhere, has been the site of various intellectual challenges, critical
debates, and institutional tensions since its inception in the 1970s.
The questions being posed by the field's practitioners continue to be
provocative ones. That the historical foundations and underlying
assumptions of the field have been destabilized or decentred since
the 1970s – be it the category "woman/women" or the assumed
political and activist commitments of its practitioners – is undeniable. At the same time, new intellectual possibilities and openings
have simultaneously been created. If the task ahead is building

greater interdisciplinary/disciplinary coherence that is sufficiently contingent and fluid, diverse, and open-ended, it must also be translatable at individual and often differently structured undergraduate or graduate program levels. This process of translation is clearly contingent on a number of factors, including not only the availability of faculty scholarly expertise and relevant curricular offerings but also strong intellectual and professional investments in women's studies as an ongoing and dynamic project.

Notes

1 There have also been some losses. For example, the undergraduate women's studies program at the University of Guelph was eliminated in 2010, as was the major in women's studies at McMaster University. In the latter case, an MA as well as a PhD graduate diploma in gender studies and feminist research were established.

2 With respect to axes of difference, the academics and scholars featured in the collection included two men, one who self-identified as gay, two racialized women, and two contributors who self-identified as lesbian. The editors, however, do not directly address the extent to which the collection is representative of the "pioneers" of feminist scholarship and women's studies in Quebec and Canada. Preliminary results of this memoirs project were published in *Atlantis* in 2006. See Eichler and Luxton 2006; MacDonald 2006; Mojab 2006.

2

Canadian Feminist Anthropology: Imagining the Terrain

WINNIE LEM

This chapter explores the possibilities of identifying a distinctive field of inquiry that may be defined as Canadian feminist anthropology. In anthropology, as in many disciplines in the social sciences, the issue of what is "Canadian" as a domain of intellectual inquiry has bedeviled scholars as much as, perhaps even more than, the question of what constitutes feminism and feminist scholarship. Indeed, a vigorous discussion of the meanings of "Canadian" prevails among scholars of history, sociology, geography, and politics as well as in interdisciplinary departments of Canadian studies. These discussions did not originate in but have endured at least since the founding of the first Institute of Canadian Studies at Carleton University in 1957, and much intellectual energy has been devoted to deliberations over epistemologies, practices, currents of thought, and processes that define a field of enquiry.[1] Similarly, as is evident from the contributions in this volume, the subject of what constitutes the domain of feminist scholarship has also been mooted, in every field from sociology to law, philosophy, and cultural studies (Benhabib et al. 1995; Mohanty 1984; Hawkesworth 2004). As Annalee Lepp (Chapter 1) discusses, in women's and gender studies programs in North America, the debates encompassed a range of issues, including determining the boundaries of feminist theory, methodologies, and curriculum as well as epistemologies and praxis.[2]

Contestations over the form and substance of what might be considered feminism and "Canadian" have been no less spirited or uncommon in the discipline of anthropology. The extent to which deliberations in anthropology may be representative of paradigmatic

struggles in other social sciences is a question I will leave for specialists from other disciplines to broach. Here, I will confine my discussion to the discipline of anthropology in order to build a scholarly
record that may be used for comparative purposes.

In the 1990s, for example, a debate erupted in several scholarly
publications over what elements might constitute the Canadian tradition in anthropology (Howes 1992, 2006; Dunk 2002, 2000).
The interlocutors in the debate proffered competing visions of the
fundamental features that might define a distinctly Canadian school
of anthropology. Such visions were based on the significance that
each writer attributed to different schools of thought, as well as
historical and political process that were pivotal to defining the
identity of Canadian anthropology. While similar debates have not
broken out among feminists anthropologists in Canada, at least not
in the public domain, tensions nonetheless co-exist, sometimes productively and at times uneasily between anthropologists who position themselves differently along a continuum of theoretical schools
from materialist to cultural feminists, to Foucauldian or poststruc-
turalist feminists.[3]

My purpose in this chapter, however, is not to summarize the
complex agendas, contentions, and debates that have emerged to
define specific fields. This has been done in many volumes. For
example, such volumes as Harrison and Darnell (2006b), Smith
and Turner (1979), and Cole (2000) are among the key interventions that tackled the invidious problematics of characterizing
Canadian anthropology. For feminist anthropology, this has been
done in volumes edited by Reiter (1975), Di Leonardo (1991), Cole
and Phillips (1996), and Bridgman et al. (1999). While certain key
issues that emerge from these deliberations will represent a point
of departure for some of my observations, the task that I have set
for myself can nonetheless be distinguished from these efforts. In
this chapter, I ask if the possibility exists of imagining a terrain of
anthropological practice that is feminist at the same time as it is
distinctively Canadian. Because, as the volumes above suggest, it is
evident that the terms *Canadian* and *feminist* are intrinsically contested categories, any attempt to meld them in order to distinguish
such a field will likely compound the ambiguities, uncertainties,
conflicts, and contentions. The perils and pitfalls notwithstanding,
my efforts in this chapter are not so much devoted to identifying
and delimiting Canadian feminist anthropology. Rather, it is my

intention to problematize the nature of the intellectual process in Canada that brought forth the contentions and engagements of anthropologists as Canadians and feminists. In doing so, I draw on the perspectives of Gavin Smith (2008, 2014) and Pierre Bourdieu (1977, 2005), who emphasize through their different insights that our practical activity as scholars is to make intellectual products. Smith (2008) particularly emphasizes that such products are the outcome of a very distinctive intellectual labour process. Moreover, this labour process occurs, as Bourdieu suggests, within a field of scholarship that involves action, interaction, and struggle. By drawing on this notion and in particular the notion of a field, I begin with a discussion of the fields of anthropology, feminism, and Canada.

ANTHROPOLOGY, FEMINISM, AND CANADA

Since the 1970s, a body of literature has emerged that allows us to imagine what might constitute a field of Canadian feminist anthropology. It includes anthologies that focus on feminist anthropology, on the one hand, and expositions that feature the range and scope of what might be defined as Canadian anthropology on the other. *Ethnographic Feminisms* (Cole and Phillips 1995) and to some extent *Feminist Fields* (Bridgman et al. 1999), serve as examples of feminist anthropology as practised by Canadian scholars from both English and French Canada. The two anthologies do not explicitly or self-consciously identify their collaboration as Canadian. Yet the majority of contributors were either teaching at Canadian institutions or had been trained at Canadian universities. *Ethnographic Feminisms* originated among members of the feminist caucus in the Department of Anthropology at the University of Toronto in the 1980s. The feminist caucus consisted mostly of graduate students and explored questions of gender in scholarship and the academy, in the absence of such courses in the university curriculum. At the time of its publication, the volume contributors were all affiliated with universities in Canada either as faculty members or students engaged in postdoctoral research. Many of its members moved on to positions as researchers and instructors in institutions across Canada and the United States. *Ethnographic Feminisms* reflected the broad agenda of feminist scholarship in anthropology. Contributions extended over the conceptual terrain of materialist analyses of the gendered divisions of labour within and outside capitalism as well as postcolonialism, poststructuralism, self-reflection, and discussions of text and voice. Its contributors came from across Canada, including Quebec, and the ethnographic focus was both global and Canadian, incorporating fieldwork on Canada and First Nations.

About the same time that these anthologies were produced, several others appeared and made significant contributions to defining the intellectual space that might be inhabited by Canadian anthropology. The earliest attempts at delineating this intellectual space came in the early 1970s following on the heels of the separation of anthropology from sociology in the national academic association. Volumes edited by Jim Freedman (1976, 1977) attempted to capture the thoughts of Canadian anthropologists about their history and definitive identity. These texts followed the Canadianization movement of some years earlier that preoccupied most social science disciplines, including anthropology (Ames et al. 1972; Magill 1981), and attempted to establish Canadian interests and research as distinctly separate from American ones. Later the work on intellectual space and identity included *Historicizing Canadian Anthropology* (Harrison and Darnell 2006b), as well as a special issue of *Anthropologica* titled "Reflections on Anthropology in Canada," edited by Sally Cole in 2000. Earlier, in 1979, Gavin Smith and David Turner produced *Challenging Anthropology*, arguably the first and possibly the only textbook on anthropology produced by Canadian anthropologists and published in Canada.[4]

In *Challenging Anthropology* the editors did not set out to explore the parameters of Canadian anthropology as a primary objective. The book's primary mandate was to include the work of anthropologists who take a critical stance toward the thematics of the discipline, and this was done within the boundaries of anthropological scholarship in Canada, broadly defined. Nonetheless, *Challenging Anthropology* contains contributions by scholars who self-identify as Canadians and participate in the production of Canadian anthropology. By contrast, the anthology produced by Julia Harrison and Regna Darnell is an explicit attempt to confront the problematics of defining Canadian anthropology. It asked at the outset, what is Canadian anthropology? Who is a Canadian anthropologist? And what are the concerns of Canadian anthropology (Harrison and Darnell 2006a, 4)? While posing these questions, the editors caution against the tendency to invoke essentialisms that often accompany attempts to define national traditions. Instead, they argue in favour of a continual self-sustained examination of the complexity of the intellectual terrain. Their project is an attempt to document the practice of Canadian anthropology in its diversity at a moment in history. Each of the contributors addresses this problematic while providing examples of the history, scope, and range of concerns in Canadian anthropology. Similarly, "Reflections on Anthropology in Canada" (Cole 2000) provides a sample of the thematics of anthropology as practised by Canadians.

As exemplars, these volumes together communicate the breadth and scope of the fields of anthropology, feminism, and Canada. They also index the diverse theoretical and professional locations of Canadians. In attending to the diversity, each of these volumes also includes at least one contribution that exemplifies the concerns of feminists in the discipline and the concerns of francophone anthropology. My purpose in this chapter is to interrogate the social worlds within which such engagements were produced. I ask whether the dynamics of those worlds conditioned the possibility for the emergence of a "feminist" anthropology as a form of self-conscious intellectual praxis that could be identifiable as "Canadian." Here again Gavin Smith's (2008, 2014) notion of scholarship as an intellectual labour process is most useful. Deployed in conjunction with an observation made by Richard Fox (1991) that academic anthropologists do not make unfettered choices about the form of their work, Smith suggests such scholars are workers that take part in larger labour processes.[5] To consider anthropologists as workers, then, allows us to see how our work is shaped, why it takes on certain themes, and has different implications in different social and political conjunctures.

This contention is consonant with Bourdieu's proposition that intellectuals should position their own labour process as a practical activity similar to other people's practical activity. Such positioning is intellectually responsible according to Bourdieu because it is imperative to get beyond what he calls intellectual ethnocentrism. Transcending intellectual ethnocentrism involves a reckoning with how intellectual activity is related to what he calls "the social world." This is the world of the intellectual's social origins, her position, trajectory, and also beliefs, gender, age, nationality as well as her particular position within the microcosm of anthropologists (2003,

283). Bourdieu further argues that the anthropologist's most decisive choices of topic, method, and theory depend closely on the location or position she occupies within her professional universe. This universe is informed by national traditions and peculiarities, habits of thought, mandatory problematics, shared beliefs and commonplaces, rituals, values, and consecrations, as well as the biases embedded in the organizational structure of the discipline (Bourdieu 2003, 283 quoted in Smith 2008). This social world and all that informs it has made the anthropologist and the conscious, as well as unconscious, anthropology that she practices.

In short, this forms our habitus as academics and anthropologists. Habitus is a concept central to Bourdieu's theory of social action and it allows a way of confronting the age-old question of structure and agency without conceptualizing the two as distinct entities. By collapsing those distinctions, habitus allows an understanding of the objective and subjective dimensions of social structures through an appreciation of how agents incorporate a practical sense of what can or cannot be achieved – the "objective possibilities" – based on their intuitions gained through past collective experience. Moreover, it "produces practices which tend to reproduce the regularities immanent in the objective conditions of production of the generative principle" (Bourdieu 1977, 78). It further refers to the implicit cultural assumptions transmitted by institutions, practices, and social relations that then generate action according to certain dispositions. Habitus, therefore, is a set of internalized dispositions that mediate between social structures and practical activity (also Brubaker 1985, 75). These dispositions reflect what Bourdieu calls a "field of objective possibilities open to agents at a particular historical moment" (Lane 2000, 25). Habitus, according to Bourdieu, must always be considered in relation to the notion of "field." A "field" is a structured space of social engagements – conflict and confrontations – in which actors struggle to achieve their objectives. Every field is inhabited by tensions and contradictions, which are at the basis of conflict and so struggles over definitions or what Bourdieu calls a distinctive "field of forces." This is a space of "forces or determinations." In such fields and in the struggles that take place in them, every agent acts according to his position (that is, according to the capital that he or she possesses) and his habitus, related to his personal history (2005, 47).

As intellectuals, our form of practical activity is to make products that are the outcome of the intellectual labour process, and this is done through action, interaction, and struggle within the field of scholarship. These engagements reflect, confront, coincide, respond to, and often transcend the social and political moments or conjunctures that form the context for them.

CONJUNCTURES

First, let us briefly consider the significant historic moment or the conjunctures that inform the dispositions of feminist engagements in anthropology. In chronologic terms, this was the mid- to late twentieth century. This is a familiar historical moment. It involved a conjuncture in which there was a contest between the forces of institutionalized gender discrimination and the politics of second-wave feminism. The second wave of feminism followed the first wave of nineteenth-century feminism in North America. The first wave focused on suffrage for women, the second focused largely on contesting the institutional inequalities prevalent in the workplace and the home. In universities, women were subjected to and struggled against marginalization and the forces that excluded women from the professoriate. The practices excluding women from securing positions within the academy were reinforced by the sayings, commonplaces, or ethical precepts, or what Bourdieu calls the *doxa* that prevailed at the time and before then.[6]

Such ethical precepts are illustrated in Sally Cole's (2003) writings on the life and career of Ruth Landes. Landes was an American anthropologist who earned her PhD in 1935 at Columbia University, mentored by Ruth Benedict, another significant figure in the field of anthropology, and student of Franz Boas, who is often considered to have founded American anthropology. Boas introduced Landes as "Mrs Landes" to Benedict, whom he called "Mrs Benedict." The misrecognition of the social status of these anthropologists aside, this commonplace address, as Cole notes, reflected the norm of economic dependence on men as well as the prescriptive norm for women to aspire to be a "Mrs." It reflected the abnormality of the pursuit by women of paid work as scholars and professors (Cole 2003, 19). Women were not only advised to scale back their ambition, but also actively thwarted in pursuing their interests in securing academic careers. The Landes case is instructive. While teaching at

McMaster University, Landes revealed to a colleague that she had wanted to pursue fieldwork in Africa. This desire was quashed by Melville Herskovits, a prominent figure in African anthropology and one of her professors at Columbia. He suggested that, as a woman, she was unsuited to do fieldwork in Africa.[7]

Such *doxa* articulated the norms of the organizational bias against integrating women into the academy as equals to men. Moreover, in Canada, as in the United States during the mid- to late twentieth century, women were actively discouraged from pursuing doctoral studies. At the University of Toronto, for example, during the early 1960s and 1970s, women were discouraged from pursuing graduate studies in anthropology. It was suggested to those who persisted in the pursuit of graduate work that they enroll in a MPhil and not an MA program.[8] The MPhil degree at the University of Toronto was a terminal degree, essentially prohibiting holders from pursuing doctoral studies. Similar dynamics pervaded anthropology departments at other Canadian universities, where women were discouraged from pursuing PhD degrees, partly due to the fact that until the 1970s there was only one Canadian university offering a doctorate in anthropology. A few women were encouraged to go to American universities.[9]

Our field was configured by tensions between those pursuing the objective of teaching anthropology and those who upheld the norms of andro dominance. The prevailing social conjuncture of institutional discrimination, combined with a political conjuncture of second-wave feminism, configured the academic and anthropological fields into a structured space of feminist engagements. Women and feminists began a struggle not only to redefine and claim the academy as a place for women but also to alter the *doxa* to render the study of women in history, society, and culture a legitimate scholarly pursuit in its own right. According to Bourdieu, every field is inhabited by tensions and contradictions that are at the basis of conflict and struggles over definitions. So we find, in the writings and actions of feminists in the 1970s and 1980s, the struggle to assert a feminist epistemology and to claim a space in the academy for work on women undertaken by women. Such an epistemology focuses on the political project of bringing women and gender relations into view, but also on the theoretical grounding of feminism of disciplines like anthropology. Moreover, it also implies a critique and dissection of power that contours the experiences of women in the field and the collegium.

This epistemology also acknowledged the hierarchies of power pervading the world of patriarchal power. Some feminist voices asserted that some second-wave feminists also practice a form of imperialism, in which the "West" dominated the "rest." As Mohanty (1984) suggested, women from developed countries assumed a universality of feminist priorities and also set the political agendas for feminist practice. There was a failure to recognize that women from developing countries, the global south, were differentiated in significant ways. Such postcolonial sentiments gave rise to third-wave feminism in the 1980s, which critiqued the homogenizing tendencies of the second wave that privileged the views of Western feminists. Second-wave feminism failed to problematize gender in relation to distinctive ethnicities, nationalities, religions, and cultural backgrounds (Mohanty 1984).

While not entirely immune to the critiques of second-wave feminism, the work of many anthropologists in the 1970s was not in fact targeted for failing to consider diversity. Indeed, the exploration of transhistorical and transcultural gender roles and relations were pivotal in the paradigmatic work of such scholars as Rayna Reiter (1975), Michelle Rosaldo and Louise Lamphere (1974), Mona Etienne and Eleanor Leacock (1980), and Kate Young et al. (1980). These scholars pursued different research agendas and subscribed to different theoretical schools, but together they initiated the assemblage of much cross-cultural and transhistorical evidence against the hegemonic assumptions of gender roles and the divisions of labour. Moreover, as their interventions raised questions regarding the different practices of and possibility for contesting patriarchy and the subordination of women across diverse classes and cultures, they avoided the tendency toward essentialism and the viewing women outside the West as monolithic. Mohanty, one of the frequently cited postcolonial critics, identified the work of these anthropologists, particularly those within political economy, as exemplary in avoiding such pitfalls (see Mohanty et al. 1991). The thematic of diversity, then, was as one of the tropes that reflected another conjuncture that distinguishes the second from the third wave of feminism.

In Canadian anthropology, such diversity was a priori reflected in the thematics of feminist inquiry in the discipline. I discussed the diverse scope of *Ethnographic Feminisms* earlier. Also in the volume *Feminist Fields*, such a commitment to diversity was reflected in the fact that the contributions were not confined to Canadian authors but also included American and international feminists scholars. Yet what might be characterized as a Canadian thematic distinguishes the book, given that the majority of authors were in fact Canadian in the broadest sense of the term, having been affiliated in Canadian post-secondary institutions at some point in their careers.

These efforts in anthropology and in other disciplines, as other contributors to this volume suggest, have been transformative and possibly subversive in changing conventional wisdoms regarding the place of women and the place of studies that focus on women and gender in the scholarly universe. Such conjunctures conditioned the formation of networks, such as the Women's Caucus in the Anthropology Department at the University of Toronto and many other such coalitions across Canada. Their efforts at advocating a place for women's and gender studies resulted in changing the curricula in anthropology and in the academy in general. Courses on gender in anthropology and interdisciplinary courses that incorporated anthropology appeared in the university curricula. For example, at the University of Toronto in 1980, an interdisciplinary course called "Scientific Perspective on Sex and Gender" included sections on psychology, biology, and anthropology. This and similar courses across the country were taught by women, and gradually more women doing research focusing on gender were hired as faculty in the social sciences. These conjunctures and the biases embedded in the organizational structure of the discipline formed part of the social world in which the feminist anthropologist and feminist thematics engaged in anthropological practice.

I turn now to a discussion of the current historic moment and the conjuncture in which dispositions toward problematizing Canadian anthropology may be situated. As Harrison and Darnell (2006) observe in their collaboration, the Canadian question is in a certain respect a historical question – hence the title of their book *Historicizing Canadian Anthropology*. Building on this suggestion, I return to the mid-twentieth century and examine the politics of that period. In Canada, as in many other northern nations, this was an era characterized by radical politics that of course included strains of feminism. In anglophone Canada, such politics took on many organizational forms calling for the transformation of society and social revolution (Palmer 2009). In Quebec, it took the form of militant nationalism. This radicalism was catalyzed by anti-colonial, anti-imperial, and nationalist struggles in the global south where, after wars of liberation were won, newly independent nations engaged in further struggles to build postcolonial nations and forge national identities.[10]

Canada itself had achieved political sovereignty from Britain through negotiation, resulting in the patriation of the Canadian Constitution in 1982. Yet struggles for sovereignty in other fields continued. The economy became a field of conflict as majoritarian ownership by the United States of many of our primary resources was decried. Culture also became a field of contestation particularly in the culture industries. Moreover, education and scholarship were fields fraught with tensions and contradictions involving a struggle against colonialism and domination by other nations and nationals. For example, as Regna Darnell (1998) and Thomas Dunk (2000, 2002) note, faculty trained outside Canada dominated Canadian post-secondary institutions and anthropology departments (Darnell 1998; Dunk 2000, 2002). Apart from giving anthropology in Canada a distinctive configuration, this structural feature contributed to the production and reproduction of an institutional bias against Canadian trained scholars. As Marilyn Silverman (1991) has pointed out, this bias was evident in the colonial mentalities that pervaded committee deliberations over university appointments. The *doxa* that often circulates in such committees is that "Canadians are second rate" and that Canadian universities are places of inferior learning. Candidates for positions in Canadian universities were therefore often stigmatized for having degrees from Canadian universities and excluded from taking up positions in academic departments. As an example of such distinctive practices, Silverman noted in a case study of hiring at an unnamed Canadian university that one key factor used to dismiss a candidate from a competition was that the candidate had a degree from the University of Alberta. It was suggested by one committee member "Alberta is not Berkeley." While a statement of obvious fact, in the rarefied context of deliberations over appointments, such statements function as rhetorical devices. The significance of these statements becomes charged and often overcharged, particularly if they occur within what Ella Shohat calls the "hermeneutics of domination." The hermeneutics of domination infers that marginalized groups often do not hold the "power over representation" or the power to define meaning to control the rhetorical devices in representation (1975, 170). Hegemonic assumptions regarding the hierarchies of influence in scholarship situate

Canadian institutions as inferior to their US counterparts and such meanings reinforce prevailing *doxa*. As Silverman points out, such statements become an axiomatic and ideological formation that contours the worldview of academics in ways that reinforce the assumptions of the inferiority of Canadian scholars and scholarship.

For Canadian anthropology, the prevailing social conjuncture of such institutional bias combined with a political conjuncture of nationalism configured the academic and anthropological fields into structured space of engagements. Confrontations with the question of nation, national identities, and national distinctions implied a reckoning with colonial practices and colonial mentalities. Academic anthropologists in Canada engaged in such struggles not only to reclaim the academy in Canada as a place for Canadian scholars trained in Canada, but also to engage in a project to alter the *doxa*. These conjunctures and the biases that were embedded in the organizational structure of the discipline formed part of the social world that has made Canadian anthropologists and also shaped the thematics that are pursued in Canadian anthropology. Such thematics also involve a problematizing of the category Canadian as a form of national scholarship in anthropology.

Thus, in the volumes referred to earlier, the intellectual labour process of authors both consciously and unconsciously problematizes the trope of Canadian in anthropology. One of the outcomes is that Canadian anthropology itself has become of field of contestations over definitions. These contestations are exemplified by the debate mentioned earlier between David Howes and Thomas Dunk. Howes (1992, 2006) contends that Canadian anthropology reflects structuralist tendencies toward bicentrism. Such bicentrism, he argues, is embedded in the dualism that results from the bilingual and bicultural – French and English – constitution of the Canadian nation. A key in the Canadian paradigm is a theoretical commitment to structuralism and cultural theory. On the other hand, Thomas Dunk (2000, 2002) argues that if any theoretical tradition underpins Canadian anthropology, it is embedded in the political economy of Harold Innis. Innis, a professor of political economy at the University of Toronto, propounded staples theory. Staples theory suggests that the development of Canada and its relationships regionally, nationally, and internationally have been shaped by position of the nation's exploration and export of a series of primary commodities, which he refers to as "staples." In that debate, Dunk (2000, 2002) also argues that key in Canadian anthropology is the continuing subordinate relationships to the colonial and imperial powers of the United States and the United Kingdom as well as France. Dunk's insights combined with Silverman's ethnographic observations suggest that such continued subordination has consequences for shaping the membership and agendas of departments. Such agendas and practices reinforce the *doxas* of inferiority. Such *doxas* are reflected in the practice of many Canadian anthropologists who, while ethnographically committed to the Aboriginal peoples of Canada – an unequivocally Canadian theme – continue to present their work and create careers in the various United States fora while avoiding Canadian venues.[11]

The phenomenon of the "colonial mentality" identified by Silverman also inserted itself in women's studies programs and departments in the Canadian academy. It was conditioned, however, by a slightly different set of conjunctural forces. As mentioned earlier, the late 1990s saw the conjuncture of postcolonialism and feminism. The ideologies of the third wave of feminism had a distinctive impact on the deliberations over academic appointments in many women's studies departments and programs. As university administrations were finally granting full and dedicated appointments to such academic units, sensitivity to the postcolonial critique regarding white privilege configured hiring practices. In many departments, attempts were made to apply a policy of affirmative action in seeking candidates from ethnic minorities and women of colour. In many instances, such practices involved informal processes of screening to determine phenotype as well as place of origin before compiling shortlists. According to one informant, a political scientist, who now works at a large Canadian university, her candidacy for one such position was declined on the basis that while she did speak with a "foreign" accent, she was informed, that she somehow did not fulfill the criteria of being a woman of colour. In other words, commitments to diversity often mirrored the US logic to exercise affirmative action in hiring African Americans, to correct the historical injustices of American slavery and racism. In Canada, the commitment to diversity in women's studies programs was often subordinated to American logic. Tensions emerged as arguments were made that a distinctively Canadian version of affirmative action should focus on First Nations peoples to correct the historical injustices and racism faced by Indigenous people. But such deliberation became entangled and also reproduced essentialist logics regarding how to determine who is considered an Aboriginal, African, or Asian.

Such debates and contests over definitions what is and what is not distinctive about Canadian anthropology and feminism will no doubt continue, become more complex, and very likely remain unresolved. My own argument is that the constant nature of such deliberations, as well as their apparent irresolvable quality, serve intrinsically as markers of Canadian distinction. They manifest the bespoken character of what constitutes Canadian. This character is in fact the tendency to avoid intellectual ethnocentrism by engaging in an intellectual labour process that problematizes rather than merely assumes the category Canadian in the field of anthropology as in other fields.

CONCLUSION

In this chapter, I have attempted to problematize the nature of the intellectual process in Canada that brought forth engagements with feminism and Canadian anthropology. I wished to question if and how the social worlds within which these engagements took place might condition the possibilities for the emergence of a "feminist" anthropology as a form of self-conscious intellectual praxis that could be identifiable as "Canadian." First, I will address the question of possibility and then I will address the question of the identification of praxes that might constitute a Canadian feminist anthropology. In keeping with my focus on conjunctures, *doxa* field, and habitus, I suggest that the possibilities for identifying such a field are linked to the social world and the particular conjunctures in the Canadian past and present, which inform our work as an intellectual labour process.

Consider the present social and political conjuncture as one in which postfeminism is coeval with ascendant neoliberalism. The *doxa* of postfeminism suggests that feminism is passé, "so twentieth-century" as the saying goes. While the ideologies of postfeminism are contested and the definition of the term debated, one salient definition suggests that "feminism had been transcended, occluded, overcome" (Hawkesworth 2004, 969). As Stéphanie Genz and Benjamin Brabon (2009, 3) suggest, the "post" prefix is a multiple signifier. One of the key signals is the "pastness" of feminism, or at any rate, the end or irrelevance of a particular phase in the history of feminism. The idea, therefore, is that we have advanced so much from the days of pre-feminism, that we have surpassed feminism. The emergence of postfeminism as a *doxa* coincides with the emergence of the *doxa* of neoliberalism. Neoliberalism prevails in this age of globalism and suggests the irrelevance of the nation state in governance and the salience of the rules of the market. Neoliberal *doxa* and practice also pervade the structures of governance in post-secondary institutions. In universities, the spectre of the closures of departments and programs has been raised under the imperatives of restructuring universities to make academic units more cost-effective, results-based, and accountable.

The convergence of postfeminism and neoliberalism has contributed toward rendering women's studies departments and programs possible targets for closure. In spring 2009, the Women's Studies Program at the University of Guelph was targeted and, despite the protests of students and faculty, it was closed. As of 2012, students can still take courses in women's studies but they can no longer pursue a major in this field of study at the University of Guelph. Moreover, neoliberalism and the principle of open borders has ensured more or less open access to our resources, including positions in the university as the practice and policy of hiring Canadians first and foremost in a protected labour market has been rendered obsolete. At this conjuncture, then, the conservative politics of neoliberalism and postfeminism inform our professional universe. As Bourdieu reminds us, decisions and choices for topic theory and method depend very closely on the location that scholars occupy within this professional universe. Moreover as Smith (2008, 2014) reminds us, our intellectual labour process is a practical activity that has distinctive political implications in different periods. I contend, therefore, that the choice to continue to engage with feminist and also Canadian epistemologies in the discipline of anthropology is not only a practical activity but also a praxis that contests the prevailing politics of our times.

As a scholar addressing the question of whether Canadian feminist anthropology can be distinguished as a phenomenon, I turn to Hegel's *Philosophy of the Mind* (1977). In this exegesis, Hegel asserts that phenomena are not formed but always in the process of formation. In considering the question of praxis, I defer to the wisdom of those who perform the intimate labours, which enable our work as scholars. While such deference is unorthodox, in a world where citation to other scholars is the norm, feminist praxis nonetheless often makes public what dominant optics suggest should be hidden from view. This is often the work that is done in social reproduction – domestic work and child care. According to the *doxa* of my son's former day care, as articulated by Zebbie, a day care worker, what is most important in any activity is process, not product. Therefore, I end by suggesting first that Canadian feminist anthropology is indeed a phenomenon. It is a formation and one that is sustained through intellectual labour that critically engages in Canadian feminist anthropology. Our efforts in the workplace show that the terrain of Canadian feminist anthropology can indeed be imagined not so much as a product but most certainly as a process.

Notes

1 See for example the early interventions of Morton (1968) and later discussed by Kymlicka (2003).

2 In my own department at Trent University, as in many others, such debates have focused, for example, on the implications of changing monikers, viz., the replacement of Women's Studies by Gender Studies. Such a renaming would signal a shifting terrain that would facilitate the incorporation of transgender and queer theory into the domain of the interdiscipline.

3 This is an observation based on years of participating in and organizing activities as a member of the feminist caucus at the Department of Anthropology, University of Toronto in the early 1980s, and the Women's Network of the Canadian Anthropology Society/Société canadienne d'anthropologie, as well as the Anthropology and Political Economy Seminar in the 1990s and 2000s.

4 Miller, Van Esterik, and Van Esterik have also produced a textbook for Canadians but the volume is essentially a domesticated version of an American textbook originally written by Miller in 2002 (2010; also Esterik in Harrison and Darnell 2006b). There are other volumes and articles in print that broach these themes as well as conference panels (e.g., CASCA 2008 panel organized by Jim Waldram entitled "Canadian Anthropology Is ..."). I am necessarily selective as a comprehensive overview of existing literature and discussion on these volumes is beyond the scope of this chapter.

5 Fox critiques the reflectivity of anthropologists like James Clifford and George Marcus, who suggested that, as a discipline, anthropology should look inward. This reflection should involve a rethinking of writing and representational strategies in the ethnographer's position in relation to her interlocutors (see also Marcus 1998, 198). Fox remarked that we should not configure the academic anthropologist as some kind of artisan making free choices about the form of her work, but as a worker taking part in a broader labour process (See Smith 2008, 2014).

6 According to Bourdieu (1990) *doxa* are the spontaneous beliefs or opinions that shape people's view of the world derived from a reciprocal relationship between the ideas and attitudes of individuals and the structures within which they operate.

7 J. Solway, personal communication, 2010.

8 Ibid.

9 E. Whittaker, personal communication, 2011.

10 These struggles were occurring, for example in Algeria and Southeast Asia, and also in parts of sub-Saharan Africa (Guinea-Bissau and Mozambique) and South America (Colombia, Peru, Bolivia, and Chile).

11 E. Whittaker, personal communication, 2011. Whittaker's observation is corroborated by my own experience as editor-in-chief of *Anthropologica*. During my tenure, I noted that, while many anthropologists were in principle committed to publishing in a Canadian journal, they continued to turn toward American journals. The making of careers on the American scene is also noted by organizers of the national association on the viewing of missing names on membership and meeting participation lists.

3

Constructing Knowledge for Equity in the University: What Do the Categories Tell Us?

JOAN M. ANDERSON
IN DIALOGUE WITH NOGA GAYLE

Canada has become the destination of people of diverse backgrounds from around the globe. No longer privileging specific source countries, Canada's immigration policies have been deliberate in recruiting those best suited to Canada's labour market needs. In reflecting on the situation of women in the academy since the early 1980s, one must therefore take into account how the face of the academy has changed – from being comprised mostly of people of northern European descent to a more diverse ethno-cultural workforce and student population. Discourses of equity and equality, which once focused on gender, must now be inclusive of other social relations, such as race, which, within the Canadian state and everyday discourse, is signified by the category "visible minority," to refer to groups of people that are identifiable by skin colour and physical features as "different" from people of European heritage. In fact, Canada has taken proactive measures to address inequalities that may result from perceived "difference" and gender inequalities. Under the Federal Contractors Program (FCP), people who do business with the Government of Canada are expected to maintain a workforce that is representative of the Canadian workforce population. The FCP was established in 1986 to further the goal of achieving workplace equity for four designated groups: women, Aboriginal peoples, persons with disabilities, and members of visible minorities. Under the original program, organizations that wanted to bid on a federal contract were required to sign a Certificate of Commitment to implement employment equity, and establish an employment equity program that fulfilled the compliance reviews (HRSDC 2011). Iris Marion Young convincingly argues that "identifying inequalities according to group categories helps identify *structural* inequalities... Public and private bodies charged with collecting and analyzing data about the status and well-being of society's members, and their relative well-being, should continue to organize such data in terms of social groups and compare the standing of groups to one another" (2001, 2). Following from Young's position, one might argue that the categories constructed by the Canadian state provide guidelines for complying with government policies to recruit a workforce representative of the Canadian population.

However, the categories we use are not unproblematic. They often treat groups as homogeneous and therefore mask complex social relations. For example, the category "visible minority" and other categories that are used in equity discourses render invisible women of Colour within the university;[1] they also render invisible Aboriginal women and women with disabilities. These categories erase gendered structural inequalities as they intersect with race, class, and other social relations that organize the experiences of women within the academy. Thus, while the categories are well intended, and do indeed provide so-called hard data about the recruitment of designated groups, they fall short of telling us what we need to know about women from diverse backgrounds within the academy. Several questions, then, come to mind: How many visible minority women, Aboriginal women, and women with disabilities are there in the academy? What are their career trajectories? What are the structural barriers that organize their everyday experiences? How is "privilege" produced and reproduced in ongoing social interactions not only between men and women, but also among women? What are the nuanced institutional practices that position different people in particular ways? Let me emphasize that raising such questions is not intended as an indictment of equity policies and efforts that are being made to have a workforce representative of Canada's population. In fact, the federal government in power at the time this policy was initiated and implemented is to be applauded for taking such initiatives. Rather, I argue that if equity is to be achieved in academic settings, we need to know how many women are situated within the so-called designated groups, as well as the texture of their everyday experiences within the academy. Such investigation would not only refine how we count but, perhaps more importantly, it would shed light on institutional practices that organize women's everyday lives. There is much to be learned from the work of early feminist scholars, such as Dorothy Smith, who examined women's experiences as they are "embedded in the particular historical forms of social relations that determine that experience" (1987, 49), and scholars, such as Patricia Hill Collins (1990), who analyze the intersecting social relations that organize the lives of women from varied social locations.

In this chapter, I tackle how we might proceed to such inquiry as it pertains to women in the academy. My modest aim is to open up a dialogic space as we collectively work to achieve equity and social justice for all women in the academy, not only faculty women in tenure-track positions but also women who are employed in contractual and staff positions and as research associates or assistants, many of whom are women of Colour.

I begin with a story from the news media to illuminate some of the issues that are foundational to this discussion, and I examine the economic position of immigrants in the Canadian labour market. In the second section, I briefly discuss the Federal Contractors Program – an equity policy with which all institutions that receive federal funding exceeding a certain level, including universities, must comply. In the third section, I examine the ways in which the discourse of employment equity renders women of Colour invisible within the academy, and, in the fourth section, I discuss the need for dialogue to illuminate equity discourses along the axes of race, gender, class, and other forms of difference, as they intersect in everyday actions and interactions to reproduce structural inequalities. As Young points out, "social structures exist only in the action and interaction of persons; they exist not as states, but as processes" (2001, 13). Critical, reflexive analyses of these processes, I argue, might produce the kind of knowledge that will move us closer towards responsible social action and an equitable workplace. Throughout the chapter, I also draw on an interview with my colleague Noga Gayle, a sociologist and women's studies scholar who has over thirty years experience in academic life.[2]

BACKGROUND

On Saturday, 25 July 2009, a weekend special in the *Globe and Mail* on the recovery gap in the 2008–09 economic recession caught my attention. The story reported, "While tens of thousands have joined the ranks of the unemployed during a nerve-racking recession, new-comers to Canada are losing their jobs at more than three times the rate of workers who were born here – and may suffer much longer-lasting repercussions, even after the economy starts to recover" (Grant and Yang 2009, A8). A fifty-year-old South Asian man who had gone from being an experienced chemist to working a forklift to make ends meet was profiled to highlight the plight of immigrants. When immigrants can find a job, it is usually well below their skill level (Anderson et al. 2010). As this man, a participant in one of our research studies, puts it, "They always encourage me to do the dishes in a restaurant, or my wife to work in a sewing factory, I think this is very bad" (Anderson et al. 2010, 108).

The incomes of immigrants fall short of the Canadian-born popu-lation with a similar level of education. The 2006 Canada census statistics (Statistics Canada 2008) show significant income dispari-ties between Canadian-born and immigrant women, both with and without a university degree. For those with a university degree, the median annual earnings for immigrant women were $30,633, com-pared to $44,545 for Canadian-born women (or 45.4 per cent more than immigrant women). The median annual income for immigrant men with a university degree exceeded that of immigrant women but, at $42,998, was less than that of Canadian-born men, which stood at $62,566 (or 45.5 per cent more than immigrant men). The statistics reveal the continuing income disparities between men and women, but they also show that immigrant women are worse off than Canadian-born women. These income disparities prompt us to examine the multiple axes of differentiation (Brah and Phoenix 2004) along which analyses need to proceed.

But who are these immigrants? One might rightfully argue that "immigrant" status should not be conflated with persons who have been positioned as "visible minorities." We should note, however, that changes in Canada's immigration policy have resulted in a shift in the source countries from which immigrants have been coming since the 1980s. Since then, a majority of immigrants have come from Asian countries and the Philippines. Many are highly educated. After all, they were selected to meet Canada's labour market needs. Yet they cannot get the jobs they thought they would find in Canada.

New immigrants are not the only ones experiencing difficulties in Canada's labour market. So also are the children of earlier immi-grants. Monica Boyd's research with second-generation young adults shows that wide variations exist among different ethno-cultural groups in terms of earnings. Second-generation young adults who are black or Latin American do not do as well as other people of colour or other Canadian-born young adults, which "raises the possibility that the visible-minority second generation also will face greater challenges in the labour market compared with the non-visible minority second generation or the third-plus generation" (2008, 21).

The current labour market conditions are not new. They bear a striking resemblance to the issues that were paramount in 1985 when I was part of the BC Task Force on Immigrant Women. Reports at the time, including *Beyond Dialogue: Immigrant Women in Canada, 1985–1990* (Seydegart and Spears 1985), which arose from a national consultation commissioned by Multiculturalism Canada, document similar employment conditions to those in the 2006 Canada census statistics. In the 1980s, we advocated for more English-language training for women (in English-speaking Canada). We thought that language and education would open doors for immigrant women but the statistics tell us that this has not happened. Boyd's research (2008) suggests that the children of this earlier generation have not fared well in the labour market. The Federal Contactors Program has been in place since 1986, yet the statistics tell us that not much has changed in the lives of immigrants to Canada in close to thirty years, and so we must ask, why? I turn now to a brief review of the FCP especially as it pertains to women in the university.

DISCOURSE OF EQUITY: THE FEDERAL CONTRACTORS PROGRAM IN THE UNIVERSITY

Do members of designated minority groups with credentials to work in the academy fare better in academic settings? What are the employment opportunities for women of diverse backgrounds to acquire tenure-track teaching and research positions? What are their career trajectories when they compete successfully for these positions?

Some universities post their equity initiatives on their websites. For example, the University of British Columbia's (UBC) data for the four designated groups – women, Aboriginal peoples, persons with disabilities, and members of visible minorities – are comprehensive, accessible, transparent, and prominently displayed in the UBC

Workforce Data (2010). These data provide important information for all four categories across the university. I draw on these data *not* to focus on the practices within UBC but rather to open up a space for examining the knowledge produced from the categories constructed by the Canadian state to "further the goal of achieving workplace equity" in federally funded institutions. While the statistics available to the public on the UBC website are comprehensive, the limitations are discussed in the university's 2009 *Employment Equity Report*:

> This report represents a new chapter in the implementation of equity at UBC. This is the first report that exclusively uses the new data gathered from the UBC Employment Equity Census Questionnaire initiated in November 2008. As a result, no previous data is included for comparison purposes. This report will provide benchmark data for future years and a snapshot of the representation of the four designated equity groups across occupational groups, faculties, and administrative units at UBC. In addition, this report comes at a time when UBC has revised the Employment Equity Plan, which now falls under the university-wide, Equity and Diversity Strategic Plan. (UBC 2009)

UBC's second *Equity Report* (2010) continued to reflect equity as an evolving process, with a broader focus on diversity and inclusion, and tying in with other important planning initiatives at UBC. One suspects that subsequent reports will be further refined to show comparisons with earlier reports.

I draw on a small sample of statistics to show the kinds of statistics that were being used by UBC as a benchmark for future years. The statistics show four equity groups, crafted along the federal guidelines: women, Aboriginal peoples, persons with disabilities, and visible minorities. One example from the data of 2009 shows that, of the respondents to the questionnaire that was sent out to faculty and staff, among deans and principals, 28 per cent were women, 14.3 per cent were visible minorities, and 7.1 per cent were people with disabilities; among associate deans and principals, 40 per cent were women, 2.8 per cent were Aboriginal peoples, 5.6 per cent were visible minorities, and 2.9 per cent were people with disabilities. Among assistant deans, 56 per cent were women; there were no Aboriginal peoples, people with disabilities, or visible minority people in this category (UBC 2009, 15). The data from across Canadian universities – in compliance with the equity categories that have been designated by the Federal Contractors Program – do not distinguish between visible minority women and white women, or between visible minority women and visible minority men. As Noga Gayle suggests, the four employment equity categories are problematic. She reflects on whether the category "women" means white women. If we follow the guidelines for naming equity groups, what do these data tell us about women of Colour in the academy? How are they counted? Are they counted in two categories – "women" and "visible minority"? Or are they counted only in the category for women, thereby erasing differences between visible minority and white women? Or are they counted in the category visible minority along with men? If so, is it assumed that men and women in the visible minority category share similar experiences? Are gendered structural constraints erased among people designated as visible minority, Aboriginal peoples, and people with disabilities? For all we know, the visible minority persons hired could all be men; those in administrative categories could also be men. What do the categories tell us about ongoing social interactions that structure life opportunities for women of Colour, Aboriginal women, and women with disabilities? Ironically, the categories created by the Canadian state render invisible visible minority women in the workplace, at the same time that the state recognizes "women" as a category of persons who may experience discriminatory practices along the axis of gender. I suggest that these categories, as constructed by the Canadian state, are grounded less in an understanding of the complex and invisible ways in which race, gender, and disabilities intersect in the everyday and more on treating people within each of these groups as homogeneous. Gayle argues for the need to explore the inner workings of the categories, and what is happening in the day-to-day lives of people in the workplace. She makes the point, "From what I have seen, it would appear that life continues in the same way – and there are no ongoing discussions about the categories, and how people have been historically positioned. The infrastructure is not in place to bring about the changes that are needed for employment equity in the workplace." She later alludes to the curriculum as a possible site of change. I will take this up in a subsequent section of this chapter. So, while statistical knowledge about the categories, and the categories themselves provide one perspective on how different groups are positioned within the workforce, we need to question the assumptions that underpin the naming of categories and how we count within the categories. I turn, now, to a discussion of the category "visible minority."

"VISIBLE MINORITY": A CONSTRUCTION OF THE CANADIAN STATE

Terms such as "visible minority," Linda Carty argues, were "developed by the state in its attempt to ignore our heterogeneity and to marginalize us by erasing our different histories and cultures and their significance" (1991, 18n1). Carty uses the term "women of Colour," which "acknowledges our ethnic differences which is why Colour is capitalized, denoting more than different shades of skin colour" (18n1). She uses it to indicate "a common context of struggle based on shared systemic discrimination in the Canadian social and political context ... the term has a particular political relevance" (18n1).

I draw on Carty's work, and I use the term *women of Colour,* to show that the category "visible minority" as used by the Canadian state not only ignores heterogeneity; it subsumes women's subjectivities under those of men. And it erases systemic inequalities between men and women of Colour, and between women of Colour and white women. Such inequalities, I suggest, might begin to be detected by a critical analysis of the intersections of history, gender, class, race, and other social relations as they structure life opportunities, which may not be visible in the tools provided to employers by the Federal Contractors Program that are meant to address discrimination in the workplace.

Although the Federal Contractors Program aims to be comprehensive (HRSDC 2011), the subtle processes that hinder employment opportunities go well beyond objective indicators. The practices of hiring, retention, career advancement, salary increments according to rank or merit, are assumed to be rational and neutral processes, based on objective criteria and arrived at through transparent deliberation in committees. It is taken as a given that these decisions are not tinted by subjective factors. Yet individual subjectivities can play out, unwittingly, in what is defended as rational and transparent decision making. Everyday social interactions in the workplace, which might have their origins in the wider community from which some might be excluded by virtue of their histories, social location, and earlier life opportunities (e.g., membership in private clubs or places of worship that provide opportunities for mingling socially with colleagues) are not just "social activities" or "gatherings" that have no relevance to decision-making processes within institutional discourses. These are the contexts in which impressions begin to be formed and managed, and networks developed. Judgments about competence and other constraining and enabling factors (Young 2001, 6) within the formalities of the workplace, while not deliberate, may be influenced by these extraneous factors. While equity policies and directives can address issues that are accessible to interrogation (e.g., harassment in the workplace, or counting numbers in each category), the minutiae of everyday life that underpin structural inequities may be more elusive. We therefore need to open up a discursive space to critically examine the workings of the everyday that are hidden from view in the official policy discourse. I argue that making visible what is often invisible, and reflecting critically on how we might be complicit in reinforcing inequities, might move us towards the production of complementary knowledges for a more equitable and inclusive workplace.

OPENING UP A DISCURSIVE SPACE: THE SOCIAL PRODUCTION OF COMPLEMENTARY KNOWLEDGES

How might we open up a conversation at the policy level about the politics of difference in the university from a critical feminist anti-racist perspective? And how might we engage with policy makers about the categories that render invisible those who are labeled as visible?

As we reflect on the 2006 Canada census statistics, it is clear that immigrant women (read women of Colour, given the source countries from which people now come) are at the bottom of the income ladder in Canada. Their incomes are not on par with either Canadian-born men or women, or with immigrant men with comparable education. Are women of Colour in the academy (who likely immigrated to Canada, or are second or third generation) also at the bottom of the income pyramid? Where are they positioned in the academy? How do their salaries compare with that of their white colleagues with a similar level of education and experience? And, if there are income disparities, how are they justified? One can ask the same set of questions for Aboriginal women and women with disabilities. How are Aboriginal women positioned in universities? How are women with disabilities positioned?

I have alluded to the highly nuanced interactive processes within the workplace that often remain hidden from view yet need to be uncovered if we are to address the constraining and enabling factors (Young 2001, 6) that equity discourses are meant to address. Critical, decolonizing, feminist methodologies (e.g., Smith 1987; Collins 1990; Razack, Smith, and Thobani 2010; Bannerji 2000; Monture 2010; Altamirano-Jiménez 2010) that enable us to produce knowledge from the standpoint of white women, women of Colour, Aboriginal women, and women with disabilities in the workplace, and that critically analyze the context of their experiences may move us closer toward understanding the complex ways in which intersections of race, gender, class, and other multiple positionings work in hiring and retention practices and career progression. These methodologies should also help us understand how privilege is reproduced by those in positions of power within institutional settings. Such methodologies would not only include counting numbers or interviewing women in the university about their experiences. While women's experiences are a starting point, critical ethnographic methods are also needed to observe the positioning of women of Colour, Aboriginal women, and women with disabilities in the university (e.g., in contract positions, staff positions, or tenure-track positions), and to critically examine the decision-making processes related to their hiring and career progress. The analysis of such data, grounded in critical inquiry, goes beyond a politics of recognition (Taylor 1992) to make transparent the institutional practices and processes that organize women's experiences.

But who is best suited to conduct such an inquiry? Can we, as researchers and academics, critically examine the very processes of which we are a part? The caveat is that those of us who are steeped in the workings of the academy may unwittingly reproduce the very processes we may attempt to critique. Collins reminds us of the tension for feminist anti-racist scholars between an emancipatory scholarship and the difficulty of implementing this scholarship while using the language and implied worldview of dominant discourses. Collins observes that this dilemma confronts all of us who want to transform the "inner circle" of power and control: "One must first learn the language of the inner circle in order to understand what is being said and to gain credibility. Yet, assuming the language of dominant discourse, even using the language of objectified knowledge to critique its terms, weds the thinker to the relations of ruling supported by objectified knowledge" (1992, 79).

Collins reminds us of Audre Lorde's cautionary note that the master's tools will never dismantle the master's house (Collins 1992, 79). The issue for most of us in the academy is that, as we go about our everyday work, we too buy into the categories without critical questioning, as we participate in the highly nuanced political relations that organize the processes of hiring, retention, and progress within the academy; we too might fall into the trap of counting the numbers of "visible minorities," people with disabilities, and Aboriginal peoples as an indicator of the progress made by women of Colour, Aboriginal women, and women with disabilities.

Gayle reminds us that "the hiring process itself usually selects people whom the members of hiring committees assume will do well within the university structure. This is where proactive measures are needed in order to engage in a conversation about what it means to have a more diverse campus community. The hiring process is only a starting point. It is what happens after that is important." Indeed! Not only do some of us participate in the hiring process, we also participate in constructing what constitutes merit – and may unwittingly construct it as a "neutral" process. We participate in deliberations about who warrants getting tenure and promotion, and often see these as based solely on academic merit. This is not to question the integrity with which we approach our work. Rather, I turn the reflexive gaze onto myself as I look back on my participation in the academy since the 1980s. The conundrum is that we are part of the very structures we may attempt to critique, and in our everyday activities, we risk reproducing these structures. As Iris Marion Young reminds us, "structural injustice is produced and reproduced by thousands or millions of persons usually acting within institutional rules and according to practices that most people regard as morally acceptable" (2011, 95). When a woman of Colour, or an Aboriginal woman, or a woman with a disability is not hired for a position for which she seems qualified, when she is denied re-appointment or tenure, or when she is having difficulty navigating "the system," for example, we too might construct these as "objective" processes based on "evaluation" of her performance, without questioning the hidden dynamics that may be at work. So, is there a way out of this dilemma?

To return to my question, can we, as academic insiders, study the very processes of which we are a part? I would suggest that we must, and we can – from a particular methodological perspective, underpinned *by critical reflexivity*. In other words, we must continually turn the reflexive lens onto ourselves, and to our historical positionality, as we examine how various intersections, including class, race, caste, sexual orientation, and religion, work to control entry into positions of privilege and to silence some voices. We might want to ask ourselves, do we privilege one kind of analysis over the other, such as gender over race or vice versa? What assumptions do we make about people whom we perceive as "different"? How do these assumptions play out in everyday life? How has history and the racialization of the colonized Other shaped our viewpoints of who is "competent" and who is not? What are the markers of "fitting in," a phrase so often used, unreflexively, in our evaluations of the Other? Are we really informed about one another's worlds?

These might seem like trivial questions, but it became apparent to me in a conversation with a highly respected senior faculty woman some years ago that we should not take the understanding of one another's worlds for granted. This person, a white woman who had excelled in a scientific field dominated by men, found it surprising that women of Colour might not necessarily share her positive experiences of the changing climate for women in the academy. She had assumed that all women would have a similar experience, which suggested to me that she might not have been aware of the complex ways in which different social relations intersect to create our experiences. This encounter demonstrated that we are not always tuned into one another's worlds. As a privileged academic woman of Colour theorizing about intersectionalities, I know that I too may not fully grasp the complex intersections of gender, race, class, for example, as I work with women who are less privileged because of class positioning. This is not because theorizing eludes me, but in the workings of everyday life, it is sometimes difficult to fathom how these intersections play out. The issue may not be a single factor, but a number of factors may come together to form the web of structural constraints. Marilyn Frye's (1983) metaphor of the birdcage of oppression reminds us that while no one wire might be constraining, the wires are arranged in a specific way to imprison the bird. Likewise, multiple forces intersect with one another to constrain life opportunities. By drawing on research methodologies that are underpinned by critical self-reflection, and reflection on the historical processes that have shaped life opportunities, we may gain further insights into how systemic inequities work within the academy, and we may produce knowledge that might complement programs such as the Federal Contractors Program. Based on what we learn, a further step is to engage with the leaders in the institutions in which we work to explore proactive models of equity that would complement current practices.

Gayle suggests that the university curriculum should also be a site for fostering a genuine understanding and practice of the processes of employment equity, and an inclusive university community. She argues, "These concepts should also be reflected in the curriculum within the university – what we are really talking about is how to bring about change within the entire campus community because one would expect a university to provide leadership on such issues. This is the university's place within the community, and it is what citizens would expect of a university." More specifically, she explains, "We need to understand how the intersections play out in everyday life. For example, we have laws that make it illegal to discriminate on the basis of race, age, sexual orientation, and the like, yet the subtleties of everyday life can unmask how people can be denied access to certain positions, and therefore influence their class position in society. This is what people need to understand. We have come to talk about intersectionalities in unproblematic ways. Words are thrown around without contextual analyses."

CONCLUSION

Since writing an earlier draft of this chapter, Bill C-38, formally known as the Jobs, Growth and Long-Term Prosperity Act, an omnibus bill that amended dozens of pieces of legislation, was passed into law in June 2012. Marjorie Griffin Cohen points out that Part 4, Division 42 of Bill C-38 states that subsection 42(2) of the Employment Equity Act is replaced by the following: "The Minister is responsible for the administration of the Federal Contractors Program for Employment." Cohen notes that while this may appear innocuous, it "essentially does away with the legal requirement that contractors apply Employment Equity Act standards in their workplaces"

(Cohen 2012). We will have to wait and see how this plays out in the workplace.

It has been argued that the categories as presented in the Federal Contractors Program for Employment Equity, though well-intentioned, are problematic. While they are a starting point in addressing issues of equity in the workplace, as I have noted elsewhere, we need to make situated experience the starting point of analysis, instead of the "categories" in which we are positioned. Referring to Skeggs, I suggest that this is not to deny that the "social space we occupy has been historically generated" (1997, 8). Rather, understanding how the mediating circumstances of everyday life shape opportunities should be the focus of any inquiry (Anderson 2004, 14). This makes it all the more important for universities to provide leadership in the area of employment equity and to address some of the fundamental issues that have been raised in this chapter. As privileged academics, we have a social responsibility to produce knowledge for the greater social good; we also have the responsibility to communicate this knowledge in ways that can be taken up by policy makers. Although we have come a long way in producing knowledge about gender relations and have shed light on gender inequalities, enormous work lies ahead if our analysis is to embrace the multiple social locations from which we all live and work. We need to grapple with epistemological, theoretical, and methodological issues to critique the very processes we may be complicit in reproducing. And we need to learn from one another. As Homi Bhabha reminds us, "it is from those who have suffered the sentence of history – subjugation, domination, diaspora, displacement – that we learn our most enduring lessons for living and thinking" (1994, 172). Lessons learned, as we engage with one another to interrogate the experiences of women from multiple social locations within the academy, may be at the core of transformative praxis.

ACKNOWLEDGMENTS

I gratefully acknowledge funding from several sources that allowed colleagues and me to pursue a particular line of research addressing issues of equity and social justice over the years. I am indebted to the Medical Research Council/Canadian Institutes of Health Research and the Social Sciences and Humanities Research Council of Canada. We are especially indebted to the men and women who allowed us into their lives and shared their stories with us. I am grateful to the co-authors of the manuscript cited in this chapter, Joanne Reimer, Koushambhi Basu Khan, Laura Simich, Anne Neufeld, Miriam Stewart, and Edward Makwarimba.

Notes

1 The rationale for using the term *women of Colour* instead of *visible minority* becomes evident later in this chapter.

2 Gayle received her PhD in sociology from the University of British Columbia. She taught women's studies at UBC, and women's studies and sociology at Capilano University. She has co-authored a book, *Ideology: Structuring Identities in Contemporary Life*; and, co-edited *Sociological Theory: Essential Reading*, and *Learning to Write: Women's Studies in Development*.

PART TWO

Identities and the Everyday

Identities and the Everyday

ELVI WHITTAKER

Identity is a fitting discourse for understanding the diversity of experiences reported in this volume. Scholars now generally agree that identity is multiple and intersectional, that it is a construction of discourses that interact over time. Part One discussed attempts to bring new discourses and identities into existing frameworks. While this earlier section showed the drafting of identity through text and policy, the chapters in Part Two portray identity as the product of everyday living, continually manifested and tested in that context.

In all identities there is a presence of others. With these others, through mutual everyday interaction, identity is shaped. "Who we are to each other, then, is accomplished, disputed, ascribed, resisted, managed and negotiated in discourse" (Benwell and Stokoe 2006, 4). Identity is always a work in process, and each exchange, verbal or silent, is a form of identity talk. An identity portrait, therefore, is only possible because of the existence of others. Hélène Cixous observes, "the other in all his or her forms gives me I. It is on the occasion of the other that I can catch sight of me, or that I catch me at reacting, choosing, refusing, accepting" (1997, 13). A master of the emerging identity, Merleau-Ponty gives another compelling, if amusing, description of identity interactions: "I look at him. He sees that I look at him. I see that he sees that I look at him. I see that he sees it. He sees that I see that he sees it. The analysis is endless" (1964, 17). Such textual pointillism is reification beyond any call of duty. He crafts a fictive identity, an abstraction of a person who is much more excruciatingly aware of self than life actually encourages or even allows. Becoming, however, cannot "be wholly fictive. It must continually integrate events which occur in the external world, and sort this into an ongoing 'story'" (Giddens 1991, 54), a story that we tell about ourselves, or that others tell about us.

The university makes ascribed identities available through basic categories, such as work classifications or specific statuses. The institution is structured through these. As Jennifer Robertson suggests, identities are "packaged as 'ready to wear' consumables guaranteed to clarify one's location or position ... products of an identity politics that has been especially endemic to American universities" (2002, 788). Specific identities share properties, concepts that unify, and a common purpose. They make and protect boundaries, and manage behaviour. Newcomers to categorical enclaves cloak themselves in the desired attributes of belonging – the building blocks of identity – the required skills, proper language and jargon, the dress and demeanour, the worldview, the awareness of others in the same category and outside of it. In her chapter, Cecilia Moloney shows how scientists learn the right ways to claim and confirm their identity. Identity building is an ongoing preoccupation, to claim and demonstrate belonging (Lester 2011). Identities also know the perfunctory entitlements of their positions, which never prove to be as absolute as promised. Furthermore, universities have established ways of dealing with these identities, directing them, listening to them, simplifying them to basics.

Identity, whether ascribed or essentialist, is a daily preoccupation, and identity work is labour intensive. Identity boundaries, while providing some certainty, also make for solitudes that demand recognition. Such solitudes are usually not anticipated, nor are the many rituals of status affirmation or denigration, through small acts and small talk, that keep individuals in their assigned place. Linda Alcoff cautions that it is the "refusal to acknowledge the importance of difference in our identities that has led to distrust, miscommunication, and thus disunity" (2006, 6).

As we live intersectional lives, or exist, as Alfred Schutz (1967) would suggest, in "multiple realities," we also have co-existing identities, both inside and outside of the workplace. The multiple identities and the conviction that entitlements are being denied play a crucial role in narrative self-portraits. Each narrative reveals a preferred or cherished identity, kept alive by the cultural notion of an infinitely perfectible self. Kersti Krug, in her chapter, reports on the dissonance that occurs between her work identity and the entitlements that her educational accomplishments decree. For the mature graduates who Lelia Kennedy writes about in her chapter, an envisioned yet missing educated identity, thus a lingering solitude, drew them to the university in the first place.

UNIVERSITIES AS TRADITIONAL
AND CHALLENGED WORKPLACES

Universities, like all institutions, are coordinated conglomerates of enclaves and identities. They seem to follow a Linnean impulse to categorize, to cement these divisions into everyday behaviour to facilitate administrative control. Workplace slots and even their attendant stresses are considered the necessities of all successful operations.

These primary necessities have been exacerbated by the now well-known challenges and pressures facing universities in the twenty-first century: ever-present tuition hikes, cuts in public funding, diminishing endowments, salary freezes, cutbacks on services such as child care, and the continual charges of elitism. There are other challenges: that the great successes in the digital world have often been achieved without university educations; that the products of graduate schools have no ready employment markets; that universities exist because of the cheap labour of graduate students and under-employed academics (Taylor 2009, A23) who serve as an underclass of "support staff" (Wernick 2006). Linda Cohen's chapter shows how universities have integrated excluded populations who live uncertain lives economically as formal and permanent parts of their structure. Similarly, Patricia Kaufert's chapter shows how the work of research assistance is seldom permanent and lacks formal recognition in the production of knowledge. In addition, the university has been corporatized with profound consequences for the university as a workplace (Reimer 2004, McGettigan 2013). New descriptions appear – academic capitalism, privatization, market orientation, managerial capitalism, contractualism, global knowledge economy, commodified knowledge, McDonaldization, among many others. In short, universities become problematized institutions.

The essays in this collection are testimonials to the stress of living with diverse and demanding workplace cultures. Some argue that this is the manifestation of the remnants of a male-centred tradition and the all too slowly shifting accommodation of women. Also evident are the stresses of the restructuring university, which reveal an organizational life of pressure and dissidence. Amidst these stresses a wider question about the epistemology of the university rises. What epistemologies lay behind the traditional university and what worldviews and epistemologies are developing behind the emerging one?

INSIDIOUS WEBS OF POWER
AND TROUBLES TALK

The term commonly used to isolate the source of discontent and also to account for the maintenance of organizations is *power*. It upholds categories, just as it explains solitudes, loss of entitlements, and other workplace stresses. In a fundamental sense, as argued earlier, power does not exist. As Foucault explains, "Power in the substantive sense, *le pouvoir*, doesn't exist ... something which is a 'power' seems to ... be based on a misguided analysis" (1980, 198). It can be known only in interactions, and by its symptoms and metaphors. As Dorothy Smith suggests, "relations of ruling" hold the key to understanding power (1987, 1990). *Power* is a gloss for the complicated relationships that work to sustain it. Residing in the relationships between categories, participants themselves contribute to the maintenance of power. Regular workplace routines nourish it.

Identity responds to the manifestations of power. As Judith Butler notes, there is no status or existence without the acts that consolidate its reality (1990, 25). Without these symptoms, power has no presence. The narratives attest to the obfuscating nature of a power that contributes to "collective insecurity" – to use the term introduced in the chapter by Abramson, Rippeyoung, and Price. The sense of powerlessness hangs heavily in the air. Testimonials of repression by power, as well as an awareness of its vulnerabilities, are reflected in the proliferation of discourses of "empowerment," "enablement," and "entitlement."

All those who know the university as a workplace have heard assertions from various groups that "there would be no university" without them. Students claim that they make the university possible, that it is primarily for them and would cease to exist without them. Faculty makes the same claim. Administrators assert that the university only works because they organize it and thereby ensure its mission and continuance. Administrative assistants assert that the university would fall apart if they did not keep it functioning. Custodians and security staff claim that, without their work, the whole place would be uninhabitable. The title of the Wagner, Acker, and Mayuzumi book captures these claims – *Whose University Is It, Anyway?* (2008) – as does the photographic essay by Greg Halpern, *Harvard Works Because We Do* (2003). Spoken from positions of vulnerability, such proclamations are not uncommon in any workplace.

Few complaints about workplace exclusions are passed through the hierarchy to university governance. Official grievances are relatively rare. Everyday unofficial strategies, however, are common. The daily practice of troubles talk – the ever-present isolating of problems, sharing them, and making them public – is one of these. Another feature of ordinary discourse in universities, as in all institutions, is a collection of aphorisms, cautionary stories, morality tales, and other lore from the past. Fictional or historically verifiable, they make up a familiar underground culture. These tales are often the work of generations and are summoned as solace in cases of identity uncertainties and other deprivations. Aubrecht and Lay, in their chapter, report that at stressful times students resort to what they call "story time," the sharing of experiences. The feminist archive is rich with accounts about the lowly position of women, from both authored and unauthored repertoires, bearing witness to what was once considered the proper order of things. Stories help to calibrate contemporary problems and assess progress. The following stories come from authors who are part of this volume, or an earlier related project.

In the 1950s, as a recent widow with a young son, Lelia Kennedy enrolled as a new undergraduate and sought accommodation on campus. The university had special quarters for married students with children but to qualify as a single mother she had to be interviewed by the head of student housing, a position held by a high-ranking male dean. In the course of the interview, she was closely questioned about her husband's death. She was given no immediate answer about whether she qualified for quarters on campus and was sent back to the main office to which the dean phoned his decision, to be relayed to her by the clerk. She was informed that the dean would not permit her to live on campus because it would be "too dangerous, too enticing for the young men there." She was left to make what she could of this.

Anthropologist Judith Brown relates her experiences as a new graduate student at Harvard in the 1950s, when women doing graduate work at men's universities were an anomaly (2010). Some schools, such as Princeton, did not accept women at all. Harvard accepted them with provisos, housing being one of them. There were new dormitories for male graduate students; co-ed dormitories had yet to be invented. Accompanied by her mother, to give her credibility, she tried many Victorian rooming houses where landladies justified excluding women because "they make coffee and wash clothes." Finally, she was accepted into a mixed household of boarders, mostly non-students. The next shock was that some academic facilities were closed to women, including the Lamont Library. Further, a woman invited to lunch at the Faculty Club was expected to arrive by the back service entrance. Perhaps the greatest obstacle to her academic career was finding a mentor to supervise her work. The reasoning was familiar – men had careers, women had marriage and children. The career part was not at all surprising; women could seldom find academic positions. Nor were there any female role models at Harvard. Only one woman with tenure, the anthropologist Cora DuBois, occupied an endowed chair to be specifically held by a woman. There were no other women with tenure or even on the tenure track. Finally, the Harvard degrees of MA and PhD were not granted to women. Judith's choices were to receive a doctorate from Radcliffe or a Harvard Ed D. In contrast to this almost feudal past, it needs to be mentioned that, in 2015, the president of Harvard is a woman, two out of twelve deans and six out of ten vice-presidents are women, and there are other female senior administrators.

Canada was not much different. As Stalker and Prentice inform us, Bishop's University barred women from entering the faculty commons room by the front door, women students could not be on campus after mid-afternoon, and some professors stated that higher education for women should prepare them to teach high school. Women were reminded of the choice before them – marriage or graduate work. The University of Western Ontario obliged women faculty to retire at sixty while men could work until sixty-five. They also had an informal departmental protocol of having less than one woman for every five faculty (Stalker and Prentice 1998, 19; see also Gillett 1981). Of course, the preference for appointing male faculty, as women "get married and have children," has been widely practised through many generations.

The final story is one of my own. In the course of a graduate theory seminar, I described to my professor the impenetrability of two texts by Talcott Parsons. In my untutored opinion, they did not capture the social structure as I experienced it. The professor paused, obviously seeking a way to reassure me, while remaining true to the writings he had chosen, and responded quite gently, "Girls can't do theory." I was the only "girl" in that seminar. Knowing his intention to reassure me, I was puzzled and depressed by this total and completely impenetrable exclusion, and it remained with me long after as an enigma, unbelievable and yet to be unravelled. He clearly thought abstract reasoning was not within a woman's domain. I bear him no ill will; he was a creature of his times. A few years later, at a time when not all universities in Canada offered doctorates in every subject, the same professor and his colleagues sent outstanding male graduates to Berkeley, Princeton, and Harvard, and a female student, deemed worthy of continuing, to Duke.

Such narratives are, in the main, oral histories, found here and there. The history of women's experiences in earlier university settings remains to be written. Those already reflecting on these issues are academics, including Manda Cesara (1982), Laurel Richardson (1997), Esther Newton (2000), and Carolyn Ellis (2004). See also the collection edited by Robbins (2008). The early university lives of non-academic women also have yet to be gathered. Isabella Losinger, however, writes of Dorothy McMurray, who as a secretary to four McGill presidents over thirty-four years, is a legendary figure in the administrative world.

The themes of identity and power, as they manifest themselves in everyday interactions, are the other side of the coin to formal and documentary knowledge covered in Part One. Yet the policies and structures discussed in these foregoing chapters are the essential context for the experiences described in the chapters that follow.

Threats to career and security are detailed by Patricia Palulis's recounting of the situation that followed her introduction of a challenging new theoretical perspective, *écriture féminine*, that collided with a tenure decision. In her ambiguous position, the relevant details of documentary and everyday knowledge were hidden from her, even as they were part of daily interactions around her, leaving her to struggle with obscure inferences. The elusive interpretations of merit are basic to her narrative. Her account recalls the traumas of an earlier generation that introduced feminist writings to universities.

The chapter by Cecilia Moloney clearly shows the place of formal knowledge in the shaping of scientific identity. The complexities of claiming such an identity are dependent on acquiring formal engineering knowledge, being able to produce documentary evidence of it, as well as displaying the everyday voice that validated the belonging. The status of academic women scientists is discussed, raising familiar issues about merit.

Solitudes among university students as described by Katie Aubrecht and Isabel Mackenzie Lay tend to congeal into new solidarities and the emergence of a collective consciousness. They highlight the familiar solitudes of gender, disability, sexual identity, motherhood, and ethnicity among students and how such solitudes create safe havens, which, in their turn, create solitudes of their own. The student experience is replete with rites of denigration from male students and professors.

Lelia Kennedy raises the question of whether age is a determining variable in university education. She chronicles the identity experiences narrated by mature women who chose a university education later in life. Their initial decisions, their experiences as students, and their coping with dual responsibilities of school and family are considered. While their pre-university solitude is the initial motivator, their position in the exclusionary category of "older student" seemed without tension.

In her chapter, Isabella Losinger reports on the experiences of "support staff" or administrative assistants. She refers to the feudal nature of the academy and to faculty and administrators' descriptions of this part of the workforce as "after-thoughts" or "non-thoughts." Despite proclamations of inclusivity, despite their presenting the public face needed to run the university, these workers are rendered invisible. Their wide technical and historical knowledge is ignored.

As a non-academic administrator, Kersti Krug writes of conflicting identities. Her experiences are shaped by policy, job categories, and guidelines. She describes how the documentary, and even the everyday knowledge, that determines her welfare in the workplace, is hidden beyond her reach. She refers to her experiences as those of a "caste system" with its expected by-products of status denigration, confusion, and threatened self-esteem.

Workplace insecurity is a dominant theme in Linda Cohen's chapter about teaching on limited contracts. Part-time faculty, necessary for a university's ability to deliver its product, are academically qualified, yet financially and emotionally isolated and forced to deal with continuing underemployment and uncertainty. They are further marginalized by faculty and by students. As women outnumber men in these positions, the category is sometimes referred to as "the penalty for rearing children."

Patricia Kaufert describes how research nurses, working on medical research projects, are the public face of their projects in their responsibilities for acquiring subjects, explaining the research, dispelling patients' uncertainties, and obtaining signatures to the all-important informed consent forms, without which no human research can proceed. In contrast, they have no intellectual input on interaction with patients, ethical issues, or on the nature of the very forms they administer. They are a "missing link" – necessary but unrecognized in knowledge production.

A "collective insecurity," an undermining of status and self-confidence, still exists for women faculty at some universities as Zelda Abramson, Phyllis Rippeyoung, and E. Lisa Price report. They belie the argument that significant gains have been made by women in universities, arguing that women remain disadvantaged in many parts of university life, in formal policy and in everyday interaction. The authors point to hiring policies, salary negotiations, promotion applications, heavy service loads, influence in committee work, and the problems of child care to make their case. These conditions evoke memories of an earlier age.

4

Tenure (Un)Secure/d:
As Words Go Into Labour

PATRICIA PALULIS

All of the residents of Academia are naturalized, none was born there, all are refugees from somewhere else, and, like most refugees, they have a simultaneous love and loathing for their new home, a place where their foreignness can suddenly confront them, just as they were feeling settled.

Pam Shurmer-Smith, "Hélène Cixous"

TROUBLING TENANCIES
IN THE LAND OF ACADEMIA

In setting the stage for a mise en scène in an imaginary land, I begin with an epigraph by Pam Shurmer-Smith. Working with the entry of feminist scholar Hélène Cixous into Academia, Shurmer-Smith maps out the cartography of a land where the residents are designated with refugee status. I have long struggled with that sense of foreignness – a refugee, transporting a discursive space from elsewhere. As I was preparing my dossier for tenure and promotion, I was writing a paper to submit to a special issue of the e-journal *Educational Insights*. I was drawn to the call for papers on academic pathologies. I wanted to work at deconstructing myself as a resident of this strange new land, querying my desire to seek entry into a space of increasing estrangement (Palulis 2009). At the same time, it was an enticement to work within a multiplicity of solitudes to open spaces where something else might happen. In a refugee camp, you begin to construct a home, a hut papered with words and images. Acker, Webber, and Smyth (2012) address the "acute levels of anxiety"

(745) related to the tenure experience. As a *bricoleur*, you work with whatever is at hand, weaving in the multiple strands of anxious threads. In questing for tenure, are we not seeking a refuge for academic freedom? I was drawn to the notion of "refugee status" in the Land of Academia because it draws attention to the horror and terror of what happens when things go wrong.

Reading Shurmer-Smith, I had finally found a home not within my faculty but in this space of a mise en scène in the Land of Academia. A mise en scène can be conceived as "the staging of a scene for the camera" (Dexter and Bush 1994, 3). I am setting the stage for the reader to imagine a wayward journey in the Land of Academia. I do not know how to tell my story and so the fragments are always open to rearrangement. There are stories that cannot yet be told and so the reader is invited to write them in. David Bate constructs mise en scène as a place of work, as a work site: "*Mise en scène* emphasizes more than just adding together elements of staging in any literal, technical sense as 'mere technique' or a question of 'good composition,' it is rather the basis of what *constitutes* the actual place and space of the image, of what it signifies. In this sense, *mise en scène* offers a concept which recognizes the image of a place of *work*, a site of meaning and production, of precisely *staging*" (1994, 5, emphasis in original).

Within this place of work, I situate my lived experiences as a site of production with fragmented meanings. I re-enact the difficulties of obtaining tenure and promotion to stage a mise en scène as to what it signifies for me to continue my story as a resident in the Land of Academia. As refugees gain landed immigrant status, they become the gatekeepers for reviewing new refugees. This is where the trouble began. As the gatekeepers began to do their work, I was held accountable. I found myself entangled in the discursive spaces that had journeyed with me from the University of British Columbia on the West Coast – spaces that have sheltered me and inspirited my writings. A discourse became a contentious space for "what it signifies" (Bate 1994, 5) for a group of jurors, that is, estranged and alien. Troubled and troubling.

Within the imaginaries of Academia, from the days of my doctoral studies at UBC, I have been seduced into the language of *écriture féminine*. Hélène Cixous contends that women "become" through writing (1986). Reading Trinh T. Minh-ha, they "become" intransitively: "To write is to become. Not to become a writer (or a poet), but to become, intransitively. Not when writing adopts established keynotes or policy, but when it traces for itself lines of evasion" (1989, 18–19). No objects in sight. For me, *écriture féminine* became an escape from the caged templates of pedagogical discourse – a space in which experimentation with and away from genre was welcomed. It was another way of being/becoming through language – where words were not archived with sacred meanings, where you did not know in advance what was going to happen as words went into labour. It was about the excitation of the unknown, the wandering trailers, the heady theoretical spaces, the entanglements with fiction, and the embodiment of lived experience. I was working and writing as a school psychologist when I stumbled into this other space of writing. Frustrated with assigning numbers and labels to students, I was drawn to other ways of being and becoming through difference. So powerful were these discursive spaces that I left school psychology and returned to a position as classroom teacher.[1]

I have worked with this way of becoming through language – finding ways to keep it alive with my students in the Land of Academia. And, yet, I cannot ignore the credentials of the gatekeepers of Academia. And so I circle the text and seek other exits and entrances. There are now many journals calling for innovations in genre and presentation. To dwell in solitudes became a space rich with generative possibilities. In the Land of Academia we are all trafficking in words. We can get into trouble evading the templates and the preferred destinations. And where do the lines of evasion go? Towards and away from tenure.

Every land has a language. In Trinh's words, "For academics, 'scholarly' is a normative territory that they own all for themselves, hence theory is no theory if it is not dispensed in a way recognizable to and validated by them. The mixing of different modes of writing; the mutual challenge of theoretical and poetical, discursive and 'non-discursive' languages ... all these attempts at introducing a break into the fixed norms of the Master's confident prevailing discourses are easily misread, dismissed, or obscured in the name of ... 'scholarly work'" (1992, 138). The mixing of these modes of writing works well for a *bricoleur*. A colleague and I wrote a performative auto/ethno/graphy about our teaching lives in the Land of Academia (Morawski and Palulis 2009). I wanted to open these spaces with my students and was excited by the creative assignments and theses they produced. Although students were initially resistant to my invitation for composing auto/ethno/graphies, at the end of a course, I was instructed to "never" not offer this assignment.

At the same time, I was beginning to feel the consequences of experimentation with genre. Administrative attempts to remove me from a doctoral committee became a paper (Palulis 2012). Assertive knocks on my office door requested how a student's thesis title was related to education. Another paper to be written. Each battle incensed my desire to persist and to resist. Returning to Trinh: "Academics, infatuated with their own normalization of what constitutes a 'scholarly' work, abhor any form of writing that exceeds academic language and whose mode of theorizing is not recognizable, hence not classifiable as 'theory' according to their standard of judgment" (1992, 154). If Trinh persevered, so could I.

Often a land has more than one language. I am working in a bilingual university situated in-between two official languages – in-between two solitudes: French and English. But in the corridors and on the grounds, the cadences of a polyglossia resound with the rich resonances of multiple languages. My working language is English but English is not my language. I have lost my languages. I draw once more from Trinh who startles us with a reminder that we "profoundly" speak "different languages" as we speak in English (2005, 121). For those at the entry level of Academia, perhaps the standard dialect is imperative. In their study of tenure in Canada, Acker, Webber, and Smyth contend, "The novice academic must conform to the norms of the institution, the department and the discipline" (2012, 745). For some of us, it becomes a site of active resistance. Arriving late in Academia as I did, it was impossible to be obedient to dictations and templates. Acker and co-authors, in their readings, evoke "an uneasy although vague suspicion that something about the procedures is not working for particular categories of people" (756). Quoting Foucault, they contend that the tenure review is an examination combining "the techniques of an observing hierarchy and those of a normalizing judgment. It is a normalizing gaze, a surveillance that makes it possible to qualify, to classify and to punish" (Foucault 1977, 184).

Shifting suddenly from an elementary school site on the Pacific coast to an academic site in the nation's capital, I found my "self" situated within the colonial legacies of two imperial languages in a bilingual university. Arriving in the Land of Academia in advance of

my collection of books, I remember my excitement in locating an
air-conditioned corridor that took me to the university library.
Carrying armloads of books back to my office space, I burrowed
into the shelter of texts. I was hungering for the writings to begin to
emerge from the readings – consuming and consumed by the readings. Already drawn to Julian Wolfreys (1997) translating fragments
of Sylvie Germain, I located the original French version of her text
in my new library. Reading between languages, I was reading as
Wolfreys translates. I was seduced into exquisite spaces of difficulty.
Insatiable affinities draw me to the French writers and scholars and
to those who read and write nearby. I am writing in English(es) while
prowling around the French book. I could identify with the phantom
woman, imagined by Germain:

> Elle est entrée dans le livre. Elle est entrée dans les pages du livre
> comme un vagabond pénètre dans une maison vide, dans un jar-
> din à l'abandon (1992, 13).

> She entered the book. She entered the pages of the book as a
> vagrant steals into an empty house, or a deserted garden (1993, 27).

MAILBOXES, MOUSETRAPS, AND AN ELEVATOR
RIDE TO THE FOURTH FLOOR

It is the month of May, the beginning of the spring session, and I am
preparing to meet a new group of students in a graduate course.
I check my mailbox on the third floor before taking the elevator up
to my office on the fourth floor. I open the white letter size envelope, begin to read the cover letter and I am stunned. I am alone in
the elevator reading the text. The cover letter is reminding me of
Article 13.3.1 of the Collective Agreement and advising me that a
member may forward a letter of disagreement to the employer's liaison officer within ten working days ... Tenure and promotion have
been deferred.[2] The Faculty Teaching and Personal Committee
(FTPC)[3] unanimously decided: "Assistant Professor Palulis' contribution to scholarship and expansion of knowledge within her area
of specialization is not satisfactory. Nevertheless, the members of the
FTPC are fully aware that their assessment of Dr. Palulis' scholarly
performance does not coincide with the generally positive assessment of her research accorded by the three evaluators."

I have almost always been in school as a student and/or teacher. I had just turned sixty-five; I started teaching when I was eighteen. Suddenly, I am declared not satisfactory. There are no words to describe the sense of degradation. My life as a fraud passes before me. Horror sets in. I somehow got through the opening session of that new class. The horror persists. Time does not heal. But words do become a workout. Words go into labour.

Not wanting to go into this tenure process blindly, I had attended a workshop on tenure and promotion. I remember a liaison officer being there from the Association of Professors of the University of Ottawa (APUO) who told us to come directly to the APUO office if we received an unfavourable response. I had measured myself against recent colleagues who had successfully gone through the process. I had paid attention to the comments on my contract renewals. I had been encouraged to work on my French. My concern was being assessed for passive bilingualism. I had been taking group lessons and I had a private tutor. I was told that I was the first person required, for purposes of tenure, to take a French test at the Second Language Institute. To my relief and my amazement, I obtained the level of scores necessary for passive bilingualism. And, of course, I had considered the worst possible scenario and was imagining other options.

The white envelopes bearing the university letterhead create a communal enterprise. We collect mail for each other; we ask our colleagues to read our letters for us; we ask them to be with us when we read; we fear being alone with these letters. There are furtive phone calls, coded messages, cups of chai, frosted mugs of beer, carafes of wine, tears, and blasphemy in both official languages – as signs and signals of our movements, stalled delays and detonations. And sometimes there is a chiming of champagne glasses at Zoe's in the Chateau Laurier to celebrate a victory.

It is not just the personal shock with which you must learn to live, you must also learn to cope with how your colleagues begin to treat you. You hear driftings of conversation – from a dinner table in Toronto – that not just anything goes – in the corridors – the reviewers were her friends – and waiting for the elevator – you have to have some standards – and the most stunning – the jurors could read between the lines – they knew the reviewers didn't think that you were ready. Just as Trinh refers to anthropology "better defined as 'gossip' (we speak together about others) than as conversation"

(1989, 68), I found myself the object of gossip never drawn into a conversation on my situation. Trinh's contention: "Scientific gossip, therefore, often unveils itself as none other than a form of institutionalized Indiscretion" (68). As Martha Piper contends, "Well, we tend to eat our own" (Thorne, in this volume). I was a doctoral student when Piper became president of UBC.

I have my own gossip to disperse. I was a volunteer in Spartacus co-operative bookstore on Hastings Street. We had a diverse cliental from street people to politicians to university professors. One day, I overheard two professors standing in front of the philosophy section "gossiping" about the new president. As the word "woman" was evoked with some disdain, one glanced over at me – a woman behind the counter, and one who had been in one of his seminars. I lowered my gaze in embarrassment. And still I was not a feminist. It has taken more than a decade to be able to maintain my gaze – here in a mise en scène. I became a feminist when I entered the Land of Academia.

Some of my colleagues began their farewells on the stairwells and in the corridors. Some were preparing to replace me on their graduate student committees. But most were silent. A few were supportive and that was how I survived. But the solitudes deepened. My estrangement became more isolating. Unless I had to teach or attend meetings, I stayed away from campus, going in at night under cover of darkness to check my mailbox waiting for another mousetrap to snap at my fingers. It was difficult to be on campus. I needed to be: Medicated. Drugged. Sedated. I found solace in my at-home library. And I read the personal stories of tenure denials in the *Chronicle of Higher Education*. I became obsessive in tracking down and following the stories of those lived experiences. I wanted to know how people survived the dreadful sense of failure.

TEXT, LIES, AND (MIS)REPRESENTATIONS

In the process of peer review for tenure and promotion, we await judgment from several levels of jurors sifting through multiple layers of text. Our dossiers are sent to three external reviewers. Although we are invited to submit three names to a pool of possible reviewers, we do not know who is selected by the FTPC. As the evaluations from the external reviewers began to arrive, in accordance with procedure, copies were forwarded to me by the dean.[4] They were stronger than I could have hoped for. I was expecting to get tenure after the third letter had arrived. I have struggled with my recollections of anticipation. After receiving all three letters, I had accepted supervision of two more graduate students and I was horrified that I had placed them in jeopardy. Put in my place, I was informed that they were not "my" students, they were "our" students. I took this to mean that I was easily expendable. But I was grateful that the faculty would take care of the students. In the meantime, my contract was extended for the time of the proposed deferral. As I began to plan out a strategy for my defense, I was attentive to the language of the reviewers and how it was interpreted in the minutes of the FTPC. One of my external reviewers commented,

> Dr. Palulis' chosen field could be described as post-reconceptualist curriculum theorizing with a particular emphasis on the post-structural understandings of language (and literacy). From this stance, all theorizing is communicative specifically linguistic and textual, and thus all radical re-formulations of curriculum and all forms of educational theorizing required for democracy and the urgent rebirth of public schools and the re-energizing of the work done within them, require challenging the hegemony of the very language used in educational discourse and in discourse about education. (Reviewer #1)

Pleased to be recognized in this space, I was shocked with how it would be interpreted by the members of the FTPC as stated in the minutes: "The three external evaluators all comment on the relatively marginal nature of Assistant Professor Palulis' scholarly work." The minutes then focus on the reviewers' comments that depict examples of marginality. The FTPC startled me with the word "despite":

> Despite these observations, it should be noted that all three evaluators generally regard assistant Professor Palulis' work in a favorable light. One evaluator observes that "Dr. Palulis has demonstrated a commitment to scholarship and a level of productivity and quality that is equivalent to other scholars of her rank and stage of career ... [and that] the originality of thinking and presentation in her scholarship is excellent and beyond that of most scholars at her stage of career." Another reviewer has observed that Dr. Palulis' conceptual work "is impressive in its

theoretical rigor" and demonstrates her "ability to challenge the grand narratives of academic discourse." The reviewer concludes by stating "she is making an important contribution to the scholarly community in curriculum theorizing in North America."

How is it then that my contribution to scholarship was designated not satisfactory? If the members of the FTPC did not understand the connections between the marginal positionings and the ways in which words went into labour in those spaces, how would they understand an even "stronger contribution?" I confess to being spiteful here. (Des)spitefully so. I apprentice myself with Avital Ronell: "Certain things unhinge, attack, terrorize, enrage, and for me certain more-or-less invasive philosophemes, common or undetected, provide an adequate interpretive guide – they get me going" (2010, 23).

The word "despite" became the hinge that drove my response. The word that unhinged me. The word that enraged me. That drove my desire to take on the fight. What was troubling was the separation of marginality, subversion, nonlinearity, and disruption from the "required for democracy, and the urgent rebirth of public schools and the re-energizing of the work done within them" articulated by a reviewer. I am left questioning the intentions of the FTPC. A further irony was that the Faculty of Education would soon be hosting the Provoking Curriculum Conference. The keynote speakers were members of my "marginal" community. An assessment becomes, in my reading, a (mis)representation of text.

I have worked for decades in school systems in both urban and remote places in Canada spanning spaces from urban Vancouver to the hamlet of Pond Inlet on the north end of Baffin Island, and internationally, as an expatriate, in England, Japan, and Libya. Teaching bachelor of education students, I am mindful of the children they will be teaching. The impact of what we "do" and how we "teach" in the Faculty of Education is immense. I have always been drawn to the outliers – to the margins – to the differences. I have often been horrified with how we assume that children can be read, marked, contained in schooled grammar – in schooled templates: "I have only begun to recognize the complexities of the colonization mechanisms in the Land of Academia. As professors colonized by the institution, we colonize our students who are eager to perform on their students what has been done to them. There are those who refuse the colonization process and who return from practicum shattered by what they see happening to children. This is a gap that is still alive and this is where the work must be done. Not to close the gap but to work in the gap. To work in the space of the wound" (Palulis 2009, 4).

Somehow we must retain these student teachers because this is where radical hope resides. Perhaps I persist in pedagogical spaces to work with the wounds of my complicities in practices that I have come to resist. It has been a very long journey. My many years of working with primary/junior students give me the courage to resist the mandates of Academia. My young students taught me that school sucks. That provocation became my working space. I am learning to work with the transformative possibilities of failure. Drawn to difficult spaces with Trinh, I take shelter in her words: "Here, the fact that one is always marginalized in one's own language and areas of strength, is something that one has to learn to live with" (1992, 156). These difficult spaces are both sites of struggle and sites of production in the workplace.

The journals that have published my papers are those of the reconceptualization movement – a movement that draws from the social sciences. A journal in which I had a co-authored paper published was declared not a peer-reviewed journal. The co-authored paper included a postscript about the reviewers' requests for revisions. I myself had reviewed an article for this journal. Who determined it was not peer-reviewed? Based on what evidence? Was this a "lie" on my part? Was this rigged evidence against me? I do not know what happened or why. I write to the editor, who replies, "Isn't academia a bummer?" I receive a detailed explanation of the peer-review process to include in my step one grievance brief.

It was no longer about tenure and promotion. It was about language and (mis)representation. I was introduced to the procedural language of a collective agreement. I declined the deferral and the generous offer of a time extension for re-application following the pre-grievance meeting. I felt that my liaison officer was trying to rescue me and was doing it very well. I did not want to be rescued. My application would now proceed to the Joint Committee (members of the Senate and the Board of Governors)[5] and I had been cautioned that the Joint Committee would likely agree with the FTPC, which is what happened.

I begin to prepare for step one grievance procedures. I request from the APUO a change of liaison officer; I seek out a lawyer in a law firm dealing with labour issues and human rights. The lawyer was recommended by a colleague in the Faculty of Law. Interdisciplinary connections are at work here. I present my case to a new liaison officer. I bring copies of my writing. Viewing the work, the liaison officer immediately understands that the genre of writing is integral to the work. I present my situation to my lawyer. I need confirmation beyond the support of friends and colleagues. I request that the lawyer read my external review letters and the FTPC minutes. My contention of misrepresentation is supported. I become union representative for my faculty – a member of the board of directors for APUO. I begin to prepare my brief. My initial writing is a rant. I am angry and need to write my way through that anger. My rant is filed away as a therapeutic production. With guidance from my new liaison officer, I begin again.

PEER REVIEW (REDUX)

My external reviewers refer to my venues for dissemination. The reviewers' positionings determine the degree of marginality – the tenor of marginality – the momentum of marginality:

> Her positioning with the larger field of curriculum studies, and language and literacy education (whether first or second language, adult or early literacy) in particular, is neither popular nor mainstream. The ramifications of this are that periodicals that may be deemed marginal by the mainstream have published her work. (Reviewer #1)
>
> Writings that attempt to deconstruct the linear and subvert norms of academic discourse are often more challenging to publish. It is encouraging to see that Pat Palulis's collaborative writing with Marylin Low has found a valuable academic home in several refereed curriculum journals that are well respected in the field of curriculum studies and have a wide readership. (Reviewer #2)
>
> JCT is considered to be a good journal. One possible caveat is that Dr. Palulis is on the board of this journal. However the audience for this genre of writing is quite small and it is understandable that she does not have a lot of publishing outlets. It is likely that this is not a conflict of interest as there are 20 academics on the editorial board. (Reviewer #3)

The peer reviews are, in turn, reviewed by the FTPC. I sense that I am "rejected and retrieved by different communities" (Trinh 1992, 156). I was reassured by being located in marginal spaces. I would drink my morning coffee – organic fair trade (Bohemian Dark Roast) – cocooning in marginality. I would reread my letters seeking these affirmations for my struggles, my insecurities, my doubts about my "self" about the space of my "work" about the intentions of my work. I was comforted with my positioning by the reviewers. I did not want to be considered mainstream. I have never been popular. I wanted both more and less than that. I wanted intransitively with Trinh and Cixous. I wanted whatever there was to want with no object in sight. I am still curious about the possibilities yet-to-come. Rereading now from the outside in, I am both more and less sympathetic toward my faculty jurors. The concept of marginality is complicated. Mainstream is there. It cannot be ignored. However, taking notes on the margins of mainstream would seem to be a task worthy of scholarly activity in the Land of Academia. I wanted to do fieldwork as homework with Kamala Visweswaran (1994). I felt the gravity of my intentions heeding Gayatri Spivak "to keep responsibility alive in the reading and teaching of the textual" (2003, 101–2). And following in the "rootprints" of Cixous I want to say: "my texts recycle themselves, but I don't think they repent" (1997, 64).

Mainstream has a complicated relationship with the margins. Handel Wright, in an article in *Educational Researcher*, one of the peer-reviewed journals of the American Educational Research Association (AERA), contends that the "*Journal of Curriculum Theorizing* (JCT) continues to lead the way in showcasing … avant-garde work" (2000, 5). He further locates the space of JCT as "cutting-edge curriculum theorizing" (5). A mainstream journal from the prestigious AERA, then, acknowledges the "marginal" journal JCT as cutting edge. Wright acknowledges the confluence of multiple discursive threads: "Heavily influenced by the discourses of feminism, postmodernism, poststructuralism, and psychoanalysis, and the participation of increasingly influential feminists such as Patti Lather, Janet Miller, Deborah Britzman, and Elizabeth Ellsworth, the JCT conference … is one site one might be tempted to identify as a space where 'reconceptualization' has become the virtually uncontested norm" (2000, 5).

Wright continues the conversation as he cites from Janet Miller on "a riotous array of theoretical approaches," all of which, Wright contends "need to be held in productive tension with one another" (10). My mentors in the Faculty of Education at UBC had introduced me to this space of tension. Enticed, I strayed from the Faculty of Education to take graduate courses in human geography, critical ethnography (with Elvi Whittaker), and Asian studies. In time, I found my reading space in texts and textures that evoked an unsettling of stability. Trinh's work encouraged me to persist in these spaces: "As feminists have insistently pointed out, women are not only oppressed economically, but also culturally and politically, in the very forms of signifying and reasoning. Language is therefore an extremely important site of struggle. Meaning has to retain its complexities, otherwise it will just be a pawn in the game of power" (1992, 154).

How might it be possible for a jury to retain the complexities of meaning? Or had words become pawns in the game of power? How is the complexity of meaning undermined by the imperative of counting? Did a journal become a pawn in the game of power? The article declared not peer-reviewed was one in which my name was first in the linearity of positioning (Palulis and Low 2005). Removing it would disrupt the intended turn taking of co-authorship. I have learned painfully that the count is an imperative. But if numbers were the mainstream game, why had I been requested to remove from my CV a paper that had been submitted for peer review?[6] I was told that everyone had to do this. However, as I spoke with my colleagues, this was not the case.

The mise en scène is a metaphor. Behind the scenes of a metaphor there is always an absence – what is left unsaid. I cannot tell all the stories. Some of them are not mine to tell. Some of the stories would have other versions. The silences and solitudes have their own voices. There are stories yet to be told.

Introduced to the French poststructuralists in doctoral studies at UBC, I attended to the ways in which French words maintained their tenancies in the context/company of English words. Without translation, the anglophone becomes semi-illiterate. It was difficult to understand why these spaces should be troubling in a Faculty of Education in a bilingual university. To work within the complexities of language in the everyday life of Academia is difficult but must be done. My journey through rough passages has me entangled in the language of the collective agreement, the language of labour law and human rights issues, the language of the Ontario curriculum, the children's stories, and authors who inspirit my teaching, and the exquisite poetic prose of literary narratives whose characters and their phantoms help me to survive. I work at becoming multilingual in English – all the while, desiring after French. With Marla Morris I want to fight the fight in resisting the institution as intrusive mother. Morris contends that we are fighting "a war of words" (2009, 217). And with Bill Readings (1996) I want to resist the corporation as omnipotent father.

There were long delays in-between the grievance procedures. I had extended my responses until the ends of deadlines as I waited for a change in the vice-presidency – for the one who would attend the step one grievance meeting. I was hoping that, perhaps, someone from the social sciences would understand my work. And finally the event happened. With my new liaison officer, I met with the vice-president and the university liaison officer. I had prepared to make a case based on the strengths of the external reviews and through addressing the misrepresentations in the FTPC minutes.

I arrived with my backpack of books, papers, photos, and my well-prepared brief. I arrived as a bag lady. Papers and books began to clutter the conference table as I worked my way through my defence. My liaison officer queried the reasons for the deferral from the perspective of the Joint Committee. We were informed that a deferral would give me more time to establish my independence as a researcher. I had thought that the co-authored performative writing went well beyond independent work. We wanted to perform what we were theorizing. At the end of the meeting, it was acknowledged that I had put a lot of work into the defence. The vice-president academic and provost would discuss the case and get back to us. After a rather extended waiting period, we were informed that my case would be taken back to the Joint Committee. This was what we had hoped for. I was requested to respond to two additional questions. Queried as to what it meant to be first author, I responded that to be first author was to be co-author. I was queried about the doubling of textual performance in my co-authored papers. Text fragments identified by name or initials performed a two-way flow of dialogue around a multiplicity of themes and topics. I submitted the table of contents from journals to demonstrate that this was a happening space. Another agonizing waiting period and I received confirmation. I had been granted tenure and promotion by the Joint Committee. It was not a unanimous decision. But I was able to cross the tracks.

The mise en scène was staged for stories to be narrated through a juxtaposing of fragments querying what happened in the event of a tenure and promotion application. For me, it was a journey of impasse and breakthrough. With multiple levels of gatekeeping, there is perhaps a chance to cross the tracks. The Land of Academia remains an imaginary world with its own constructions of excellence and some serious gaming with words. We are all players in the gaming with words. We are also the weavers of texts and lies, and (mis)representations. I am inviting the reader to weave a reading into this text. What happens in a mise en scène as a work site? Each player in the decision making and in the network of support would have another story to tell. And crossing the tracks can invite more trouble.

SHE, AS TRINH'S INAPPROPRIATE/D OTHER: A MÉLANGE OF GENDER AND AGE[7]

A year following the tenure and promotion decision, I submit my application for academic leave. In December, just before the holiday break, another mousetrap awaits my arrival and I receive a white envelope in my mailbox. The FTPC has not approved my academic leave on the grounds that my plans are not feasible. No explanation is provided. I know the routine now and submit a letter of disagreement, attend the pre-grievance meeting, have my lawyer write a response to the administrator's response to my brief, and I wait. The Joint Committee approves my leave and I do not have to proceed to step one grievance. Was there an underlying agenda? Again, I am questioning: What is wrong with me? Is ageism involved? My lawyer had previously discussed the possibility of a human rights grievance based on ageism. Who is marking? Who is marked? At one point in the pre-grievance procedures, I am informed that I might be granted an academic leave if I agree to resign/retire at the end of it. I am reminded of Trinh's (1992) title: *Framer/Framed*. Between the framer and the framed, radical feminism must be put to work. Words go into labour once again. Rehabilitation has risk and promise.

Having been drawn into spaces of marginality with Trinh T. Minh-ha, I listen to the cadences in her words: "Living at the borders means that one constantly treads the fine line between positioning

and de-positioning" (2011, 54). Trinh refers to the "fragile nature of
the intervals in which one thrives" (54). Risking failure may be what
is most fragile. While age may have been a factor in some of the decisions handed down to me, I also believe that age and experience gave
me the strength to resist those decisions. My life did not "hinge" on
the results. I could retire and/or find work elsewhere. I had a rather
nomadic history in the workforce. I could move on but I could not
live with being branded with the designation: Not Satisfactory.

TRANSGRESSING BOUNDARIES ...
IN FINE COMPANY

Following the decision of the Joint Committee to grant tenure and
promotion, the May 2010 issue of *International Review of Qualitative
Research* arrives with an article by Christopher Poulos who speaks
of "the courage to transgress, to reach across the boundaries that
threaten to contain us – or even shut us down" (2010, 67). Poulos
stages a performative (auto)ethnographic documentary about his
"trial by fire" during tenure and promotion. While the circumstances
of his experience were somewhat different from mine, it was the
final decision coming from above that resonated with me. In Poulos's
performance, it is the narrator who announces a reversal of his fate:

Narrator: "The university committee has voted to overturn the
previous committee's vote" (2010, 84).

I took pleasure in multiple rereadings of this performative documentary. Poulos's chorus in black robes, with hoods shrouding their
faces, fed my imaginaries. Brought some *noir* humour to the events
that had happened. Poulos entitles his article "Transgressions." I had
thought that transgressing boundaries was the work of postcolonial scholars, of poststructuralists, to open possibilities for thinking
beyond a Eurocentric framework. A worksite as a place of possibilities for transformation. Just as Poulos transgressed and trespassed so
did I in my breaking away from traditional genres. As radical feminists we must be willing to fight. I continue to mentor myself with
Avital Ronell, who attempts "to secure the space of academia as a
sheltering place of unconditional hospitality for dissidence and insur-
rection, refutation and undomesticatable explosions of thought"
(2008, 98).

The Poulos article was there in the margins performing my trials
through tenure and promotion. But the difficulties did not begin

there, nor did they end there. What to do now? Does one walk away? Or does one stay and continue the fight in a work site of tensioned productivity rich with possibilities of redux? The Land of Academia is territorial. Cartographies of gender persist. Significations of excellence abound. Roadmaps must be negotiated around and about research units: Occupation 101. How does one set up a hut of one's own in the outskirts – staging a fringe festival of words – away from the blinding spotlights of excellence and distinction? Perhaps, it involves renovating space and place as an architectural restructuring of solitudes.

A lingering assault drifts into a future of solitudes – that those who obtained tenure through the Joint Committee will never have the respect of their colleagues. Words are at-work to construct another barrier of exclusion. Accused of crossing the border illegally, I have been designated an illegal immigrant. I have been referred to as a pariah. A colleague declares that I am being shunned. I could sense Ronell's "SWAT team of academic proprietors closing in" on me (2008, 98). Was it because I followed the advice on those cover letters? I followed the procedures of the collective agreement: a member may forward a letter of disagreement to the employer's liaison officer. Once again I draw from Trinh: "Borderlines remain then strategic and contingent, as they constantly cancel themselves out" (1992, 138). Having obtained an academic leave as well as tenure and promotion through the Joint Committee, I am now assured that I will never have the respect of my colleagues. From another angle, came another message – they do not understand my work. To stay in the game, I must learn to play more than one game. I am learning from a trio of architects, Lewis, Tsurumaki, and Lewis, to dwell "in the messy tension that exists in the middle of the playing field, being, as it were, caught up in the game" (2008, 11).

And reading again with Trinh: "Power, as unveiled by numerous contemporary writings, has always inscribed itself in language ... Power, therefore, never dries out: tracked, pursued, worn-out, or driven away here, it will always reappear there, where I expect it least. And language is one of the most complex forms of subjugation, being at the same time the locus of power and unconscious servility" (1989, 52). I confess that I am not innocent. I am guilty of playing my own games and making up the rules usually in retaliation for some perceived injustice. I felt suffocated between the demands of administration and the dictations of the Ontario curriculum. I did not expect to not get tenure. I expected to get tenure and then to resign with a new position in my sights. A double backfire took place. I did not get tenure and promotion. I was given a deferral. I was given the interview at another university, prior to receiving the tenure verdict, but not the job. Humiliation becomes humility and one begins to grow again from the humus. As Annalee Lepp articulates in this volume, we are always working within the tensions of destabilized terrain, which can create new possibilities. During the decade of my work in the Land of Academia, many traumatic events took place. How can we work in the fault lines of this destabilized terrain so that generative possibilities might emerge?

SOLITUDES ON LOCATION[8]

Sylvie Germain contends "texts too are places ... places where anything can happen ... places where solitude and absence light up, where emptiness chirrs and silence sings" (1993, 94). I seek a habitat within Trinh's "refuse and refuge" (2011, 43). You pack your wounds in your backpack and, as you travel on, you begin to work at patching them up. I am taking my solitudes with me. A mise en scène vacates the premises of the Land of Academia to set up a temporary tenancy in island topographies – to chase after ink-winds with Germain's phantom woman:

> Le vent, le vent de l'encre se lève à son passage et souffle dans ses pas (1992, 15).

> The wind, the ink-wind, rises at her passing and blows beneath her steps (1993, 28).

In a studio apartment, in a guesthouse near the old harbour of Reykjavik, I begin my year of academic leave – my year of writing – weaving in the phantoms of stories past with the mythical characters I am pursuing in the lava and ashes of Icelandic tales. What was declared "not feasible" is happening. On location in Reykjavik, I poach from a title by Trinh and I seek an "elsewhere within here" (2011). Characters and their phantoms hover nearby as I circle the pond in the old town – a bird sanctuary "where emptiness chirrs and silence sings." I re-enter the poetic prose of Sylvie Germain. For once you have tasted the ink, you can never settle for template(d) conditions.

Le goût de l'encre se levait sur les pas. (Germain 1992, 13)

She entered suddenly. But she had been circling the book for years. She would brush against it – though it did not yet exist – she would leaf through its unwritten pages, and some days, she even made its blank expectant pages rustle faintly. The taste of ink would rise beneath her step. (Germain 1993, 27)

ACKNOWLEDGMENTS

I wish to thank my colleague Cynthia Morawski for her thoughtful comments and suggestions regarding this chapter. I would also like to thank Elvi Whittaker and Kersti Krug for their help to bring the work into the contextual domain of the book and for editing suggestions. A special thanks to Elvi for opening feminist ways of becoming a book, we were invited to read and comment on each of the chapters.

Notes

1 I began my doctoral studies while working as a school psychologist. I took a one-year leave of absence from my school district in order to satisfy the one-year full-time residency required in the doctoral program. When I returned from my leave, I declined a school psychology position and returned to a teaching position. After I had completed the doctoral program, I continued in my teaching position while applying for tenure-track academic positions.

2 The tenure dossier is evaluated according to research, teaching, and academic service. My teaching and service were deemed to be satisfactory. My research was judged to be "not satisfactory" by the Faculty Teaching and Personnel Committee (FTPC).

3 The FTPC is composed of five tenured faculty members nominated and elected by the tenured professors in the faculty of education and chaired by the dean of the Faculty of Education.

4 The covering letter from the dean states, "In accordance with Article 5.2.1.4 of the Collective Agreement, please find enclosed a copy of the evaluation of your scholarly activities received from an evaluator." We are informed that we can then, if we wish, during the next ten working days, send to the dean our written comments concerning the report. The comments will be sent to the members of the FTPC along with the report itself.

I did not submit comments as I was pleased with the evaluations. We are not informed about the identity of the evaluators. I attempted to guess who authored them based on the style of writing. As two evaluators disclosed to me later at a conference, I had guessed correctly on one and not on another and could not identify the third evaluator.

5 The Joint Committee consists of elected members of the Senate and the Board of Governors. The mandate of the Joint Committee includes tenure and promotion decisions as well as academic leave decisions.

6 The Ontario Council for Graduate Studies (OCGS) guidelines for CV format stipulate a space for papers that have been submitted but have not yet been accepted: "When giving details on individual publications, be as specific as possible in the case of forthcoming publications (e.g., in press, submitted, accepted, etc.)."

7 I have often found refuge in Trinh's titles, especially so in "She, the Inapropriate/d Other" as an going site of tension in a mode of resistance. One cannot appropriate the inappropriate "She" as Other. I am grateful to find a mentor in Trinh as I am drawn to her discursive trangressions across the boundaries of academic genres.

8 I initially engaged with mise en scène as a worksite for this chapter to recreate an imaginary space for myself in the margins of Academia. During my sabbatical year I took a documentary film course, met a radical group of activists, joined a co-operative of videographers, purchased a video camera and have footage awaiting editing. Back on campus, I can now stage a scene for the camera. Stories always begin somewhere in the middle and this one has not yet ended. Documentary soundtracks begin to chirr as silence sings in the solitudes.

5

Seeking Scientific Voice:
Strategies for Emerging Scientists

CECILIA MOLONEY

INTRODUCTION

This chapter examines scientific "voice" or expression and "her scientific voice" to highlight the challenges that women students and professionals continue to face in the natural sciences, in particular in academia. It will be argued that an individual scientist employs many different "dialects" in her scientific work. At the same time, the scientific community continues to promote the ideal of the strictly impersonal scientific voice. Yet seeking her own voice is crucial to a future scientist's success. The disconnect between the ideal impersonal voice and the scientist's desire and need for individual expression confounds many aspiring scientists and engineers, and women in particular. This chapter will envision the possibilities that could emerge with the more balanced development of "her scientific voice," in part through a fuller understanding of scientific voice.

VOICE DEFINED

Much has already been written about voice and the importance of finding one's voice, as a woman, as an artist, as a scholar, as a scientist. What is meant by "voice" and "finding one's voice" differs from context to context, but all of the various meanings are consistent with how the woman on the street would understand them. All definitions and uses of voice have something to do with expression.

In everyday usage, we understand voice as vocal utterance, literally, of words or song, giving expression to what is inside us, our feelings, thoughts, ideas, and opinions. Metaphorically, voice is understood as expression in a wider sense, expression coded in word or song, but also in gesture, touch, mood, and works of mind or hand. Thus, we understand the following sentences: "She was in fine voice today." "I had no voice in the matter." "She voiced the thought that ..." "She has lost her voice." Voice need not be attached only to an individual, but may be a collective attribute, as in "We spoke with one voice." Voice can also be attributed to the material or natural worlds, as in "the voices of the violin and cello," or "the voice of the sea."

Voice is used with particular meanings in given contexts. For example, in creative writing classes, aspiring writers are advised to seek their own voice in their written words, not to copy the voice of a favourite author. It can take years for a writer to find or develop her own voice. Similarly, artists in other media seek their own voice, their unique expression, in paint, stone, form, and so on.

To underscore what is meant by artistic voice (and subsequently its contrast with scientific voice) consider the first sentences of two well-known novels: "It is a truth universally acknowledged that a single man in possession of a good fortune must be in want of a wife" (Austen [1813] 1985). "Once upon a time and a very good time it was there was a moocow coming down along the road and this moocow that was coming down along the road met a nicens little boy named baby tuckoo ..." (Joyce [1916] 1976). Even if the reader were not immediately able to name the novels from which these opening sentences are quoted, he or she may be able to estimate their periods or styles and guess at the differing themes that these two novels might explore.

On the other hand, there are almost no clues about the identity of the author or authors of the sentences below, which begin a scientific paper. Moreover, without expertise in the specific field of the paper, it would be extremely difficult to date the paper or to estimate the objectives the author(s) had in writing it: "The T-DNA transfer process of *Agrobacterium tumefaciens* is activated by the induction of the expression of the Ti plasmid virulence (*vir*) loci by plant signal molecules such as acetosyringone. The *vir* gene products act in trans to mobilize the T-DNA element from the bacterial Ti plasmid. The T-DNA is bounded by 25-base pair direct repeat sequences" (Wang et al. 1987 quoted in Montgomery 1996, 1).

THE NATURE OF SCIENTIFIC VOICE

Although the concept of a scientist's voice may not be explicitly discussed in scientific circles as in the artistic world, we can nonetheless refer to scientific voice. Scientific voice is different from the voice of the artist. Unlike artists, aspiring scientists are not taught about this voice overtly, nor directly advised to seek their own voice. Rather, a student in the natural sciences picks up scientific voice during her apprenticeship, partly indirectly by reading scientific papers and by listening to other scientists, more directly through feedback on her presentations and written work from supervisors and peers in graduate school and later. The scientific voice, like the artistic voice, can take years to acquire.

What distinguishes a scientific voice from other voices? It could be argued that because the scientist is cautioned to factor out the personal as much as possible from her work and communication, there is no individual scientific voice but rather a common or collective one. This scientific voice is a highly constructed voice. It is a spare, economical, clear, precise, and often understated voice. It uses simple language when possible, along with the highly developed vocabulary of a specific scientific field, all to the end of speaking as precisely and objectively as possible about the scientific phenomena at hand. It is as if the scientist were a mere conduit through which the scientific data speak. In the words of Scott L. Montgomery, geologist and essayist about language in science, "from its beginnings in the 16th century, modern (Western) scientific speech has taken on a single, breathtaking, linguistic purpose: that of giving the material universe a voice" (1996, 59).

For these reasons, a young scientist may not be conscious of herself as seeking an individual voice. She may be aware of a collectively held ideal of the strictly impersonal scientific voice, and strive to attain it. However, I hold that this ideal scientific voice is not realized in practice, nor is it, in fact, ideal. Individual scientists do have their own voices. Moreover, to seek and acquire her own voice is crucial to a scientist's success, since employing her own voice will lead to creativity and innovation, releasing her whole person's potential to discover and create. This is the argument for voice in any field, and there is no reason to expect science to be different in this regard. As the noted Canadian science communicator Jay Ingram expresses it,

[Scientists] are not unemotional, robotic generators of data ... Many of them are absolutely crazy about science, and experience the same highs and lows as any creative person. Yes, there is that difference: they have to be able to defend their results, usually in a numerical, statistical sense, in the community of their peers.

That process does not limit creativity, but it appears to. In public, scientists are often cautious, choosing their words carefully, taking care not to claim too much for their work, knowing that it must stand the test of time and replication. (2011, 10)

The perceptions that outsiders may have of scientific expression as impersonal are not incorrect. However, we need to understand the origins and continuing reasons for the archival or published form of scientific expression, and also to understand this form as a final product based on deeper levels of human activity and of human emotions, and – we might dare to go on to say – of human passion and love. Sherry Turkle notes in her self-styled "book about science, technology and love" (2011, 3) that "traditionally, scientists have been reticent to talk about their object passions or, one might say, about passions of any kind. There was a canonical story about the objectivity and dispassion of scientific work and scientists stuck to it" (2011, 8).

One way to start to uncover the individual scientist's voice is to notice that scientists speak multiple dialects.[1] One is the highly formal and stylized dialect of archival communication, most typically in written form. Somewhat less formal can be the dialects of conference presentations and the lecture room; less formal still the dialects of the laboratory, emails, and small-group conversations with peers and students; much less formal may be the dialect which the scientist "speaks" with herself on paper as she works out problems and devises experiments, or in her head as she reflects on her work. Thus, there may exist a range of dialects in any specific scientific "language" of any particular scientific field. The less formal and constrained the dialect, and the smaller and friendlier the group with which the dialect is spoken, the more this language can be personalized or can become blended with other usage of language, including metaphorical figures of speech and everyday or street language.

AN EXAMPLE OF SCIENTIFIC "DIALECTS"

This section provides an extended example of how scientific dialects are used and how they change across audiences and time. The material is drawn from electrical and computer engineering, in which I teach and do research, in order to trace an example of voice from those of undergraduate students through to archival expression in a research paper. The example is written as a composite of voices heard, remembered, or internalized over a career of study, teaching, and research supervision in fields that use the material of the example.

Preamble: A Scientific Paper and Its Context

To set up the example and to establish the formality of archival scientific voice, the example starts with a quote from a journal paper in information theory, a theoretical field in mathematics that has application in modern communications engineering. Next, the context of the scientific quote is traced back to undergraduate courses, and a set of dramatic vignettes shows how a key idea in the quote might be discussed in different scientific voices by students, professors, and researchers.

The quote is comprised of the first two sentences of a scientific journal paper:

> Versions of the central limit theorem for continuous random variables have been shown in the sense that the divergence between an n-fold convolution and the Gaussian density with identical first and second moments (non-Gaussianness) vanishes as $n \to \infty$ ... Although long suspected that the non-Gaussianness decreases at each convolution, it was not shown until 2004 (in the equivalent version of increasing differential entropy) by Artstein [et al.] ... by means of a tour-de-force in functional analysis. (Tulino and Verdú 2006, 4295)

What caught my attention about this quote was the use of the word *convolution*. Students of physics and of electrical and computer engineering (ECE) encounter convolution in connection with the time-domain behavioural modelling of linear circuits, where the output signal across or through a part of the circuit, denoted generically $y(t)$, is modelled as the convolution of an input signal $x(t)$ with a characteristic function for the circuit so viewed, known as the impulse response *h(t)*, that is,

$$y(t) = \int_{-\infty}^{\infty} x(\lambda)h(t - \lambda)d\lambda$$

Convolution would typically be introduced to ECE students in a second- or third-year course on linear systems, usually titled Signals and Systems. This is often considered to be a difficult course, and the topic of convolution regarded as one of the most difficult topics in the course, both as an abstract idea, and as a process, that is, to work out the above integral (Nelson et al. 2010).

Later, students might see convolution again in connection with probability and random processes, as for applications in communications engineering. For example, the innocuous looking equation

$$Y = X_1 + X_2$$

where X_1 and X_2 are independent continuous random variables, requires the convolution of their probability density functions (PDFs) in order to determine the PDF of the summed random variable Y, that is,

$$f_Y(y) = \int_{-\infty}^{\infty} f_{X_1}(x)f_{X_2}(y - x)dx.$$

It is a generalization of this situation (i.e., where $Y = X_1 + X_2 + ... + X_n$) that the well-known central limit theorem refers to, when the X_i are all mutually independent and distributed with the same probability distribution. Students in many areas of science and engineering will encounter the central limit theorem in this context in a university-level course in probability and statistics. In addition, many of us are familiar with the idea of grades in a course having an approximately bell-shaped histogram; this shape is consistent with the central limit theorem and the contribution of many part marks from tests, assignments, and so on to each student's final grade.

The Tulino and Verdú paper reveals, in part, how science works, but not how the scientists who had the long-held idea finally came up with the proof of the central limit theorem. Nor does it address at all the difficulty that many students encounter in seeking to understand what convolution is and how it is used. In fact, I find it interesting that the word *convolution* is used at all in the Tulino and

Verdú paper as the role of convolution in the PDF of sums of random variables would be so well known by readers of their paper that it could have been left out. Moreover, it is worthy of note that no actual convolution integrals appear in the Tulino and Verdú paper.

Now consider the following series of dramatic vignettes that build from a first encounter with convolution in a second-year class to researchers reading and planning to use the paper by Tulino and Verdú in their research.

A Dramatic Interlude in Five Voices: Behind the Scientific Paper

VIGNETTE I

In the context of a Signals and Systems course, with two students studying in the lab.

Student A: Hey, do you understand this convolution business? I mean, what's the point of the shift-and-flip? *(Referring to $h(t-\lambda)$ in the integral.)* I can see the shift – you want to work out what happens for every t. But why flip? $h(t-\lambda)$ on the λ-axis means you draw the impulse response backwards. But the circuit is causal, going forward in time. So why have its impulse response going backwards?

Student B: The prof said that that shows the memory of the system.

Student A: Memory? In a circuit? Wait … you mean, like how a capacitor charges to capacity and then discharges when the voltage is shut off?

Student B: Right.

Student A: But that's a really short period of time. I mean, think about a picofarad cap. That would just zip away.

Student B: Yah, but you can see it on the 'scope, with a standing wave.

Student A: You're right. You can see it. And it looks like the step response for this $h(t)$. But it's going forward in time, not backwards. I just don't get this backwards part of it.

Student B: Well, if you don't like it that way, turn the integral around and convolve h with x. That's the same thing. I mean convolution is commutative. Then you have $x(t)$ going backwards at every t.

Student A: Are you going to tell me that now the input signal is some sort of memory?

Student B: No. But I will tell you, you better *remember* this for the exam. And that's in the future, not in the past ... in case you're wondering.

VIGNETTE 2

In the context of a subsequent Communications Engineering course, with Student A in class, after having mastered the process of convolution in Signals and Systems.

Prof X: (Pointing to a slide which shows $Y = X_1 + X_2$ *followed by the derivation of the result that* $f_Y(y) = \int_{-\infty}^{\infty} f_{X_1}(x) f_{X_2}(y - x) dx.$*)* So, you can see that we end with the result that the PDF for Y is a convolution of the two PDFs for X_1 and X_2. Now you are all familiar with the convolution integral, which you will recognize from Signals and Systems.

Student A (to self): Not convolution again! I thought we left that behind for good in 2252. Turns out it has no application at all, it's just a model, based on some "function" $\delta(t)$ which doesn't even exist in the real world. And here it is again. And with no circuit in sight, just a sum of random variables! How on earth does that lead to a convolution? ... And is there any memory here? ... I better go home and work on this one.

Prof X: So you see in this example of adding the independent uniformly distributed random variables X_1 and X_2, we get a hat-shaped PDF for their sum Y. And if we were to keep on adding more such random variables together, the convolutions would smooth out more and more and eventually we'd get something approaching a Gaussian curve.

Student A (to self): A Gaussian? That's the same as a bell-curve. Ok, I think I can see it, especially if you graph it visually. Yes, that's not too bad. I think maybe I can get it. Still not sure if I can *do* a convolution and get it completely right, but I can see how it's starting to smooth out the PDF.

Student B (as class ends): This is boring.

Student A: Actually, it's pretty cool. And finally, an application for convolution.

VIGNETTE 3

Five years later, as Student A meets with her PhD supervisor to discuss her research in wireless communications.

Student A: I found a paper by two researchers, Antonia Tulino and Sergio Verdú, proving the differential entropy increases with each new variable in the sum. I don't understand their proof completely, but it's important. ... I know my simulation results are pretty good, but it will really help to have this theoretical claim behind them ... And the central limit theorem can still apply, even if the component signals have different distributions.

Prof Y: Looks good. Convolution, eh. I'm teaching that tomorrow to my second-year class ... the students usually find it pretty hard.

Student A: Yes, I found it hard at first, too.

Prof Y: Did you? That's surprising. But this is interesting ... the non-Gaussianness decreases at every convolution ... uh, huh ... I see they end with a nod to engineering intuition getting to the core of mathematics. You'll like that.

Student A: Yes, finally an application for convolution!

Prof Y: Ha! Ha!

Deconstruction: What the Paper and Drama Reveal about Scientific Voice

This extended example shows that the scientist's voice at the most formal level of a journal paper appears to be very different from that of everyday communication. At this formal level, the scientist seeks to speak in a universal voice. But that level is a mere codification of what has already happened, and has already been voiced differently at other levels of work and discourse. Scientists are well-known for their after-the-fact explanations of results that were worked out laboriously and over time, sometimes serendipitously, and occasionally intuitively or in symbolic form.[2] In the natural sciences, after a phenomenon has been discovered or explained by a hypothesized model, the possibly lengthy effort to discover or explain is no longer considered worthy of note, and the discovery or explanation is viewed, in hindsight, as coded in its logical connection to or derivation from previously known results. Thus, scientific results are often stated as obvious, even trivial, in the form presented. I think this complacent coding of scientific results in their final form, and not by the forms in which they were realized, discourages a lot of would-be scientists who do not feel that they can measure up to such austere standards of knowledge generation.

HER VOICE

Although I have used the feminine pronouns, "her" and "she," in my references to artistic and scientific voice, our cultural tendency is to think of the masculine as normative of collective groups. That is, we hear the artist's voice as "his voice" and the scientist's voice as "his voice." When we speak of "her voice," "her artistic voice," "her scientific voice," our sense of the voice changes. In particular, "her voice" may not seem to exemplify the disembodied, detached, objective sense of the scientific voice. It may not be heard as a universal, dominant, or representative voice. It may even be heard as a deviant voice. In fact, it may be interpreted as a personal voice, the voice of some particular woman. All of us, women and men, hear a woman's voice as different from a man's. We embody and personalize her voice much more than we embody and personalize his voice.

And in science, an embodied and personalized voice is frowned upon, as different, as weaker, as not holding up the impersonal standard of science. And yet, that embodiment and personalization is in the mind of the listener (or reader). It need not be manifest in the speaker, especially if the voice is in a written form.

THE FEMINIST VOICE

A significant body of feminist literature about women and voice has emerged in recent years. Carol Gilligan uses "voice" to refer to "ways of speaking about moral problems" (1982, 1), distinguishing the moral reasoning in women, often via an ethic of care, from that of men, often via an ethic of justice. Following Gilligan, many other feminist scholars have used voice to refer to women and their development on a variety of dimensions. For example, Belenky et al. consider the connections between voice and knowing, and between voice and agency (1986). There have been criticisms of the Gilligan and Belenky et al. approach, as some feminists criticize the essentialism in such women-versus-men developmental models, and postmodern feminists are not comfortable with searching for a single, true voice. Yet it must be admitted that Gilligan's metaphor of voice has been enormously influential, even well outside feminist and academic circles.

Key to Gilligan's work is her tendency to equate voice with personal characteristics such as authority, agency, self, and authenticity, and to equate silence, or non-voice, with passivity and powerlessness, with being controlled, subordinated, or victimized. To be silent, in her view, is to be silenced, to be without knowledge or agency. Voice, on the other hand, gives a woman power, although not necessarily the male type of power – "power over" – but rather more relational forms of power – "power to" or "power with" – in which power gives (shared) capacity rather than the domination of others (Freeman and Bourque 2001).

To understand why Gilligan and voice have had such a resonance in feminist and women's circles, we need only make a short reference to the historical context in which Gilligan published her work. The women's movement of the late nineteenth and twentieth centuries followed millennia of enforced collective silence of and about women. Western culture is built on the twin cultures of ancient Greece and Judeo-Christianity, and we can find defining texts for women's silence in each of the foundation cultures. For example, Aristotle wrote, "Silence gives grace to a woman – though this is not the case likewise with a man" (quoted in Glenn 2004, 5). Expressing similar sentiments, Paul of Tarsus wrote, "Let a woman learn in silence with full submission. I permit no woman to teach or to have authority over a man; she is to keep silent" (1 Tm 2:11–12, [New Revised Standard Version]).

To understand the lingering effect of such texts in Western culture, we need to view these quotes within the context in which they were written. Both the Greek and Judeo-Christian cultures were cultures of the word: "In the beginning was the Word," is the first phrase of the Greek-influenced Gospel of John (Jn 1:[NRSV]). In those ancient cultures, speech was a cherished and characteristic human ability. In ancient Athens oratory was the path not only to authority and power (i.e., power over) but also to understanding and truth, to civilization itself. However, women were debarred from speaking, both individually and collectively. They were not citizens of the state, they were not Athenians (Fantham et al. 1994). They were silenced. No wonder twentieth-century feminists have claimed the right to speak so fiercely. No wonder they have traced development in terms of the ability to claim voice and to speak in their own voices.

Yet, despite our newly claimed voice, the picture is still not rosy in the twenty-first century. Expression is not merely a matter of a speaker giving voice to what is inside her. There also needs to be a listener who listens with attention and hears with fidelity. Psychologist Virginia Valian discusses what she calls gender schemas, the unspoken and often unconscious beliefs we have about women and men (1998), and presents many examples to show how significant and pervasive these schemas are. For example, research shows that the same resumé presented for a scientific position will be evaluated differently in terms of the competence of the candidate, the salary he or she merits, and so on depending on the assignment of the applicant's name as male or female (Moss-Racusin et al. 2012). In terms of voice, this means that the gender of listener and speaker influence what happens in communication. It would seem that quite apart from finding a voice, women have a hard time simply being heard.

HER SCIENTIFIC VOICE

What are the implications of this gender bias for women scientists? In the 1980s, sociologist Gerhard Sonnert and science historian Gerald Holton conducted the Project Access study, which examined the career paths of a large sample of women and men academic scientists in the United States (1995a, 1995b, 2002). One of their goals was to identify and explain any gender disparities in science paths within the sample group. The sample group scientists were considered to be similar in that all of them had been initially promising and equally advantaged at the start of their academic careers: they had all been recipients of prestigious federal agency postdoctoral fellowships over the 1950s to 1980s.

While studies of this kind can be out of date even by the time they are written,[3] Project Access can provide us with insight into the scientific voices of women and men, as manifest in their published papers. That is, for academic scientists, published papers manifest and measure voice, both by their number and their quality. Project Access found that the women scientists in their sample group, averaged over all fields, had about 20 per cent fewer publications per year, and that the women tended to publish book chapters and conference proceedings over the more prestigious (in science) journal papers more than the men.

Sonnert and Holton conducted a further small study of biologists, both women and men, to try to understand these gender differences in publications. They found that while the women biologists had published on average fewer papers, their papers tended on average to be more substantial and comprehensive contributions. Moreover, the women's contributions tended, on average, to be cited more frequently than the men's in work by other scientists. Thus, it could be claimed that, on average, the quantitatively less strong output by the women scientists was actually of higher quality and hence of more value to their fields. In the voice metaphor, we might say the women spoke less often, but when they did speak they had something more significant to say.

In addition to examining publication rates, Project Access asked its study group what they considered to be good science, and analyzed the scientists' reports of their standards. Holton noted that this part of their reported results could have been titled, "What you thought is good science may be dangerous to your career, especially if you are a woman scientist" (2005, 181). Project Access found that the women scientists tended to define good science in terms of integrity and comprehensiveness, while the men scientists tended to cite creativity and good presentation.

Although the gender differences in such studies are often small differences in means, there are implications worthy of note. The women in the Project Access study come across as the "purer" scientists, valuing the production of high quality work. However, it is easier to assess quantity than quality, and there is a tendency for committees of hiring, promotion and tenure, grant selection, and the like to fall into doing so. Then, the "purer" scientist may accumulate a disadvantage that will stay with her throughout her career, like interest compounding at a lower rate, compared with other scientists who started with the same initial capital. Similarly, the women scientists who came across in the study as less careerist than the men, and less politically adept, also experience "an accumulation of disadvantages throughout their academic careers" (Stout, Staiger, and Jennings 2007 quoted in Abramson, Rippeyoung, and Price, this volume).

DIALECTIC OF VOICE AND SILENCE

Many women who are working academic scientists today may recognize the "quality versus quantity" issues highlighted by the Project Access study. Some may infer from such data – as well as from their own experience – that they should seek to increase their voice output by publishing more research papers to attain voice parity with their male colleagues.

However, there is another, and potentially liberating, perspective within which to situate a response to results such as those of Sonnert and Holton, one based upon a valuing of silence as well as of voice. I agree with the several feminist scholars who critique Gilligan's view of silence, and who suggest rather that silence is not only an indicator of powerlessness and passivity, but when it can be freely chosen, silence can be part of power and agency (Glenn 2004; Mahoney 2001). There are various contexts in which it is the one who is silent who holds the power, while the voiced have less power. One example is a university examination, in which the candidates must speak (whether orally or in written form) while the examiners remain silent in a position of judgment and power. Similarly, in legal proceedings in a courtroom, or in negotiations in a corporate board-room, the most powerful participants tend to be more silent than the less powerful who must speak to plead their case.

Thus, voice and silence are seen to be in a dialectical relationship with each other. This dialectic is manifest in the quote,

> Every decision to say something is a decision not to say some-thing else, that is, if the utterance is a *choice*. In speaking we remain silent.
>
> And in remaining silent, we speak. (Scott 1972, 146 quoted in Glenn 2004, 13)

The expectations of academic scientists today are very high. They are expected to produce voiced output in many forms, including lectures, student supervision and mentoring, research proposals and papers, conference presentations, committee memos and reports, reference letters, and emails. Moreover, academic women are often asked, and sometimes agree, to more than their share of academic service to their institutions,[4] especially in some science disciplines in which the percentages of women faculty are low. With all of these demands on their time and voice, women scientists may need a more comprehensive strategy than simply working harder at increasing their publication output. I suggest that "being silent" may be good for their careers and part of such a strategy. What I mean by "silence" in this context is a judicious keeping back for one's self, not always doing and saying what one is expected to do or say all of the time, not necessarily even being a "good" scientist according to a lofty but hard-to-attain ideal. I suggest the deliberate combination of "being silent" with "being voiced" as a strategy to thrive.

For example, for one woman scientist, it may be an important part of her silence to write one paper for a prestige journal than to write two conference papers or to serve on the organizing committee of a local conference. For another, her silence may include chairing a committee that matches well with her talents and available time, and sending her regrets to other service requests. For yet another, her silence may be to spend time organizing good teaching methods and materials so that the teaching semester will go smoothly, thus freeing up time and energy during the teaching semester to craft a winning research funding proposal.

This dialectic of voice and silence will result in a balance individually defined for each scientist, one that allows the scientist to "feel real,"[5] to be caught up in joy and wonder at the world of nature, logic, and people, and also politically astute; to be both non-conformist and doing her own thing, and a full member of the body academic; to be both innocent and courageous, contemplative and active, voiced and silent. In short, to speak with her own voice – whatever this voice may be for a particular woman, in her particular circumstances. Let us refer to this balanced, personalized voice of the scientist as an authentic scientific voice.

Yet, while I suggest an optimistic view of a possible future for individual women scientists, we must remember that there remains the need for institutional change, not only of policies in the academy and in scientific establishments but also for new levels of awareness (or simply for awareness, in some cases) that there still is a problem of a gendered voice differential, and especially in the sciences. As long as there are listeners who do not hear women well and clearly, there is work still to be done.

TOWARDS AUTHENTIC SCIENTIFIC VOICE

How do we assist institutions to listen with more fidelity, and to allow and validate their members to express themselves with more authenticity, and how do we help women (and also men) scientists to grow into their individual, unique voices?

One critical aspect of balancing scientific voice is to moderate the austere requirement for scientific distance and objectivity in scientific publications. Approaches to mitigate the harshness of that voice are based on diversifying and expanding students' and others' perception and understanding of what can constitute scientific voice. Examples of well-balanced scientists can serve as role models (e.g., Feynman 1989; Franklin [1990] 1999), as can examples of artistic scientists and scientific artists who illustrate a range of ways of expressing both science and art (Moser 2011). In addition, students' deeper understanding of the role and purpose of objectivity in science and in scientific method can be fostered through reflection exercises that help students to become more aware of how they operate when they are engaged in scientific activities as well as in everyday activities. For example, an activity such as ordering a meal from a menu can be simulated in a workshop setting and then deconstructed in order to help students become aware that the thought process of such an otherwise ordinary activity is similar to scientific method; the intention is that such an exercise can tend to allay students' concerns about engaging in new scientific procedures and topics of study (Moloney 2007). Other strategies could encourage women scientists (and indeed all scientists) to use the individual and the subjective in their various scientific dialects (as the characters do spontaneously in the dramatic vignettes in the extended example above), even as precision in written publications is upheld.

Nurturing the scientist's awareness of the importance of her subjectivity and of her sense of herself as scientist is another important component in balancing scientific voice. The general approach for this component is based on the somewhat obvious observation that being a scientist is not just the doing of science but also living life as a scientist – and living is individual and subjective. However, the personal and the professional spheres of a scientist's life may seem to the scientist to be lived on different planets, and strategies are needed to assist the scientist to allow her a better understanding of herself in her two (or more) spheres. Artistic expression is one way in which concrete possibilities can be imaged and understood. In particular, artistic expression can enable us to examine our lives as scientists, and to imagine other ways of being scientists and other ways to organize the scientific establishment. Some preliminary work has been undertaken in developing materials to enable artistic expression by professionals in science, engineering, and other disciplines (Samson and Moloney 2008). Closely related is the literature on narrative and other techniques, for example, with medical professionals (Charon 2006), and with engineering students (Ellis, Mikic, and Rudnitsky 2003). However, the application of narrative and other artistic techniques to liberate expression in scientific and related fields is relatively new, with significant scope for future work.

In 2011–12, a group of researchers at Memorial University of Newfoundland conducted a project titled Thinking Creatively about Research, which encompasses both of the components outlined above: the moderation of the burden of scholarly objectivity and the nurturing of the subjectivity of the scholar. The project offered a co-curricular workshop-based course for graduate students in the humanities and in engineering, which focused on the creative aspects of research writing in these disciplines, on writing as a process, and on writing as a social practice within a community of discourse (Badenhorst 2007; 2010). The aim of the project was to support the development of creativity of thought and writing, process skills, and attitudes that could have lasting impacts on the writing productivity of participants, not only in their graduate programs but over their careers. Results show that the approach is effective at freeing the writing "voice" of the participants (Rosales et al. 2012; Badenhorst et al. 2012).

CONCLUSION

In this chapter, I have argued for a more balanced perspective on scientific voice, one that encourages voiced expression combined with silence, and objective precision combined with subjective self-awareness of the scientist as scientist. While various examples and strategies illustrate approaches to liberating more balanced and authentic scientific voices, much work remains to be done, particularly if the entire scientific enterprise is to be changed. However, efforts in this direction are worthwhile, as they can help to make the sciences into more welcoming fields of study for university students, and more satisfying professional homes for academics, women as well as men (and would also produce better science, although that is the subject of a far longer work). The reader is left to reflect on what science could be like, would be like, if all of us, women and men, were validated in growing into our own unique, authentic voices from our student days and beyond.

ACKNOWLEDGMENTS

This research was supported in part by grants from the Natural Sciences and Engineering Research Council of Canada (NSERC) and Petro-Canada through the NSERC/Petro-Canada Chair for Women in Science and Engineering, Atlantic Region, 2004–09. Portions of this chapter were presented in earlier versions at Women on the Atlantic Academic Tundra: Thriving and Surviving, Mount Allison

University, Sackville, NB, 3–4 March 2006; and Breaking Boundaries, Forging Connections: Feminist Interdisciplinary Theory and Practice, Mount Saint Vincent University, Halifax, NS, 11–13 April 2008. I acknowledge, with thanks, the "voices" that inspired the dramatic vignettes in this chapter, notably my former students in Engineering 4823 and 5420 at Memorial University, as well as my graduate students and research collaborators.

Notes

1 Scott L. Montgomery writes of dialects specific to particular fields of expertise within science (1996, 7), while I am referring to the various dialects any one scientist speaks within her own field of science.

2 Famously, the ring nature of the benzene molecule was discovered symbolically by German chemist August Kekule after a dream (Csikszentmihalyi 1997, 101). Other discoveries have been mediated by the relationship between the knower and the known. For example, geneticist Barbara McClintock reported an experience she had shortly before she made a significant discovery, in which, while looking at chromosomes through a microscope, she had the sense of being down inside the sample and part of the system she was studying (Keller 1985, 165).

3 It can also be said that this study reflects an older and different generation from today's; nonetheless, the studied generation of scientists is still active and influential within academia.

4 Service load and various other career demands on academic women are further explored in Abramson, Rippeyoung, and Price, this volume.

5 "Feeling real" is a subjective state in the psychology of communication and non-communication of D.W. Winnicott, discussed in the context of women, silence, and power by Mahoney (2001, 78).

6

Solidarity in the Solitudes of Student Life: Contemporary Women Students Discuss Life and Work in the Academy

KATIE AUBRECHT AND ISABEL MACKENZIE LAY

Sharing imprisoned secrets both creates solidarity and destroys it. The academy teaches us to binge – on food, readings, intellect, stories, and bodies and to purge of them in the form of an essay. Bodiless papers written in empty curves don't engage the metaphysical with the material. But when our hearts are open we can feel stories moving through us, with us and beyond. The spirit of inner mumblings, grumblings, leaky thoughts and corporeal orientations to the world awakens an internal magic that sparks our drive to share, to care, and to heal.

Isabel Mackenzie Lay, "Ravenous Cow"

INTRODUCTION

This chapter seeks to disrupt binary understandings of solitude and solidarity in the life and work of contemporary university students. We engage with the contemporary woman university student experience through reflections on our own lives as students and in conversation with colleagues. We made use of our informal networks to recruit women students, issuing invitations via email, at the International Disability Studies Institute held at Ontario Institute for Studies in Education in July 2011, within campus groups, and by word of mouth. Networks consisted of other students we knew through our paid employment, activist and artistic commitments, and mutual academic programs. Invited participants were informed that their stories would be occasions to reflect on the gendered organization of university student life. Stories were shared in-person, via face-to-face conversations, on the phone and through Skype, and through email correspondence.

Because we are both students in equity studies programs, which take a critical interdisciplinary approach to studying social justice issues, the nature of our networks meant that many participants were familiar with critical feminist theory and therefore attentive to issues of sexuality and heteronormativity. However, we did not perceive this as a "bias" in the research. Rather, it added another layer of complexity to the meaning of "woman" student. Although unrepresentative of all "women" students, such narratives needed space to be told. At the same time, not everyone we spoke with had a background in equity studies or was familiar with contemporary theoretical frameworks or social critiques.

Over the course of August and September 2011, we spoke with thirty-five students who were studying or had recently studied at a Canadian university (Alberta, British Columbia, Ontario, Nova Scotia, and Quebec). Of this group, nineteen students were pursuing graduate degrees (MA and PhD), twelve students were in undergraduate programs (BA and BSc), two were in professional programs, and two had recently graduated. Participants ranged in age from twenty to forty-eight years. The academic interests and backgrounds were in varied areas, such as education, health professions, sociology, journalism, cultural studies, and women and gender studies – all programs traditionally dominated by women (McKillop 1994). The students constituted a heterogeneous group that included international, disabled, non-disabled, heterosexual, queer, transgender, childless, single-parent, "traditional" and "mature," students of colour, and white students. Although we recognized the importance of identifying the differences that constituted this group, we also wanted to examine how binary thinking regarding university students, such as traditional vs. mature, reproduce false dichotomies and fail to capture the situated nature of student life and work.

Since our interest was in understanding how, when, and where solidarity emerges in the "solitudes" of student life, interviewing both undergraduate and graduate students had no specific consequences for our study and reflected the realities of many Canadian universities where these groups interact in the same cultural environment. Our aim was not to capture the "true reality" of a particular demographic – "woman student" – but to give voice to lived experiences of being typified as such.

This is a collaborative work recognizing those who have contributed to the conversation, whether explicitly or implicitly, named or unnamed, or as co-authors (see Acknowledgments at the end of this chapter). Although our focus is on women students, our discussions and exchanges were often animated by a resistance to the cultural imperative to identify in strictly gendered terms, *as women*. While this was by no means always, or even often the case, we nonetheless encountered difficulties in framing our invitation to others. Some participants expressed a fundamental ambivalence concerning the meaning of the phrase "women students," with a few noting that asking for women's answers may exclude replies from a spectrum of lesbian, gay, bisexual, transgender, transsexual, intersex, queer, questioning, two-spirit, and ally (LGBTTIQQ2SA) experiences and from those who identify as gender neutral, gender queer, or gender fluid.[1] There were some queer and trans students who experienced a hesitation to identify with the category of "woman" student even though they had prior experience living as women, were identified by the university as women, or had most recently transitioned from male to female.

There was an undeniable hesitance to identify as women, regardless of political engagements or disciplinary background. A few participants that told us that they identified simply as students, rather than as women or women students. Others asked us, "What is a 'woman' student?" which raised the possibility that the category excluded some LGBTTIQQ2SA students. Therefore, within the context of this work, we refer to the "woman university student" as typically understood in the contemporary Canadian university setting to mean a young, cisgender[2] woman enrolled in classes on campus, and as this figure is conceptualized in counternarratives that question this identity.

This tension animated our conversations and led us toward the adoption of an anti-colonial perspective. According to Dei and Asgharzadeh, "The anti-colonial stance fosters the idea that intellectuals should be aware of the historical and institutional structures, and contexts which sustain intellectualism" (2001, 301). They maintain that "in the absence of an understanding of the social reality informed by local experiences and practices, decolonization processes will not succeed" (299). An anti-colonial perspective offers conceptual tools for unpacking the meaning and significance of women students' lives and labours in the university setting.

The contemporary Canadian university is a vestige of a history of colonial expropriation of lands, cultural genocide of Indigenous people, and imposition of Eurocentric systems of governance (Aubrecht 2012). In this chapter, we aim to re-appropriate the "woman student experience" as a "social reality informed by local experiences and practices" (Dei and Asgharzadeh 2001, 299). Through a sharing of stories, which one author refers to as "story time," we explore what it means to be situated, and to situate oneself, as a contemporary student in the "gendered terrain" of the university (Wagner, Acker, and Mayuzumi 2008). We engage women students' narratives of the solitudes of university life as textual encounters with the alterity of the woman student body. As Steans reminds us, "differences among women do not necessarily preclude the possibility of solidarity. On the contrary, respect for difference is a necessary condition for forging solidarity. Moreover, while conflict is apt to be viewed as the negation of solidarity, conflict need not be divisive and can be creative. In the struggle to forge solidarity, conflict can serve to generate critical reflection upon what divides groups and individuals" (2007, 730).

Our findings are not generalizable or representative of all contemporary women university students in the conventional scientific sense. The stories included in this chapter are of women who "claim their education" (Rich 1995, 231), of students asserting their right to be in the university, despite the assumptions they encounter that contradict this claim. Recognizing the historical misappropriation of the stories of marginalized and oppressed groups and the imbalance in power between the researcher and the researched (Costa et al. 2012), we made sure that all of the participants in the study had the opportunity to review and respond to how their stories were framed. These stories provide one way of situating the existence of the woman university student as a collective engagement. Our narrative encounters brought us in touch with the often unexamined relations of how students are taught to read and rewrite resistance. We treated our stories as beginnings to think about apartness together, and as "tools used in understanding and describing the world of human experience" (Myers 2000, 1).

The solitudes of student life are approached both as historical moments and sites of solidarity in and through which the patriarchal contours of contemporary communities can be negotiated and rethought. Although the narratives presented deal with particular instances when the gendered dimensions of university student life became apparent, there is also the recognition of the situation, "woman student," as a historical development. Sexism and gender-based discrimination are interwoven in the very fabric of university life. Attention to the ways that resistance is enacted within the university is therefore of central importance to our analysis.

WOMEN STUDENTS:
A PROBLEM OF "TOO MANY"?

The historical exclusion of women from education, especially higher education, has contributed to their subordinated social status. Today, however, there seems a tendency among students to accept women's rights as a naturally emergent historical given, rather than a recent and arduous accomplishment. Studies by Statistics Canada confirm that there are actually now more women than men students in the university. According to a 2007 Statistics Canada report by Frenette and Zeman titled "Why Are Most University Students Women?" it appears that the problem facing today's women students is not one of inequality but overabundance. Frenette and Zeman explain, "In recent history, universities have been the domain of male students. Over the last 30 years or so, however, a dramatic reversal has taken place on Canadian university campuses. According to the 1971 Census, 68 per cent of twenty-five to twenty-nine year-old university graduates then were male. Ten years later, women had more or less caught up to men as only 54 per cent of graduates were male. By 1991, universities had clearly become the domain of women, as they made up 58 per cent of all graduates" (Frenette and Zeman 2007, 6). In 2008, 62 per cent of all university undergraduates were women (Turcotte 2013).

The discrepancy in the numbers of female to male graduates is described as a "gender gap" (Frenette and Zeman 2007, 4). The report alludes to the high numbers of women as unnatural. Further, it attributes this so-called gender gap to "academic performance, study habits and parental influences" (Frenette and Zeman 2007), making women's presence in the university less a question of a struggle for equal rights than one of good rearing and patriarchal benevolence. We cannot just dismiss the power that statistics have over the ways we understand the historical moment. As Scott reminds us, "Statistical reports are neither totally neutral collections of fact nor simply ideological representations. Rather they are ways of establishing the authority of certain visions of social order, of organizing perceptions of 'experience'" (1999, 115). Crediting patriarchal culture with tolerance and enlightened, progressive treatment of the "second sex" (de Beauvoir 1973) conceals women's struggles to gain university admittance and sustain enrollment.

In his work in disability studies, Rod Michalko uses the term "excessive appearance" to describe the production of disability as "too much and not enough" (2009, 66). This concept applies also to women in university. Depicting women in university as an "excessive appearance" reduces their presence to a question of numbers that need to be brought down and regulated, further illustrating the patriarchal assumption that women are not biologically fit for higher education (McKillop 1994, 126). This is apparent in the family planning initiatives reminding women of their "biological clock" through workshops on fertility, and reports on stress and suicide, and the disproportionate numbers of women "sufferers."

However, in our storytellings, motherhood appeared paradoxically. Motherhood occurred in the shape of significant others offering care and strength, but it was also easily dismissed, which invalidated women's claims to resources and opportunities. For instance, one student experienced herself as "storied as not having a story as a mother," which she situated in a "disjuncture between what I knew about myself and the space I was allowed to occupy." Some students challenged the romantic tropes of motherhood, which emphasize femininity and domesticity. Resisting masculinist rationalities and heteronormativity, they queered ideas of motherhood and family, emphasizing the need to interpret caring, feminism, gender, and sexuality as labour.

The following description is an alternative narrative of caring and education. It speaks to building greater solidarity through feminist interrogations of the academy and demonstrates how an anti-colonial healing rage is linked to battling systems of oppression (Johal 2005, 270–2). As one participant noted, "I learned how to be a feminist, and an intelligent woman, from watching my mom fight through discrimination and harassment as a single parent, and as a woman in the sciences ... The activism that I learned from my mom was the audacity of doing things that you think should be unremarkable, and then realizing belatedly that you have to fight for them ... If activism is a form of education – telling people about what we see as a problem, and why – then maybe education is a form of activism. Maybe."

At the same time as students recognized the important role that their mothers played in their relations to higher education, there was also a fear of becoming a mother. One married graduate student frames this fear in terms of a question of "being where one needed to be": "Despite the fact that the students in our program are pre-dominantly female, and that I knew of women who had children while in school, the thought of getting pregnant terrified me. Invitations to employment and professional opportunities had a way of appear-ing on late nights at local pubs after university events and talks. I was scared that if I had a baby I couldn't be where I needed to be."

UNIVERSITY: A CULTURE OF BELONGING?

In *Belonging: A Culture of Place*, bell hooks writes, "I believe that we can restore our hope ... by building communities where self-esteem comes not from feeling superior to any group but from one's relationship to the land, to the people, to the place wherever that may be. When we create beloved community, environments that are anti-racist and inclusive, it need not matter whether those spaces are diverse. What matters is that should difference enter the world of beloved community it can find a place of welcome, a place to belong" (2009, 183). In hooks's imagined "beloved community," a critical understanding of one's relationship to place can foster strong coun-ter-hegemonic movements of peoples in solidarity, which results in building greater spaces of welcome. For hooks, creating commu-nities of radical acceptance and inclusivity involves reframing mem-ory as a collective process, which she calls "journeying" (see also Chapman 2012). Conventional travel stories can produce dehistori-cized understandings of place that assume a self-evident relationship between individual and collective experience. Such self-evidence is problematic in its reliance on a notion of the individual as universal and natural, and its suppression of the terror of many women's jour-neys within the university. As hooks says, "it is crucial that we rec-ognize that the hegemony of one experience of travel can make it impossible to articulate another experience or for it to be heard" (2009, 100–1).

Enlightenment narratives of the rational and autonomous individual are continually mapped and remapped onto university bodies. However, taking time to reflect, shifting "off course," changing majors, and/or temporarily leaving the university are discouraged and widely understood as a kind of failure. This reinforces the student-subject-consumer ideal, which assumes that students have the financial means to enter into and leave the academy at their leisure. Erasing the actual work it takes to find (and reclaim) spaces of belonging at the university (or to go to university at all), these ideas further manifest an exclusionary image of a "non-university" student as educationally or intellectually "deviant."

There is a cultural fiction that the transition to university requires an adjustment, and that this adjustment is an experience common to all students. Networks of support built into the university (such as psychiatric services, health care, social clubs, caring professors, and students) are there to welcome particular students deemed worthy and capable of scholarly excellence. A sense of entitlement and easy travelling (into and out of academia) underpins the success story that drives Western capitalist culture. The glorified narrative about the academy quickly changes with the realization that the institution can still establish solitude and exile just as much as a place of belonging and home.

Although becoming a university student can prompt a "journeying" toward solidarity, spaces of belonging are typically structured by social clubs, campus groups, and cliques that are part of the university apparatus. As one queer white woman noted, "I'd heard about the queer club on campus. Not only was I looking to be more comfortable with myself, but I was a human rights activist – whatever that means – and wanted to become more involved in queer activism, too. But whenever I walked by the queer club, I just couldn't go in no matter how hard I tried. Every time I walked by I saw the same scene I'd always witnessed in high school: the same people banded together in a little group, looking at everyone new who came in there with suspicion. It was hard, from what I'd heard, to break into the centre and feel accepted."

Reflecting on how the institutionalization of solidarity can foster more spaces of solitude and oppression, many cisgendered women, queer, transgender, and gender-neutral students expressed how, in their desire to journey out of aloneness, they were often met with more discrimination in what they had believed to be supportive communities. One queer woman of colour described how a university student services group, comprised only of three members, went about marking the "positive" spaces on campus to designate anti-queerphobic and anti-transphobic places of equity, belonging, solidarity, and safety for students: "I wonder where my body as a queer woman of colour fit in to their 'positive space' initiatives. I sit beside a familiar face, another token, needing desperately the warm smile that screams, 'You are safe!' I anxiously scribble down notes while contemplating whether or not to take the risk of saying anything in opposition to their plans."

Ironically, in the attempt to raise public awareness of queerphobia and transphobia on campus and delineate spaces of community free of harassment, the indiscriminate sticking of positive space stickers across campus could produce a false impression of inclusivity. Greater visibility of "positive" space cannot simply be accepted as a sign that the university is more welcoming and respectful of difference. The student felt that because the positive space campaigners could not ensure that university staff and students were adequately trained in anti-oppression education around queer/transphobia so as to safely designate spaces as queer- or trans-positive, it was safer *not* to put the stickers up. She feared that the positive space campaign might mislead students to think that these spaces were safe and thus position them in potentially violent situations.

This student felt that her concerns about potential dangers were unheard and silenced by other members of the group. She shared how it was not until other students in the group, who she described as white, echoed these same fears that people began to hear the validity of this argument. Non-recognition of the diversity of bodies that move through spaces marked as safe meant that the stickers could lead LGBTTIQQ2SA students toward racist queer/transphobic spaces while, at the same time, project an image of the university as "tolerant" and "progressive."

McClintock reminds us that, in the colonial encounter, "white women were not the hapless onlookers of empire but were ambiguously complicit both as colonizers and colonized, privileged and restricted, acted upon and acting" (1995, 6). Although the group was composed of other queer women, race made some voices *more* heard and accepted than others: "Nobody acknowledged my comments to have any sort of validity. Being one of the few students of colour at the meeting you would think they would listen to me to understand the experience of a queer student of colour accessing services. They moved on to continue talking about the aesthetics of the positive space sticker. I sat frustrated at their lack of respect and dismissal of my comments." She encountered a "lack of respect" not only for her comments but also for her perspective as a queer woman of colour.

The ghost of imperial projects continually haunts community building in the form of consumer activism, and disguises stories of decolonization and anti-oppression struggling to exist in the university. In turn, activist hierarchy supports the easy travelling and shifting of white bodies in and out of activist spaces, while the work of people of colour in the LGBTTIQQ2SA community is silenced. Solidarity is often falsely represented under the banners of "inclusivity," "diversity," "positivity," and "safety" as a means of protecting and legitimizing white, middle-class, feminist communities, through "activist" practices that end up tokenizing embodied difference. This effectively fosters more solitude within spaces of solidarity. The leisurely act of travelling to buildings within the academy and anointing them with stickers paints a neoliberal aesthetic of (in)action and progressivity that legitimizes student apathy and erases marginalized stories of struggle in university activist communities with the illusion of equitable campaigning.

As a social and textual practice, the positive sticker campaign organizes a conception of reality as something that *sticks*. It feeds a kind of student politic that erases and silences the constant shifting, disruption, violence, struggle, strength, and dissent necessary for the oppressed to exist in the academy. Without dialogue, it can become a wounding sticker campaign that simply ends up re-positioning spaces of solitude as places in which students *get stuck*. Inclusionary practices undertaken in the absence of dialogue and the recognition of social hierarchies can provide for the appearance of what one storyteller referred to as "solidarity among tokens." At the same time, the meaning of this appearance cannot be reduced to a false or artificial solidarity but a space within which new possibilities for community materials and can be engaged.

Women students repeatedly described an atmosphere of tensions and "dismissiveness" within the university environment, and expressed their desire to be "taken seriously." One student reflects, "We were a close-knit cohort, because of the ribbing we took from other science students, and because we knew what we were studying was important to our lives, both personally and professionally. During one class a chemistry professor asked me what my major was, as I struggled with some experiment that required the careful titration of acids and bases (with no real-life applicability). I proudly responded 'Family Science' to which he quipped, 'Oh, you're going to school to be a Mom.'" Women's academic and creative labour, when it was recognized, was made to appear as frivolous and rewarded in a patronizing way. One student recalled being patted on the head; another received winks of approval from a senior male professor. Gender-based stereotypes were invoked as a way of dismissing women students' academic labour and claims to science, while at the same time demeaning women's work as caregivers.

TAKING "RESPONSIBILITY TOWARDS"

A woman PhD student recounted a conversation she had with a friend about caregiving:

> Talking to a CO-TA and dear friend about all the things weighing on my mind: an exhausting commute in order to have a job with family health benefits, things that needed fixing with the apartment, a chore list a mile long, mountains of laundry, no idea what to do for dinner, and a partner sick at home which meant that the work was all up to me – even more than it usually was. Talking about home life was getting depressing, so we switched gears to talk about our current academic work. I told her that I was looking at the concept of "care" for my comprehensive paper: "I mean, what is care anyway? It's such an abstract idea." My friend laughed at me! "Are you kidding me? Care is what you're doing every day! It's what women have to do every day, it falls on us – your research is your reality!"

This student's remarks illustrate how women are routinely asked to take responsibility *for others* through care of the home, the family, the community. Yet another student reminded us that alienation and exclusion are not "things" we always can or should take responsibility *for*. In a speech delivered at the convocation of Douglass College, the women's college of Rutgers, State University of New Jersey in 1977, Adrienne Rich frames responsibility as a communal project best understood as a collective movement *toward* new ways of enacting solidarity, and an "experience" (1995, 233). Rich describes the university as a "man-centered university" in that it privileges and prepares men for leadership and power positions, which reproduces masculinist traditions and authority within the university setting and beyond (127). Rich's assertion that the "exceptional women who have emerged from this system and who hold distinguished positions in it are just that: the required exceptions used by every system to justify and maintain itself" (127) draws attention to the inheritance of patriarchal intellectual traditions within the academy (131).

This inheritance is clear in this white student's exchange with her advisor: "In the beginning months our meetings would focus around my academic life. However, after several months passed it became apparent that our meetings no longer entailed discussions on my academic life and focused on me as a person. He would stab at my dreams in life. When I informed him I was applying to law school there was no encouragement and he asked if I would enjoy being a nurse. I would leave the meetings feeling torn up and in tears each time. Normally, I feel very confident and believe in myself as a young woman. However, in this case I certainly felt subjected to a power imbalance in a student/professor relationship. I felt so alone, belittled and discouraged by his remarks."

This narrative displays the interlocking nature of sexist and classist oppression (Barone 1999). How we perceive and respond to the violence of sexism may work to reproduce the very inequalities we claim to want to dismantle and to work to disrupt. In this situation, the professor's directive to consider a career in nursing was interpreted by the student as an accusation of inferiority. In contrast to the legal profession, which has been and continues to be dominated by men (Rhode 2001), the nursing profession has historically been considered the domain of women. This student's response could be read as demonstrating recognition of the nursing profession as a pursuit less worthy than law. This rests on cultural stereotypes about the inferiority of women's work, particularly those associated with the provision of care. That these exchanges were upsetting for the student reveals something very important about a hierarchy of value within feminist student critique. However, her distress could also be conceived as resistance to the paternalistic claim to know her and what is best for her. Given that her future career aspirations and perhaps even a letter of reference to future universities and employers are at stake, her anguished relation to being defined as a nurse could also be read as resistance to having oneself and one's fate defined solely on the basis of one's perceived gender.

The hierarchies of power on which the university is based, as reflected in selection criteria, tiered ranking systems, and differentials in status and prestige depending on one's position in the university and program of research or study, can nonetheless obstruct access to the experience Rich describes. Whether someone is an undergraduate, an MA, or a PhD student makes a world of difference in terms of institutional expectations and privileges. Naming institutional violence and appropriating stigmatizing stereotypes offers one way of taking responsibility towards togetherness. One MA student recounted how she and her women colleagues were treated as academically inferior, sexualized, and objectified by male PhD students: "What's in a name? For myself, and a group of six females aged twenty-three to twenty-seven, the one-year master of arts program provided adequate time to deconstruct the name-calling we were subjected to 'Pussycat Dolls' – an American pop girl group and dance ensemble based in Los Angeles. The Pussycat Dolls were a group of young women founded as a burlesque troupe. As their namesakes, we didn't quite fit the traditional mold. We danced, cheered one another's successes and offered kind words in the safety of elevators when it felt like the floor was falling out from beneath us."

According to Audre Lorde, "For women, the need and desire to nurture each other is not pathological but redemptive, and it is within that knowledge that our real power is rediscovered. It is this real connection which is so feared by a patriarchal world" (2000, 54). The work of interrogating patriarchal inheritances and colonial "molds" involves being held accountable for supporting oppressive systems that uphold the status quo. Many of our colleagues described experiencing a sense of belonging in classes taught by women professors and in just observing women in positions of leadership in the university. Differences in age and lived experience also impacted student solidarity.

Mature women students, however, face challenges that students who continue directly from high school do not (See Kennedy, this volume; Massey, Brooks, and Sutherland 2010). One mature student highlighted how pre-existing systems of prestige and conflicting structures of authority presented barriers to solidarity among women: "A personal hurdle I have found is matriarchal/hierarchical in nature. Professors have worked hard to attain their university position, which I wholeheartedly appreciate. However, likewise many mature students have gained positions of authority in their work life. I'm not sure that this is recognized, and appreciated what a sacrifice it is to leave such positions, even if they were unfulfilling, in order to better oneself. I have personally found being a mature student on campus a challenge with some professors of a similar age."

Contributors lamented the discrimination women students face, the barriers to their participation, and the recognition they deserve as full and valued members of the university community. It was also recognized that the shame of the perpetuation of inequality within the university *is* something "women students" are implicated in, something "we" could take responsibility towards. One graduate student who recently completed her degree situated her understanding of the privilege of attending university as inseparable from the racism of North American society: "When I was a kid, we lived in a predominantly black neighborhood. So I knew I had a race pretty young, and the older I get, the more I understand my experiences through that lens, although I didn't at the time. It was just my life, my friends, my neighbourhood. As I got older, my surroundings slowly got whiter, and that made me uncomfortable, but I couldn't figure out what to do about it. What do you do about the fact that every year, there are fewer people of colour in your class, when you're a basically upwardly mobile white girl?"

For Lorde, "Women responding to racism means women responding to anger, the anger of exclusion, of unquestioned privilege, of racial distortions, of silence, ill-use, stereotyping, defensiveness, misnaming, betrayal and coopting" (1997, 278). In remaining silent about our ambivalent relations to gendered designations we close possibilities for transforming self and society. This recognition has produced a sense of complicity in the reproduction of systemic racial and sexual violence. According to Andrea Smith, "sexual violence is ultimately structured around power relations – it entails establishing the power to control someone's life. Similarly, 'knowledge' about someone also gives one power over that person. Withholding knowledge, then, is an act of resistance against those who desire to know you in order to better control you" (2005, 119–20). Many of the women students we spoke with described feeling as though they did not have the option of "withholding knowledge" except through silence and self-segregation. One queer woman of colour undergraduate student depicts this feeling as a question of embodiment: "My body stiffens with anxiety as I walk into an old antique-looking lounge room. This feeling of stiffness is not at all one that is unfamiliar to me. It is a response my body has continually expressed since my 'acceptance' into the university. The room is filled with older white folks drinking wine and having food. I look around hoping to find another token person of colour or at least an undergrad student. 'Ah,' I sigh in relief as I discover four token people of colour in the room, one of them being me."

The lines between school and work are often blurred. This is especially true in graduate school, where scholarships and student funding can take the form of research and teaching assistant positions. With little time to pursue employment outside of the university, students are often reliant on professors for references that are not only academic but professional and social as well. Since it is often the case that students at university are away from family and friends, student groups that coalesce around a professor (who is a course instructor, advisor, or employer) can offer a key source of support and social interaction. However, the formation of such groups can also make it difficult to speak out against sexist, exploitative, and exclusionary practices without risking a loss of academic standing, income, and reputation. Consider the following narrative by a fourth-year undergraduate student:

> One day, talking with another student about courses I had suggested a course by a professor that I had been working for as a research assistant. She had contacted him about the course and mentioned our conversation. He was very angry that I had suggested his name to the other student. He asked me who I thought I was that I felt I could make "referrals." Did I think I was a doctor? My job was to answer the phone. He was the "Doctor," and I had trespassed. I had no right to pass on his name, since, like his name, I was property too; often lent and loaned out to other researchers on the team without any notice. Some part of me knew he wanted me to cry, knew that my humiliation was the whole point and purpose of this exchange. But, I didn't cry and I didn't leave. I just stood there and stared at him.

In this student's story of "returning the gaze" (Bannerji 1993), she illustrates how taking a "stand" is something that women students are often compelled to do alone and in silence. The forging of a relationship with another woman student using a professor's "name" was constructed by the professor as a breach of the student's role in the office and a distortion in her own self-understanding: "He asked me who I thought I was."

Fortunately, more stories told of learning communities initiated and supported by professors. These communities were depicted as sanctuaries within the university that fostered dialogue and collaboration. Their membership expanded beyond any one name, course, program or field, and even the university itself. Within these communities, students, professors, and staff, as well as family members, artists, and activists outside of the university fought for recognition of the historical significance of university life and work.

CONCLUSION

Frigga Haug asserts that "The personal is political – this slogan is for many women a challenge to discuss their day-to-day problems with each other in small groups. To do this would lead them out of their isolation into a sense of collective experience" (1999, 16). In troubling the identity "woman student" and the role of gender in the production of student types, this chapter offers a contribution to understandings of the solitudes of university student life. In our analysis of women students' stories, we problematized the gendered dimensions of the social processes by which students are led toward or away from small groups. Although women students acknowledged the existence of small groups as important and even life-sustaining alternatives, questions arose concerning how solidarities were practised and defined within these groups and how they were aligned within the patriarchal structures of universities.

When we invited students to participate in a dialogue about the contemporary woman student experience, some refused to tell us stories. They refused on the basis of having an estranged relation to the woman student identity and/or to the university identity. We read these refusals as resistance. We also recognized the risk that some participants faced in telling their stories that others did not due to privilege. In this way, staking a claim in and against dominant narratives of the woman student experience fostered a questioning process, which exposed how people can stake a claim in university education and work against this very claim by reclaiming counter-narratives that exposed legacies of racism, sexism, queerphobia, and transphobia, for example.

Through solidarity *in* strangeness, *with* strangers, many contemporary students are questioning the imperial grounds of what a "woman" student identity means. In that respect, their stories bring Lorde's notion of difference as "that raw and powerful connection from which our personal power is forged" (2000, 54) to life and work in the university setting. Lorde says, "Within the interdependence of mutual (nondominant) difference lies that security which enables us to descend into the chaos of knowledge and return with true visions of our future, along with the concomitant power to effect those changes which can bring that future into being. Difference is that raw and powerful connection from which our personal power is forged" (2000, 54). Contemporary student critiques display a desire to question and to take responsibility *towards* others, creating not simply a "woman-centred university," or even an "other-centred university," but a *decentring* of normative ways of thinking about movements within the university based on individualizing rather than collectivizing terms.

Within the shifting and "sticky" (Ahmed 2004, 90–2) spaces of university life, students challenged reductive and dismissive understandings of motherhood, approached care and education as sites of power and sources of healing, and named alternative creative ways of transforming assumptions about solitude through the enactment of counter-communities. Rather than something that could be found in numbers, strength appeared in the sharing of stories of transgression and disruption. This sharing is not always necessarily explicit; it can take the form of witnessing. The fundamental relation between solidarity and witnessing was expressed by an international graduate student, who said, "It reassured me to know that they had made it through some of the same challenges I was facing and in many cases, they gained new perspectives and strength through those experiences. I saw these women show an incredible amount of strength and courage (and disrupt notions about what constitutes a strong woman!) by allowing themselves to be vulnerable while consistently working towards the things they hoped to achieve."

To break through gendered relations, we need to attend to the ways in which the recognition of difference is structured by patriarchy. Talking and writing together about the violence of gendered ways of knowing identity and difference, today's university students are shifting collective understanding of the solitudes of university work. Despite the imperative to read the appearance of solitudes as proof of isolation, injury, or illness, or as signs or symptoms of the existence of "problems," our conversations revealed solitudes both as sites of, and spaces within the university for new ways of imagining women's work. We learned that the university must create space for the diverse appearances and experiences of women and non-women-identified students, and *they* are re-appropriating and renaming the university as a foundation for new ways of thinking about difference.

ACKNOWLEDGMENTS

We thank Elvi Whittaker for the opportunity to dialogue with the contemporary woman student experience and for her guidance and valuable feedback, as well as Kersti Krug, Joan Anderson, and the anonymous reviewers. We are grateful to Tanya Titchkosky, Rod Michalko, and Eliza Chandler for supporting women students' creative and poetic works, and to all of the students who spoke with us, including Alexandra Aubrecht, Christina Aubrecht, Drew Danielle Belsky, Julia Chisholm, Jodi Cunningham, Brandy Jensen, Patty Douglas, Tania Ruiz-Chapman, and to the mothers, daughters, sisters, colleagues, classmates, professors, staff, administrators, artists, activists, friends, neighbours, strangers whose daily struggles and collective projects make the social and political significance of women students' life and work in the university something worth talking about. This research was supported in part by funding from the Social Sciences and Humanities Research Council of Canada.

Notes

1 LGBTTIQQ2SA is an acronym that represents lesbian, gay, bisexual, transgender, transsexual, intersex, queer, questioning, two-spirit, and ally communities who do not conform to heterosexual or cisgender identities. The initialism is employed in Canada as a positive symbol of inclusion representative of diverse sexualities and gender variant communities that have historically been oppressed by hetero-patriarchal culture.

2 *Cisgender* is an adjective that describes a person whose gender identification matches the sex given to them at birth. *Cisgender* can be used to differentiate between other gender identity categories such as transgender. It also signals the power and privilege that comes from being socially recognized as fitting within the gender/sex binary system.

7

Changing by Degrees:
The Narratives of Mature
Women Students

LELIA KENNEDY

INTRODUCTION

Traditionally, universities have offered both social and economic advantages in the future lives of those young students deemed capable of learning at a tertiary level. In the early days of universities in England – Oxford starting in 1096 and Cambridge in 1209 – a strong relationship existed between universities and the Church, the former offering a religious education for the latter. Students, always male, entered university at fourteen or fifteen years of age. This arrangement lasted for centuries. Later in the nineteenth century, adults seeking intellectual sustenance, with the help of public supporters, formed their own educational opportunities. Mechanics' Institutes were organized in England, Europe, and North America, largely dependent on aid from business and industry, which, in return, gained highly skilled workers. In addition, the public lecture became a popular preoccupation, not only as a form of entertainment but also as an opportunity for adult education. At these lectures, the public had exposure to experts, often from universities.

By the early 1900s, psychological testing began to support the prevailing idea of the time that intelligence continued to increase into the late teenage years but gradually declined thereafter (Wechsler 1939).[1] By this time, a strong tradition of accepting into universities only students who came directly from senior secondary graduation, presumably then at the peak of their intellectual powers, had also developed. This belief endured until the end of the Second World War.

At the end of the war, the large number of veterans, compensating for the forced postponement of their education, brought an unprecedented acceptance of older students at universities. This change was temporary. Once the veterans had been educationally processed, however, the former attitude returned. This reversal happened despite the strong evidence that older returning students did better than their younger cohorts, and even better than their own earlier performances whether in secondary school or in any previous university attendance.

Universities went back to their old policies and few adults graduated. For example, at the University of British Columbia (UBC) in 1978, a couple of decades after the veterans' era, only 0.2 per cent of the British Columbian population over thirty-five years of age had enrolled full time (Statistics Canada 1978–79). Despite this low enrolment, other institutions emerged to cater to older students by offering distance education, extension departments, and community colleges.

By the late 1970s and early 1980s, once the bulge in the young population (the baby boom) had been educated, student enrolments at universities in Canada and England dropped. The reaction to this loss of students was to focus on attracting older students. Various efforts, including research, conferences, and policy reviews, were made to assess these possibilities. Universities were encouraged by the idea that adults were not, as once believed, too intellectually limited to benefit from the experience. This was further supported by the realization that life circumstances had prevented many able people from acquiring the education they had once envisioned for themselves. At the same time, "life-long learning" emerged as a cultural notion and some institutions, spurred on by this new ideology, even bestowed credits for life experiences based on the claims presented by older prospective students. In addition, fees were lifted for those over sixty-five.

Was this the proper approach to take in this troubling situation? What if the older students could not cope with university demands? Or could not cope with a return to public life? An attempt must also be made to find out whether they did well after graduating or fell by the wayside. The study upon which this chapter depends was just such an attempt, the aim being to cast light on some of these questions.

Cultural ideas about the perimeters of adulthood were evolving. Having a second chance might change the course of one's life, and even the idea of having a second career emerged as accepted wisdom. Changing jobs had once been considered irresponsible but now it came to be seen as a chance for advancement and self-improvement, and thus was now actively encouraged. These cultural trends were a lifeline for non-traditional students and a philosophical and financial boost for universities.

Furthermore, emerging feminism encouraged women to broaden their lives and make them "meaningful." They entered universities and the work force, and increasingly were accepted in their new aspirations. They opted for a second chance, for activities once thought inappropriate (Fodor and Franks 1990; Jacobson 1991). Since 1971 at the University of British Columbia, for example, the fastest growing sector of the student population has been that of mature women; by 1975, they constituted 24 per cent of all women undergraduates (Stewart 1990, 128). At many universities, the enrolment of mature women was actively promoted with special awards, bursaries, and ongoing support from organizations such as the mature students' associations.

By 1993, the enrolment of women in universities in the United Kingdom began to outnumber that of men. The educational editor Richard Garner, reporting on a study by the Higher Education Policy Institute, observes that this is true across most areas of study and all types of universities. Women are also more likely to achieve a good degree pass and have a lower dropout rate. It is apparent in all ethnic groups, even ones where education for women is not viewed positively (Garner 2009). Similar reporting has continued to appear in the media in North America as well as in the United Kingdom. Furthermore, women who had careers in the 1960s to 1980s had planned for children later in life, after they established their careers (Goldin 2004). They, therefore, planned to manage their own education and children concurrently. According to Goldin, 21 to 28 per cent of these women had realized this dual goal by the age of forty. Consequently, women of all ages filled up the vacant seats at universities.

INTERVIEWS

Data was needed about whether the university experience was beneficial to the lives of mature people. How did they assess the influences of their new education? Did they achieve their career goals? Was getting established an easy or a lengthy process? While these were the target issues, some responses by the women also provided insight into the difficulties of making the decision to go to university, the reactions of spouses and family to this decision, and the experiences of being a mature student on campus. I interviewed women at least three to eight years after they had received a baccalaureate degree in arts or science. They ranged in age from forty to seventy and were thirty-five years or older at the time of graduation. The age of thirty-five was chosen as the lower age limit to make a clear distinction from traditional students.[2]

The original study was done in the 1980s in two countries and at three institutions – in the United Kingdom at Sussex University and Birkbeck at the University of London (itself once a Mechanics' Institute), and in Canada at UBC. Birkbeck offered standard university courses in the evening hours, which created extra opportunities for mature adults. During this time, rapidly developing research ethics and a new respect for privacy were taking hold in universities, which presented a problem for me as I sought interviewees. At Sussex University, privacy regulations were not yet in place, so names and addresses of former students of the appropriate age were available to me. At Birkbeck I had access to a general institutional mailing for volunteers. Those who volunteered to be part of the study facilitated contact with other mature graduates. At UBC I was given names and addresses but I was not permitted to phone directly until prospective interviewees had responded giving me permission to contact them.

I interviewed one hundred students, about fifty of whom were women, and in this chapter I report only on the women. In 2010, in a check on more recent experiences, six women from universities in British Columbia were also interviewed.[3] At both times, those interviewed had studied in several possible ways – full-time, part-time, only at evening courses, or through a mixture of these alternatives. They were married or not, had children or none, had been employed or not, and had differing financial resources. Some had been sent to university by their employer and given financial support. Others attended without such assistance. The interviews ranged from one

to six hours, were open-ended and informal. The mature graduates were asked for narratives about their experiences using the
Flanagan Critical Incident Technique (Flanagan 1954; Butterfield et
al. 2005). This technique required that no topic could be raised
without its having been first introduced and discussed by the person
being interviewed.

Three to eight years on average after graduation, the women were
asked to tell me the story of the effect of university on their lives.
These intervening years provided them with time for reflection on
the impact that education had on their life history. The graduates
themselves sometimes remarked on the importance of the interval
between their graduation and these interviews and how the intervening years allowed reflection. Tedder and Biesta (2009) have also
emphasized the idea of "biographical learning."

DECISION TO ATTEND UNIVERSITY

Why do women attempt to enroll at university at a later age? For
some, their early plans had been to attend university but life events
had intervened. Marriage was often one of these events. Another
was employment, supporting self and sometimes family – both
important financial considerations. Among other factors that inter-
fered with university plans was the very powerful one of living with
the stigma of having been discouraged from higher education by
secondary school teachers. Sometimes parents, in traditional patriarchal fashion, gave educational opportunities to their sons while
ignoring their equally intelligent daughters. They were supported in
this preferential treatment by the familiar expectation that daughters would marry or choose occupations then considered appropriate for women, which not require a university education. In a few
cases, poor health produced grades too low for university admittance. There were other challenges, such as a lack of encouragement,
low self-esteem, financial concerns, responsibilities for families, and
doubts about the worth of a university education (Massey, Brooks,
and Sutherland 2010). These reasons appeared equally in the earlier
study and in the recent follow-up. Women were entrapped in their
own solitudes without any apparent escape.

Yet new life circumstances created new possibilities. Women in
both periods reported this. Many decided to go to university when
there was a serious disruption in their lives, or at "critical junctures"

(MacFadgen 2008, 42). Four women made the decision after the death of husbands and a few others after divorce. Others, dealing with failing marriages, prepared for the future while they still had financial support. Some with encouraging spouses waited only through what was considered a conventional time for children to mature to an acceptable age. Many women chose a less disruptive and presumably less threatening gradual approach by choosing evening courses. Others, though successful at work, reported having long endured the adverse comparison with university-educated colleagues. This was especially true in the case of teachers without final degrees. Even a few clerks at universities made use of the special educational privileges available to them.

Not all women claimed to have had a long-standing cherished idea of a university education. One woman fashioned a dramatic narrative about the occasion of her decision. She had been drying the dishes. She paused. The house was quiet. Her children were in school. She looked out the window at the trees and a thought entered her head, "you should go to university." She finished the dishes, laid down the towel, and went directly to the university to make arrangements.

Mature women students displayed personality characteristics reflective of their new endeavours – strength, adaptability, and determination. "I discovered how much I can cope with and manage without bursting into tears. It is the discovery of one's own capabilities. I keep pushing back the barriers. I have wondered when I am going to come up against my limit but I have never got there. There has still been plenty of space to play around in. It's the same as having children – you discover you can survive." This self-confidence seemed warranted as this particular woman attended university full-time, cared for an aged mother, coped with crises with her children and ex-husband, and managed a huge house and the several boarders she had taken in out of financial necessity. Such demands demonstrate the burdens faced by many women and coping strategies they have.

COPING WITH DUAL RESPONSIBILITIES: PUBLIC AND PRIVATE LIVES

The majority of mature women students, unlike their traditional student counterparts, had established adult lifestyles to maintain. Over 80 per cent of the women had been or were married or in long-term relationships. As Edwards (1993) indicates in her research on mature women at university, the private and public worlds were forced to merge when the women began to pursue education, and the question of the connection of family to the educational process came to the fore. The popular assumption socially afloat about this combination of responsibilities was generally negative, causing many women anxiety about the possibility of looming catastrophes.

Mature graduates who reported marital difficulties were concerned mainly with everyday managing of household duties. However, four women had enrolled at university in anticipation of impending marriage breakdown and economic uncertainties about the future. As one participant explained, "I went back to university because I really didn't have a marketable skill. I wanted a job I could enjoy when my husband and I broke up. I knew it was coming because I had found out he was going out with another woman." Some women initially blamed their attendance at university for the dissolution of their marriage, but later it became clear that marriage problems had led to their becoming students in the first place. Apparently blaming a marriage breakdown on preoccupation with studies was more socially acceptable than admitting to the alcoholism or physical abuse that caused the initial problem.

Many mature graduates spoke of spousal encouragement as critical to their success. "A good marriage survives any changes that occur," noted a Sussex woman. Husbands tended to children and accepted household chores, which, for some men, meant behaving quite out of character compared to their previous reliance on traditional marital expectations. In many cases, the emotional ties in a marriage were reported as strengthened by virtue of the special help extended by a spouse. One husband "welcomed me every night with a cup of tea when I came home tired. When I felt like giving up, he would remind me I would regret it forever. He was a tower of strength. His part in keeping me going was absolutely essential. I couldn't get through without a happy home life. If that part of life is okay, then one doesn't have to worry about other things besides university. I wrote him a letter afterwards, telling him how marvelous he had been to me."

Inevitably, there was also spousal ambivalence. Now a successful author, one woman reported that her husband had been supportive enough while she was at university, but later refused, rather unexpectedly in her eyes, to read anything that she had successfully published. She noted that nothing else had occurred in their relationship to cause this attitude.

Several mature graduates noted the contagious influences of their education. One husband followed in his wife's footsteps to university. Another described himself as having experienced four university educations – his own, his wife's, and that of his two children. One husband was reported as being most appreciative when the wives of several colleagues were having "nervous breakdowns." In contrast, his own wife was developing into a stronger person.

Some husbands were reported as ambivalent and uncharacteristically demanding. It appears strange and more than merely coincidental that two husbands in two different countries suddenly developed a passion for opera, playing Wagner at top volume for hours on end. Some spouses vacillated – sometimes they were encouraging, sometimes irritable. When I interviewed a few husbands, they expressed pleasure in their wives' more interesting and fulfilling lives, perhaps bowing to what they recognized as the emerging social perspectives on this issue. Thus, despite popular misgivings, the mature graduates reported their marriages to be happy, untrammeled by their educational experiences and declared satisfaction with their lives as a result (Jacobson 1991). Perhaps, after all, the integrative processes in marriage were accelerated by the stress, struggle, and the achievement university education introduced. A typical comment was "it made our married life so much more interesting. We are able to talk together. We are taking night courses together. We have a wonderful time. In fact, we don't have enough time together. We are fortunate that way." Despite prevailing expectations, more mature graduates married as a result of meeting partners at university than were divorced for being there.

Two-thirds of the mature graduates had children. Family sizes ranged from one to five children, aged from infancy to independent adulthood, although most children of those interviewed attended secondary school at the time. One son started university a day after his mother. Another mother started university after both her children had completed two degrees each. Some mature students had extraordinary family responsibilities while attending university as in the case of one, who, as well as having three children of her own, gave a home to several foster children. Another took under her care the entire family of a dead friend.

In discussing both short-term and long-term influences on children, with few exceptions, the women felt that their children had benefitted rather than suffered. They argued that children were exposed to a positive attitude towards education: "My getting a degree definitely set up in the children's minds that this was the sort of thing that women did. All my children are going to university. I really enjoyed university and I think it rubbed off on my kids." One daughter informed me, "If parents are in a learning situation, they are more real people to their children." Another mother noted an unexpected difference: "My children were okay while I went to school. I was always able to leave after the kids and get home before them. They never complained about my going to university. That reminds me, in the year I did stay home and was redecorating and getting caught up in my housework, I started to be fussy about the children leaving their things lying around and they observed, 'We sure liked it better when you were going to school.'"

The opposite could also be found. In the 1980s sample, only two mothers reported unpleasantness. "My children, who were in their teens, were resentful, especially the two who were at university at the same time as me. They didn't realize how well I would do, getting *As* and honours. They resented helping around the house. It was all right when I was working, but not when I was doing something 'ridiculous for my age.' My sons still resent that I went to university." The age of the children seemed to be a factor in their reactions. No mothers of younger children had difficulties, but not surprisingly, teenagers were frequently more opinionated.

The mature graduates were more relaxed about the timing of their own children's university education. Many believed that students need not proceed to university directly from high school. They advocated work and life experience as advantageous preparations for university. The changes most commonly reported as resulting from mothers' educational accomplishments were enhanced communication, sharing of university experiences, reducing intrusions into the children's lives, and acquiring more sophisticated child-rearing skills.

FRIENDSHIPS AND SOCIAL
EXPERIENCE AT UNIVERSITY

Most mature graduates found the university to be a goldmine for friendships (Gunn and Parker 1987) and claimed as many young friends as mature ones. While they were aware of belonging to the category of "older students," they did not report incidents of discrimination, but typically reported making friends among students of all ages and sometimes among the professors. "I'm not sure what gave the most pleasure, the actual studying or being with young people. They forget that you are older after the first few days. You forget yourself. Without the gracious young students at university, I doubt I would have survived." Ten women reported keeping their younger university friends years after graduation, incorporating them into their private lives: "I have always done a lot of entertaining, a lot of dinner parties. I mixed my husband's business associates with my school chums. I had so many friends, lots of them young fellows hungry for a meal." The long-term friendships formed the nucleus of post-university gatherings. "I made some good friends. You can't close the textbooks and say friendships are over after the finals. We've kept together. We call ourselves The Group."

Friendships with younger students proved mutually beneficial. Being parental substitutes was the crux of some friendships, and there was an amused observation about "eroded shoulders." Younger students responded by sharing familiarity with the campus, carrying books, and providing assistance on field trips. The women claimed mutually valuable contributions in dealing with essays and in discussions on lectures and textbooks.

Many made deliberate efforts to maintain links to old friends. "I retained old friends all the way through because I kept thinking one must need friends when it is all over. I would call them once in a while and they would understand why I was too busy to see them." Yet the pressures of study, the lack of time, and a loss of common interests inevitably took their toll. The strongest friendships and the most understanding old friends survived the years of study. Others did not. Many mature graduates, facing the inevitable, echoed the sentiment expressed by a woman from Birkbeck: "It was a good way of weeding out friends."

THE AFTERMATH OF UNIVERSITY:
EMPLOYMENT, NON-EMPLOYMENT,
AND EVERYDAY LIFE

All the graduates offered narratives about life after university. When they began the journey, half the women were housewives. The next most common occupation was teaching, some without the required basic qualifications, which had inspired the educational move. Several others were secretaries and artists. Other occupations listed were clerical officer, government officer, lab assistant, manager, notary public, nursery school proprietor, and flight attendant.

The search for jobs usually began months before graduation. Some returned to previous positions. At the time of the interview, many were fully employed, some were unemployed, and about half were in post-graduate studies. Four women in the earlier sample continued to a PhD. Among the expressed career interests, education, in one form or another, was the chief preoccupation. This particular interest of mature students has been reported in several studies (e.g., Woodley 1991). Sixteen women upon graduation either became or continued as teachers. Eight became instructors in colleges and polytechnical institutes, three became counsellors, two were social workers, two were lawyers, and two were employment officers. Beyond these, the occupations were as office worker, farm owner, notary public, advisor, research director, administrator, proprietor, manual worker, and play reader. From time to time, some opted for part-time rather than full-time work to satisfy their husbands' expectations about their availability to host events or to accompany them on business trips. Five were either unemployed or not seeking employment. Difficulties in the employment market for women over fifty in England resulted in some not finding desirable jobs and having to settle for less attractive employment. A similar problem existed for two immigrants to Canada, further complicated by the limitations of strong accents.

Students in the first study graduated in the 1980s, and those in the latest study graduated in the late 2000s; at both times, economic conditions were not optimal. Even those who hoped to teach faced difficulties. "There had been a shortage of teachers for forty years, and as soon as I graduate there is a surplus of 40,000," stated an English woman. Some prospective teachers, opting for interim substitute-teaching jobs, were eventually able to fill the full-time positions they wanted. All around, the advantages of post-graduate education were evident. "I didn't have a problem getting a job, luckily. I did a philosophy master's and that helped. It gave me the edge over candidates who had not done that. The headmaster admires academic achievement." There were other narratives from teachers about job satisfaction resulting from their degrees: "I do actually lecture in the subject I like learning about. I'm happy building on the knowledge I've got. I found that as I learned more I enjoyed myself more. A cheering experience! You realize you are alive mentally." Others were equally enthusiastic: "I look forward to going to school every day. Holidays can be a drag because I miss the students. It is a pleasure. I hope it always will be."

Not always, however, was there satisfaction in teaching: "I don't even like teaching. The courses are so superficial and trivial. I feel totally at odds with the school. I have always hated even the school environment. Never liked it." The pay ensured her commitment to teaching, however. Obviously, expectations had risen with university education and now seemed to rest not merely on the belief that they were fulfilling the basic demands of the job but on acquiring opportunities for themselves as well. One woman remarked, "I am making a lot more money but it isn't the financial part that is the criterion. It was at one time but now I want a job I enjoy. This is one of the changes that has occurred. I wouldn't want a job now that didn't make me work hard and be completely involved in it." This sentiment was echoed by another woman for whom work satisfaction had become a crucial issue: "I am my own department and have a secretary. I had the job sewn up in three months. I then said to my boss, 'You must expand this job as there is nothing left to do.' I had to spread five letters over two days." A new perspective on self-enrichment had emerged: "I am now committed to both teaching and continuing academic work and find satisfaction in both."

Sometimes a career goal simply could not be attained. The most disgruntled mature graduate in this study had attended university with a single profession, social work, in mind. Failing to qualify for the particular graduate studies required, she found herself unable to enjoy the jobs she eventually did acquire, even though they were similar to social work.

Although in pursuit of career goals, many were content to take stopgap employment, often slow and disheartening. An English woman, for example, worked full time as a filing clerk, as well as being given mere hours a week in her preferred field of further education. Each year she was invited to teach a few more hours and finally a permanent position opened. Being single she was able to subsist on a part-time salary. Despite such setbacks, however, a 2011 study shows that mature graduates, whether they studied part time or full time, secured paid work, graduate-level work and with a higher salary, and they did this more frequently than traditional graduates (Woodfield 2011).

At times, age was a stressful disadvantage. "There was a job advertised that was just my cup of tea – everything I could do. I got a letter back saying that twenty-five years was the maximum age for the job." Despite their experience, mature graduates claimed to accept, realistically and philosophically, the level at which they were hired: "Start at the bottom again." A few older graduates complained about delayed promotions, though most were eventually promoted: "I know that, in many ways for my career, it has been a disadvantage, certainly in the short term. When I look around me I see where others have got to."

On other occasions, gender was clearly the disadvantage. One applicant was offered the directorship of a community centre. A few days after her appointment, however, she received a letter informing her that the job had been changed to that of secretary, consisting of typing letters and similar activities. Disappointed, she refused the job, in the belief that her gender occasioned the change in job description.

It was not uncommon for mature graduates to express a necessity, even an obligation, to "repay society" for their education. A broad range of newly acquired community-oriented repayment activities followed: volunteering for organizations such as Meals on Wheels, being board members, taking part in choirs, arts clubs, and writers' clubs, and coaching sports such as grass hockey, swimming, and skiing. Several donated time and effort to their church. In addition, they used skills learned at university in boosting their communities through the field of publishing, from producing books, handbooks, and newspaper articles to professional editing, research, and teaching. One graduate, in recognition of many such efforts, was honoured as Woman of the Year.

THE GIFTS OF INTELLECT, CONFIDENCE, AND SELF-REFLECTION

As if taken from a promotional discourse about the benefits of higher education, the women described the university as "a greenhouse for intellect" and "like opening a new magnificent book." Almost half of them referred to significant intellectual changes: "I came to the concert-pitch of my brain-waves, using what was given to me." Most extolled the exposure to new ideas, and of having greater awareness

and a deeper understanding of local and world events. One participant remarked, "Going to university is mental expansion. I was introduced to concepts I didn't dream existed before. The whole sphere
increases both in regard to the content of one's own courses and in
relation to other disciplines." Another cited a familiar discourse:
"The more one does at university the less one feels one knows, yet
one can look back at former ignorance."

Abandoning a blind trust in authority was an important reported
change. Before university, one woman, while trying to educate herself in the field of art history, became concerned about the contradic-
tory statements she found in books. Once enrolled in university,
however, she learned that books merely reflected informed opinions,
that personal evaluation was paramount, and that a firm foundation
for many subjects was a rare commodity.

Self-reflection became a common reported experience. "My preju-
dices were deep to begin with, and through knowledge I came to
have more rational values. Rather than taking things for granted I
learned to look at several points of view." Another claimed, "It taught
me to think in abstract terms and to see occurrences and behaviour as
part of a larger system. Uneducated people don't see things this way."

Other intellectual gains mentioned were the discipline of thought,
thinking precisely, and learning to look with a critical eye: "Perhaps
the best part of the course was the practical criticism. I can listen to
the radio and read articles in the newspaper, I see what is wrong and
why." A great intellectual boost was having learned to use the library.
They had learned skills missing from their previous lives – to analyze, organize, and concentrate. The very discipline of thought was
often lauded: "My concentration is better and I absorb better. I concentrate on lectures all the time while other people complain of not
being able to focus their attention." They reported becoming more
realistic and more up-to-date in their subject. The graduates reported
a new appreciation of the arts, reading more sophisticated literature,
and writing and speaking in a more sophisticated way. This was
especially noted among those who had had limited earlier opportunities. "I read books and authors which I wouldn't have done on my
own, such as Homer – where everything began. Without going to
school, you don't pick up these things and read them for fun."

Perhaps somewhat perversely, several women reported drawbacks
as a result of their educational experiences. One felt her knowledge
was disappearing, referring presumably to what she knew before

the university period; another said that she did not learn much; and another woman suggested that university had knocked the magic out of her life because she had lost the ability to enjoy her own imagination.

Capitalizing on the intellectual gains, several students who continued with graduate work published their own work or facilitated publishing by others. They reported published textbooks, books on specialized areas in their disciplines, or contributions to encyclopedias and handbooks. One wrote freelance articles for a prestigious newspaper, and one was an editor of a somewhat obscure literary journal.

THE SENSE OF SELF

Perhaps the most significant consequence of earning a degree was the perceived advantages to the person, the sense of self. Not until they had discussed the more public aspects of their experiences did their thoughts turn to personal development. A Sussex graduate expressed this well: "I have a strange feeling that there is a whole side I haven't talked about at all, an intuitive bit I haven't expressed – an ability to apply, and having a seeing eye through insight gained through study, and therefore a heightened appreciation of everything you do. One is conscious of this going on as it happens." As during the interviews they had alluded to such personal changes, I was free to press them about it. Some were surprised by such questions admitting to not having thought about that aspect of their education. On the spur of the moment, however, many were able to describe these very changes. A woman, who had enrolled in UBC for personal development reasons stated, "There is no question that the primary function of a university should be personal development. I don't believe that it is a job factory. We need expertise, of course, but we also need a complete person – a renaissance ideal should be prized." However, keeping the recognizable attributes of their former selves, particularly a proper level of humility, was equally important. "People say university hasn't changed me and I am flattered. I keep thinking of my older daughter who has completed an MA in economics. It so changed her. She is so academic it gives me a pain."

Of all changes in to the person, "self-confidence" was most significant and frequently mentioned. The women reported feeling equal in situations where they had previously felt inferior. "To me, the real influence of a degree is in how I see myself. I feel as though I've got more to offer, more as a person. It differentiates me from other people. I feel I'm as good as anyone else, a valuable feeling." A gain in self-respect, self-sufficiency, and self-fulfillment helped to obliterate a previous sense of inadequacy. Above all, they valued themselves for having finished a degree: "More than anything, that is what I got out of it – self-image and assurance – a feeling of self-accomplishment, which was very valuable to me, especially as a secondary school dropout. I had felt incomplete all through the years." One participant described her lack of self-confidence as so severe that she could barely force herself to sit waiting for an interview for admission to university: "It was a shock to my family to have me change from a non-person to someone with enough confidence to do anything I wanted." There was a new confidence in their own judgments and beliefs, in realizing their own capabilities, and in believing that they had actual contributions to make. They reported more independence, emotional strength, and increased poise in dealing with groups, in expressing opinions in front of others, and in persuading a group to accept their ideas – all seen as valuable not only in life but also in committee work and public speaking. One woman noted, "I became more assertive, having learned how to talk about things."

Reports of being rejuvenated were another way of reflecting these new powers. "I still feel eighteen or nineteen. This was one thing university did for me. I think there is a great gain for an older person, a new lease on life. I was revitalized." They reported new strength in dealing with adversity and trauma. On the death of her child, for example, one woman handled her grief by increasing her studies from part-time to full-time. She firmly believed her mental health had been preserved by preoccupation with study instead of dwelling on her loss.

Barbara Merrill (2009) emphasizes the changes in adult identities resulting from experiences in education. Biographies or self-histories help us realize that adult learners experience the instabilities of social, economic, political, and technological changes. Changes, and even transformations, can be absolute, almost oppositional reconstructions of the personality, such as, in one case, moving from being a nun to being a businesswoman. Although changes and transformations were certainly met, the fragmentation to which she referred was not seen. The graduates in this study had been successful and used the time after graduation to become settled. An example of this fragmentation is shown in the following comment: "You lose all your reference points at university. It changes all your values – turns you right upside down. Education caused us to challenge what we knew but there was nothing to take its place. Somehow, you just end up feeling you were right and don't lose your original values." A nun left the church and went into business. Although this particular conversion took a long time, she reported happiness once the full change was finalized. This new grasp on power was often tempered by more sensitivity to the feelings of others. One graduate narrated a greater willingness to be dependent on others and supported this claim by marrying and giving birth to a child.

Comments on emotions also revealed the influence of university education. Mature graduates most often mentioned tolerance, which increased, and prejudice, which decreased. More Sussex students than others reported increased tolerance, a greater understanding of the problems of others. In almost all narrations, higher education is seen as the enriching ingredient: "It is a deepening of experience, a heightened appreciation of everything you do." To this was added the liberation and broadening of life opportunities, an ability to select the most rewarding choices, and generally a greater quality of life: "All the parameters and boundaries to life vanished. I learned that if you want to do something, you *can* do it." As many had done before them, they admitted that, in applying the skills learned at university, they were actually able to "appreciate knowledge for its own sake." A recent interviewee stated emphatically, "Going to university is absolutely worthwhile. I will tell anyone to take a later degree. It lasts the rest of your life and adds to your enjoyment of it."

Out of over fifty mature graduates, 98 per cent were pleased and sometimes ecstatic about their experience at university and beyond. In comparison, in a university survey at UBC, Laliberte (2006) found that 95 per cent of students were pleased or very pleased with their university experience. Sussex had percentages that increased from below 85 per cent in previous years to almost 90 per cent in 2014 (University of Sussex 2014). And the evening university, Birkbeck (University of London 2012), had the highest student satisfaction scores among London universities – in the 90 per cent range consistently since 2005. Only one woman, seventy years of age, who was interviewed for the original study was completely negative about the experience and seemed depressed. Another woman only complained of feeling overworked.

DISCUSSION

That mature women learn well at university has been known for many years. What was not readily apparent was their ability to use their education to cope with the wider world. It was found in the study that among those who desired employment, for example, there appeared to be no age limits for the capacity to change, or to move beyond university into the working world. In economically strained times when work was relatively hard to find, age did not seem to impede success or full-time employment. These women sought jobs with complexity, variety, and challenge, and on the whole reported high job satisfaction. Their experiences in the job market revealed that they appeared to have no greater difficulty than traditional graduates. Most found satisfying positions and improved their economic situation considerably.

Intellectual changes in viewing the world, and changes to identity and the self were noted by the large majority of those interviewed. Greater cognizance of world events, a new engagement with the social and cultural world, an inclination that was previously more remote, now emerged. This was coupled with a growing awareness of self, a confidence in this newly evolving self, and a newly discovered tolerance for others. While no doubt these changes are also claimed by regular graduates, the somewhat unexpectedness of this new knowledge typified the mature graduate responses. It was as if it were a surprising bonus beyond that of improving their economic situation; it was as if a world opened, one hitherto hidden from them. They spoke of enrichment, broadened horizons, and a love of learning. Some of these changes were radical enough to be seen as conversions. The responses did not appear to be occasioned by matters of class or socioeconomic status and appeared in all the interviewees. Rather these changes seem to speak to earlier solitudes, both intellectual and in perceptions of self and identity, that characterized the lives of the mature graduates in the period before they entered university.

Besides these intellectual changes, the social solitude, as they once experienced it, also appeared to evaporate. While they did not complain of any earlier lack in social connections, they did enter into new relationships. Despite different countries of origin, universities, and times of attendance, the mature graduates had a new strong foundation of community, much as if, as one put it, "they had been raised in the same village." This foundation of community created a

sense of belonging and a feeling of being at home with themselves
and the university (Kennedy and Vaughn 2004). Expectedly, the
mature students who had the most similarities with each other were
those who had been sent to university to complete their education by
their employers. They also maintained their business friends throughout the university period and after graduation.

The mature students did not complain of ageist treatment from
the traditional students. It is clear, however, as Aubrecht and Lay
point out in their chapter in this volume, that traditional students
belong to a clear category of "older student." The mature students in
this study, even if they sensed the exclusion that might occur with
this categorization by age, seemed to avoid the possibilities of any
stigma by adopting, overtly and without prompting, a mature stance
– an unchallenging posture that avoided friction. They proclaimed
their maturity clearly and did not attempt an age kinship. Nor did
they seem to consider the younger students as a reference group in
their lives or studies. Good-naturedly, they performed motherliness
or alternately presented themselves as novices in need of help.

A contrast exists between the mature graduates in this study and
in the studies of students still at university. The mature graduates'
comments concerning their education were of a high positive nature,
even more positive than the 90 per cent satisfaction with the arts and
science programs shown in many years of surveys. The critical attitudes reported by Aubrecht and Lay come from students still at university and burdened by race, sex, and disability. Another difference
between mature graduates and the students studied by Gouthro
(2009) is that the latter expressed concern about the state of the market place and its effect on future jobs. In addition, the cost of education was an ongoing problem. Lavell (1998) reported that educational
costs were a major source of anxiety for single mothers. She also
noted that these students reported a middle-class bias against the
working-class students. While these factors affected many students
during university, they seemed to have no effect in the reporting of
mature graduates in the years after their graduation. Furthermore,
the mature graduates in my study did not have the burdens of race or
disability. The pressures and platforms of contemporary university
student cultures no longer applied to them as students. If they once
suffered from solitudes, they appeared to be free from them once at
university. They also seemed unaffected by the ageist solitudes characteristic of most student cultures.

When interviewed, almost all the mature graduates had achieved professional status, changed their lifestyle, and found satisfaction for their achievements. Despite popular opinion that they must be disadvantaged by their age, they find themselves situated at least as well as, and often better than, younger students vocationally, financially, socially, personally, and intellectually.

ACKNOWLEDGMENTS

Much gratitude is owed to all the women in England and in Canada who participated and gave freely of their time and experience. Also thank you to my former PhD supervisor at Sussex, Tony Becher, a model of a man, who encouraged the biographical approach.

Notes

1 The belief about decreased intelligence lingers in popular knowledge. There is, however, a large body of literature and research on this issue, dispensing with it as a myth. See, for example, Horn and Donaldson 1976; Allman 1988; Schaie and Zanjani 2006.

2 The category of "mature student" varies widely from university to university, from researcher to researcher. Some university classifications place the age of mature student as early as twenty-one. In contrast, most statistics provided by governments on the age span of university students give separate age categories, thereby avoiding the labelling of maturity. MacFadgen, in her study of mature students, describes mature students as "25 years of age or older taking degree-level courses and who had adult life roles and circumstances, flexible enrolment status, and varied educational goals and intentions" (2008, 5n1).

3 The latter students were from UBC and Simon Fraser University.

8

The Non-Nons: Secretarial and Clerical Staff

ISABELLA LOSINGER

For the uninitiated, the lure of the university as workplace is irresistible. From a societàl viewpoint, the production, transmission, and exchange of knowledge is a stimulating and highly valued activity. Many prospective employees value the academy as a workplace and indeed see for themselves a productive role in student services, research management, and a myriad of administrative positions, for instance. At a very basic level, it is hard not to be captivated by the student experience: the perpetual youth of individuals who fill our classrooms at the beginning of each academic year, their emotional and intellectual growth over many years of study, and the ceremony of graduation, all of which makes working at a university an ostensibly enjoyable and rewarding occupation.

THE FEUDAL NATURE OF THE ACADEMY: INVISIBLE IN THE HIERARCHY

The university as workplace has been imaginatively described by many observers of higher education: at any one university we might find Sanskrit scholars, accountants, glass blowers, philosophers, and curators of pregnant hamsters (Wriston 1959, 7). However, the quaintness of these occupations (barring the accountants) belies the full reality of the working university in that it fails to include *all* members of the campus community. This exclusion of staff is endemic to the literature of higher education. Whether handbook, memoir, history, or self-reflective volume, writing in higher education has largely ignored the presence of the many different campus workers who do everything but teach. University staff is often an after-thought, or more practically speaking, a non-thought. Indeed, the term "non-non," surely the most cryptic of terms found in the American literature of higher education to describe university staff, reveals the university's fixation on defining a large percentage of its workforce by what it does not do: non-academic, non-faculty, non-teaching, non-professional, and non-classified (Szekeres 2004; Hohenstein and Williams 1974; Reyes and Smith 1987; Looker 1998; Freeman and Roney 1978). Indeed, there is a lack of sincerity (or perceived value) in gaining any measurable appreciation of the university employee's daily working environment. This reluctance could result from a distinct queasiness at the possible answers. While the university prides itself on its stance of political neutrality, freedom of speech, and unconditional inclusivity, the internal working realities reveal that stratification – in multiple forms – is the campus norm.[1]

Given the implacability of the faculty ranking structure, the tensions between academic and fiscal mandates, and the intense competition for internal and external resources, it is hardly surprising that the university remains a feudal enterprise. Within that enterprise, the staff predictably is placed in a "non" position as it compares with the rights (and, admittedly, the obligations) that accrue to the other members of the university. Department heads, deans, and other senior academic leaders are accorded a status akin to barons (rarely baronesses) and kings: these individuals are "held aloft by the drudgery of many common folk" (Houck 1990, 3). The craftspeople and skilled workers of the feudal society are analogous to the administrative, clerical, and secretarial classes of the university. These individuals are not part of the society; instead, they "stand apart" from it (Houck 1990, 7). And standing apart certainly implies isolation. While staff can find a collective identity in organized labour groups and professional associations, their daily working environment leaves many of them isolated, particularly in academic units where there may be only one or two staff members. Those whose occupations require them to work after regular office hours are particularly vulnerable: many university toilets are cleaned at night, when the rest of the university community has left the campus (Halpern 2003).[2] The invisible nature of staff employees – whether nighttime custodians or administrative assistants – means that their working stories are largely absent or non-existent. They do not normally publish memoirs, leave items to institutional archives, or produce other such records of their working experiences.[3] There are no large sets of data, primary or otherwise, to attest to their experiences, although some studies on student services and labour relations have been completed as part of graduate work. In the Canadian context, graduate projects have focused on the role of women staff, minority staff, professional development, and informal learning, for instance (Ruchkall 1997; Lizotte 1997; Dressler 1995; Rapaport 1997). In regards to the history and development of the university staff complement the literature is even thinner.[4] Giving the university staff themselves a voice is an intense undertaking. Universities have invariably considered their resources to be better invested in hagiographic departmental and institutional histories, with few making any real effort to include the voice of staff beyond occasional references to, on the one hand, employee dedication ("without whom the university could not function") and, on the other, the travails of industrial action from the various unionized groups on campus.

ADMINISTRATIVE ASSISTANTS
(AKA "SECRETARIES")

Of the many employee groups on campus the administrative assistant is a constant at all institutions. The administrative assistant, a job title increasingly used instead of "secretary,"[5] is invariably female. She is often the first person one meets upon entering a department or administrative unit. It has long been acknowledged that first impressions are critical to, for instance, prospective students (or parents) who are deciding on a university, prospective faculty members as they consider employment offers, and department heads or senior academic leaders in the midst of recruitment. A smile from the receptionist instantly creates an environment hopefully conducive to a successful outcome to the business to hand. Furthermore, whether amenable or not, the assistant often acts as gatekeeper and general factotum. In an academic unit, she guards access to the department head and is privy to information – often of a highly sensitive and confidential nature – that no other staff or faculty member has. A trusted intermediary, the assistant can also be the department head's prime source of information, being an integral part of the campus grapevine (Coffman 2005, 95). The belief that she is the one person who really knows what's going on has been substantiated by research in both the public and private sectors (Andrews 1995, 60), and her ability to cultivate relationships for intelligence purposes is a much-valued (and admired) skill.

Consider the university administrative assistant in greater depth. With very few notable exceptions, we know little of her working life, and even less about her feelings about the job and about the university as employer.[6] An ongoing satirical column in the *Times Higher Education Supplement* regularly features "Maureen," a departmental secretary at the fictional Poppleton University. Literary humour aside, Maureen's working life is arduous and undervalued. In her book *Killing Thinking: The Death of the Universities*, Mary Evans describes Maureen's role:

> Much of the work necessary to the continuation of the university, and the academic department, is performed by the hard working secretary Maureen. Indeed, in this case "hard working" scarcely does justice to Maureen's contribution. Maureen is always at work, when at work she is always in her office, and when in her office she is always fully aware of what is going on. As the academics stagger through their days in a haze of confusion, either internal or external, Maureen is always on hand to deal with student questions, the intricacies of assessment documents and the running of the department. A few academics take the managerial shilling and become the authors of complex business plans but in the main it is Maureen, for a salary which is probably half that of most academics, who literally services the academic world. (2004, 78–9)

SOLITUDE AND UNACKNOWLEDGED DEDICATION

In the "real" university world, Maureen has her counterpart in countless nameless individuals, of whom only a few (perhaps just one?) have left a written record of her working days. The one splendid Canadian example is that of Dorothy McMurray, former secretary to four university presidents at McGill University. McMurray worked at McGill from 1929 to 1963 and at some time during, or shortly after, those years jotted down her memories of the many years spent in the President's Office. Ironically, McMurray's *Four Principals of McGill* (1974) would probably never have survived had McMurray not received a phone call (on the very day she was culling her household contents, including these memoirs) from Stanley Brice Frost, director of the History of McGill Project. Frost was aware that McMurray had recorded some notes and his well-timed phone call was a plea for their preservation in the interests of the university's historical record. McMurray must have agreed with alacrity; and the book, once rescued from the rubbish bin, was subsequently published by the Graduates' Society of McGill in a limited print run of five hundred copies (Frost 1984). Sold at ten dollars a copy, the book's proceeds were donated at McMurray's request to the McGill Development Fund. Unfortunately, the book does not provide much detail of McMurray's specific job duties. Rather, it focuses on the work of the four presidents themselves. Nonetheless, a poignant glimpse into the loneliness of her working life is found in her summation of the total experience: "I saw these four completely different personalities attempt the back-breaking, heart-breaking job of running McGill, and possibly there is no one left today who knows as well as I do what a really heart-breaking, back-breaking job it was" (McMurray 1974, 9). McMurray's modesty allowed her but a few confessions as it related to her own capacity to do the work involved. On occasion, she conceded moments (and sometimes more) of physical exhaustion: eighteen months of having to "stumble home after a day much too long" might embitter employees today, but McMurray's capacity for work was informed by a dedication to McGill and an unwavering loyalty to the presidential incumbent. This loyalty, apart from an honorary degree, went largely unacknowledged by McGill's institutional historians.[7] McMurray's dedication was also at variance with the oft-bruited suggestion that university staff have jobs whereas faculty have careers, the inference being that the former are more motivated by compensation than the latter (Corson 1975, 83–4; Perkins 1973, 163).

CONTRIBUTING TO INSTITUTIONAL HISTORY

Yet secretaries and other university staff *do* want to be part of an institution's history. As I learned during my interviews with staff, they want to leave a legacy that will be captured by historians and writers in higher education. As Alice, the pseudonym of a secretary who worked at the University of British Columbia from 1969 to 1971, remarked, "I would like to see a lot about the contribution of the people who are working there 'cause you always see a lot about who the head honchos were ... all those guys they've had so much fame and fortune from the work they did at the university and of course it was deserved but there were so many people who were the cogs in the wheel who just never got any recognition at all" (2007, interview with the author). Brenda, a secretary employed at UBC in 2007, also explained, "I'd like to see more on, yes, the professors are important and the doctors and the research and everything but those of us behind the scenes that no one – no one really knows about" (2007, interview). At the very least, secretaries and other staff want to be recognized as being an integral part of the university, rather than a silent, unacknowledged or "back-stairs" group. This may particularly be the case for the university assistant who, as has been earlier described, is often the first person seen upon physical entry to a university unit, whether administrative or academic. Away from the reception desk, she is responsible for a myriad of tasks, activities, and priorities that all elude the casual observer. For the employees themselves, these tasks aggregate to what is often a fulfilling (if sometimes tiring) working experience. Indeed, it is striking how many assistants (i.e., former secretaries), despite the passage of many years for some of them, have retained rich, informative memories of their working environments, their daily tasks, and the people with whom they worked.

Common themes and memories emerge. These remain reasonably uniform throughout the decades: thoughts about wages and benefits (and lack thereof), enjoyment or dislike of the work, relationships (testy, friendly, or otherwise) with staff colleagues and faculty, and issues of hierarchy, status, and respect. Regardless of the circumstances of the individual, their words sharply convey, on the one hand, a strong sense of community and interest in the university, and, on the other, an equally strong sense of isolation and exclusion.

MEMORIES: EARLY DAYS AND CAMARADERIE

UBC, like many other large institutions of higher education, is viewed by the greater public as a stable, long-term employer. It has consequently attracted employees who have been prepared to serve lengthy terms. As part of my uncompleted doctoral research, I interviewed thirteen such employees at UBC: secretaries who had worked between 1946 and 2007. Most of these individuals had worked at multiple locations on campus. Collectively, they represented a total of thirty-three workplaces: thirteen academic departments, five faculties (i.e., deans' offices), four schools, six administrative units, one research lab, and four non-departmental/non-faculty academic units. All interview participants chose their own pseudonyms.

One of the oldest interview participants, Janet, hired at UBC in 1946, remembers secretaries who had been there "for twenty years, I think": "They were institutions in themselves, everyone would say, well, if you need to know something, go ask the secretary in this particular office, she's been there forever" (2007, interview). Janet worked as a secretary primarily in one department, but also spent a year typing theatre scripts and watching theatre students rehearse. She considered her wages to have been satisfactory and remembers that UBC had no difficulty recruiting staff. Janet's supervisor, a long-serving academic administrator, was an exacting employer, a "pretty severe, strict disciplinarian," and "an amazing administrator," who nonetheless always expressed his appreciation of a job well done.[8] His surprise at Janet's spelling prowess was clearly recalled. He repeatedly remarked to her that he could not believe that "someone who hadn't taken the science courses could spell" and that he was astonished she never needed a dictionary. While her supervisor might have found this skill surprising, Janet recalls that the women working as secretaries at UBC in the 1940s were university graduates or women like herself who had taken business courses.[9] In all, she feels that staff were treated "very nice, very well." While the food served at UBC's cafeteria was "institutional food," it "wasn't too bad," and lunchtime activities included bridge, "pep meets," or other forms of entertainment.

Despite what seems to have been a relatively enjoyable stint as secretary, Janet left the university in 1953, a year-and-a-half after being married: "I think I would not have stayed too much longer; the jobs at the university were changing ... They were setting up new departments such as the Department of Housing and taking away from our department the allocating of housing, the arranging to have them billed for their monthly rentals, things like that, they were also taking away, ah, other things that we had done, that were not part of our department, but they were setting up in individual departments because the university was growing so quickly ... As far as I was concerned, it was getting less interesting, it wasn't as diverse as it had been at the start, so I can't say that I would have stayed on too much longer."

STRATIFICATION AND SOCIALIZING

Janet's youth in her days as a secretary at UBC was evident in the enthusiasm and overall positive memories of her employment. Fiona, on the other hand, was older than Janet when she accepted a position as secretary in a large department in 1968 (Fiona, 2007, interview). Born in 1924, Fiona had worked as special assistant to the prosecutor in New Westminster, BC, prior to answering an ad in the paper for a secretarial position at UBC. Recently widowed, Fiona was interested in coming to work at UBC as she had friends in the Point Grey area and wanted to live there. Fiona's academic qualifications included a high-school education along with some business courses taken at a college. Arriving at her new position at UBC, Fiona found a "really hierarchical dynamic" in the department. The professors and secretaries were lodged in second-floor offices, and the lab technicians on the first floor. As secretary to the department head, Fiona was well positioned to observe the organizational climate: "It always rather amused me that the professors called the secretaries by their first names but that we were expected to call them Dr. this and Dr. that, [laughter] so I guess we felt our level was more ... with the people that worked in the lab." Nonetheless, Fiona certainly had fond memories of her one job at UBC, as she retained photographs taken of her going-away party (along with other informal photos of get-togethers throughout the years) when she left the university in 1971 upon her remarriage. Apart from the secretaries' short skirts, what stands out in the photos of Fiona's farewell party is the groupings of different departmental employees. Fiona identified the clusters of people: "professor, professor, professor, professor," "technical people," and "these, the other people, the other people that we socialized more than with the faculty were the grad students." In essence, the faculty was grouped at one side of the room, and the others clustered at the other side. Fiona remembers that she and the other secretaries socialized mostly with the lab technicians – often on Friday nights – with the "odd faculty member" joining in. Fiona met her second husband in this department: he was an electrical engineer who lectured on a sessional basis.

Unlike Janet, Fiona would have stayed at UBC had her second husband not wanted to take a full retirement, and had they not relocated outside Vancouver to live. However, she probably would not have stayed in the same job, due to the volume of work and wanting to move on to something else after a few years. Fiona worked a lot of overtime, returning to the office in the evenings for some quiet time during which to work on the budget. The department head was "quite particular" and Fiona's desk being right outside his office meant that she was frequently running in and out of the head's office. The head was very nice, "an old fashioned gentleman." Fiona remembers her wages (and no benefits) as having been equitable with her earnings in her previously held positions in the private and public sectors. Fiona probably would have enrolled in courses had she not been recovering from the loss of her first husband. Her aunt, after all, had received a degree from UBC, and had taught French for many years at a Vancouver high school: this same aunt had also participated in the Great Trek of 1922, a student march from an earlier site (Fairview) to what was to become the Point Grey campus of UBC. Fiona certainly had a personal and historical link to the university.

CAPABLE OF DOING MORE

Alice also had a personal link to the university (2007, interview).[10] After completing one year of studies at UBC she left to get married. At the time, her husband was a PhD student in oceanography; Alice worked as a scuba diver on the west coast of Vancouver Island and in a logging camp before accompanying her husband back to Vancouver. Alice supported him and their young child by working as a dental assistant in downtown Vancouver. In 1969, Alice applied for a job at UBC working as a technician at night in a laboratory. Shortly afterward, she worked as a secretary in a department in the science faculty, as a "general run-about," followed by a job as a clerk in another faculty. During the ensuing year and a half, her husband died. Alice was promoted to secretary to a dean, and worked for one more year, but "there was no union, there were no benefits, there was straight wages and I wasn't coping." To be able to provide a secure background for her daughter, Alice decided to leave UBC to pursue her nursing credentials. Like Janet and Fiona, Alice had loved the campus, but on her own she could not afford to remain working there. The financial imperative aside, it is suspected that Alice would have been reluctant to stay working within a secretarial capacity anyway. Regarding one of her jobs, for instance, Alice concluded that she could have supported the dean to a far greater extent than was allowed in the official scope of the job, had she been able to exercise greater autonomy: "I was basically a typist. Anything that came through the office – I was never asked for my opinion; I was never given any authority. Everything went to the dean. And he never seemed to think that he could rely on me for any of the tasks surrounding anything rather than just typing up what he wanted me to type, although by that time I knew a great deal about the university and could have taken a lot of the load off him." Alice's experience was consistent with that of many secretaries working in the university sector, and this feature might well have been one of the key differences between working in the private sector versus the public. Vinnicombe (1980, 38–9) describes the experiences of one woman who had worked for over eight years as secretary to the head of a university department. The secretary experienced the same frustrations as Alice; she was unable to initiate many activities (including responding to written enquiries) on her own volition as she was basically restricted to typing and photocopying.

Alice's lack of autonomy in her job is a common theme, repeated by other UBC secretaries in the 1970s and 1980s. Chantal, a secretary for a year during the 1970s, certainly found the work less than stimulating for that very reason (2007, interview). In particular, Chantal resented being "lectured at" when faculty asked her to do something. She knew the job that had to be done, and it "got her back up" when she was lectured at by the faculty member assigning her work. Another secretary, Gertrude, working in the late 1980s, also felt very stifled by her lack of autonomy, and this was a major factor in her eventual decision to leave UBC after four years of otherwise rewarding work (2007, interview). Gertrude had had many years of working experience before arriving at UBC for a three-month stint in an academic department. This led to a further four years of employment, all spent at a word-processing centre. The job was overall enjoyable, as Gertrude was often sent to many different units within Education to back-fill when secretaries were sick or on holiday. Sojourns at some units where Gertrude could enjoy a "certain amount of autonomy" were rewarding; less so were those where she felt stifled and did not have the autonomy she felt she needed to do the job well. Suggestively, Gertrude conceded that the organizational culture at UBC was "Dickensian": this very word was used by a visiting faculty member in whom Gertrude confided as she debated whether or not to leave UBC.[11] While Gertrude found the individual professors and staff to have been mostly "great," it was "just the way the whole work setting was set up at the time that was not conducive to me doing my best." Although she clearly had the qualifications to apply for management positions, Gertrude decided against it due to the "atmosphere" at UBC, which was not the type of environment she felt she could work in.

WORKING WITH OTHERS

Gertrude was (and is) not alone in her conclusions regarding the way the university's jobs are organized, and the personal and professional impact of a working environment in which some of the university's workforce are valued differently to others. It is inevitable that references to the people (often, the professoriate) be made by those who work *with* (rather than *for*) them, and these references help inform and define the staff working experiences. Every staff member has a story to tell about direct and indirect supervisors, academic program and department heads, deans, and executive academic leaders. For the most part, these stories are jocular, bringing to mind working relationships that are productive, respectful, and, on the surface, benign. As has already been seen, Janet's relationship with her supervisor was seemingly one of mutual respect. Leah's experience was similar, as she recalled one former dean, a "wonderful man" who "coloured my image of people with degrees." "I was young then – twenty, twenty-one years old – and he was middle aged when he retired and he came ... with a string of initials. When I typed out his name with all of his qualifications and achievements after, it pretty much took up just about two lines. But he was the humblest, gentlest man I ever met, and he was generous and he was kind ... I [now] work for lawyers and I'll tell them right up front, just because you went to university and got a degree doesn't mean you're smart" (2007, interview).

Alice also had positive working relationships with the head of her department, who was always "really in tune with his staff," who treated them "like equals," and who took them to the faculty club once a month for lunch (2007, interview). (This was in sharp contrast to a secretary Alice knew in the same unit who had been at UBC for over thirty-five years, but who felt very much on the fringe despite knowing the university "like the back of her hand.") Both Fiona and another secretary, Nina, remember a former president of UBC, Walter Gage, as "an amazing man because if he met you once, he always remembered you ... You know, even secretaries and the non-faculty, if you happened to meet him if you were out for a walk or something, and he'd remember your name. He was amazing that way" (2007, interview). Certainly, he was amazing for Nina, a long-serving UBC employee, who after some thirty years, still remembered Gage's love of teaching, as illustrated by the fact that he had taught Math 100 three times a year (2007, interview).

This sense of virtual camaraderie, however, needs to be considered within the overall boundaries – as gendered and stratified as they are – of working life at the university. In looking back over the years, as Nina put it, "there was a hierarchy, there was no doubt; there was the faculty, the staff, and the students ... but the staff knew their place. It was this – there was this huge gap between faculty and staff, and it changed over the years because I think we all realized that we are here; we are all here for the same reason, we just have different roles to play but we're all here to put bread on the table, bottom line, okay but our services are a bit different."[12] Nina's identification of a gap between faculty and staff is better known today as the faculty/staff divide. A practical example of the divide at UBC may be found in the experiences of Ruth, a secretary from 1976 to 2001 (2008, interview). While her experience in one academic unit was remembered with fondness (Ruth wears their parting gift of a "beautiful chain necklace" all the time), her final years at UBC at another unit were not. For some years prior to her retirement, Ruth worked with two other secretaries, in a unit where the female faculty far outnumbered the male. The faculty, however, proved not to be overly supportive of the staff: "They'd come in, you'd talk to them, there wasn't much interaction in the way of joking or interest in what you were doing, it was like you were there for one purpose and one purpose only. It got worse as time went on." As time indeed went by, the three secretaries asked for the opportunity to work flex time. The request for flex time, for some inexplicable reason, proved to be highly unpopular with the faculty, who seem to have been influenced by a rather heavy-handed administrator. Throughout the long months of negotiation between the administrative assistant, the secretaries, and their union, the faculty "were told things that were not true and so they really turned against the staff ... two of the women who were involved in pushing for flex time were let go and the reason for this was they needed to cut back on their budget ... I got punished, I went from an office with a view, an outside view, nice windows to an office that had absolutely no windows and I spent the rest of my time ... in there."[13]

Ruth, like Nina, was highly sensitized to the cultural and political issues of the university and understood the nature of the staff's position on campus. Both women clearly enjoyed their jobs at UBC, yet both also recognized the enormous shortcomings devolving from an artificially stratified working environment. (Ruth, it should be noted, was married to a university professor). In Ruth's estimation, the future does not necessarily promise better things for university staff, at least not at UBC. The university, says Ruth, has a significant challenge in terms of recognizing the contribution of its staff: "Over the course of twenty-fives years I saw the university change. Not necessarily for the better. I think the secretarial/clerical support staff has not received the recognition they should have. The salaries have not kept pace with other educational institutions. Faculty and students, as a whole, do not give their secretaries and clerks the recognition and support that should be given. They do not realize that without this support the university would not run as smoothly as it does (even if many of them are computer literate and do their own typing). Secretaries and clerks do much more than type a course outline or a research paper" (2008, interview).

A CALL FOR RECOGNITION

The experiences of a few secretaries over time at UBC constitute a mere capsule of data, yet a pattern emerges – a pattern that may be described as "imprecise, certainly; impressionistic, perhaps to a fault; but not without some validity" (Ziegler 2001, 303).[14] Surely each individual conveys a unique perspective on a complex environment. This perspective becomes critical as the institutional environment becomes ever more complex: administrative staff are indeed doing more than just typing course outlines or research papers. The permeation of technology throughout virtually every administrative activity has necessitated continual learning and adjustment, and increased the need for refined skills of communication, collaboration, and relationship management. Fiscal constraints, increased corporatization, and a heightened sense of accountability have further impacted staff by shuffling their positions and changing relationships.[15]

How staff perceive the institution in which they work, their roles within it, their daily experiences, and their ability to navigate their own personal and professional paths is important, if only for their labour to be recognized as an integral contribution to a university's success. How they can expose their particular solitude on campus remains to be determined. At the very least, however, there needs to be a concerted effort on behalf of university leaders to understand the needs of an increasingly educated, politically aware, and less deferential workforce. The systematic capture and preservation of historical and current working experiences of these workers would go a long way to mitigating the invisible nature of their contributions.

ACKNOWLEDGMENTS

This chapter owes its very existence to the women who generously participated in interviews about their working experiences at the University of British Columbia. In turn, its inclusion in this book is due to the generosity of Elvi Whittaker, who made space – literally and intellectually – for a discussion about people who are rarely noticed by university researchers. I would not have met Elvi but for a chance conversation with Kersti Krug, who continues to encourage me to write about working life in the university. Finally, the composition of the "Non-Nons," and the research preceding it, were possible only with the stalwart support of family: human (Kathleen, Simon‡, and Simon Charles) and canine (Lanza).

Notes

1 On this topic see especially Lubrano (2004) for a discussion of class at Columbia University. See also the musings of Rutgers University lecturer Kevin Mattson in his travels to campus by bus: the conversations of other university employees, "maids, janitors, and low-paid office workers ... told me something" (2003, 89).

2 Greg Halpern (2003), a graduate student at Harvard, produced a brilliant composition of black and white photographs of Harvard employees, capturing particularly those who work as custodians, cleaners, and servers. The majority of these workers are from minority groups.

3 A rare first-hand account is Ann Kristine Pearson (2008) in her review of administrative staff, particularly those involved in the delivery of student services, at the University of Toronto. Pearson draws on a rich personal experience to expose the complexities of administrative tasks that are largely unappreciated by those who have never done them. Her conclusion that the "professional persona of administrative staff is practically nil" is sobering. Joan Eveline's (2004) quotes from general staff (as opposed to academic staff) at Australian universities are equally sobering, speaking to themes of hierarchy, invisibility, and devaluation.

4 The works of Liebmann (1986) and McGrath (1936) are singular. Liebmann provides a foundation for writing the history of "non-academic employees," and McGrath traces the early growth of administrative positions at universities in the United States. Both these works are dated, and it is puzzling that there is so little interest from contemporary researchers in exploring the history of university staff. Notable exceptions are the studies of working women at the University of Toronto by Prentice (1991) and Wagener's (1996) published thesis on staff at Georg-August-Universität Göttingen.

5 In this chapter, I use secretary when referencing a published author who has used that term, or in my interview data of women who were hired into positions where the job title was officially designated as "secretary."

6 Crawford and Tonkinson's (1988) study of women staff at the University of Western Australia is a rare and important contribution to the literature, particularly their data regarding secretaries. As well, Pringle (1988) includes university secretaries in her interview data.

7 Dorothy McMurray is absent from Hugh MacLennan's history of McGill (1960). She is, however, referenced in Stanley Brice Frost's two-volume history of McGill as well as his biography of F. Cyril James (principal of McGill, 1940–62).

8 This administrator, a physicist, served in various senior administrative capacities throughout his long career at UBC.

9 Prentice (1991) found that many women at the University of Toronto in the 1940s supplemented their teaching duties with secretarial work. By 1940, women had certainly infiltrated universities in large numbers, but they had done so in response to the growing need for assistance in the laboratories, libraries, classrooms, offices, and, of course, in the kitchens and custodial services.

10 A fifth-generation Canadian born in Victoria in 1946, Alice also had an uncle who had participated in the Great Trek, along with three other aunts

and uncles who had graduated from UBC. Alice herself had finished a year of university.

11 Gertrude couldn't remember this professor's nationality, but thought that it was European, maybe British. Interestingly, the term "patrician" has also been used in describing UBC's culture (Frick 1993, 7). Gertrude's casual engagement in conversation with a faculty member might not always be the norm: for some faculty, talking with staff can be a risky business. For instance, the first woman to graduate with a PhD in classics from UBC in 1976 was recruited to a faculty position at the University of Winnipeg. This woman did not interact frequently with the other faculty members, instead drinking her coffee with the secretaries and library assistants. Admittedly this helped her form some long-term friendships, "but it didn't do anything for my career" (Cahill 2003, 194).

12 Nina was a secretary from 1972 to 1980; her position was then reclassi-fied to a management and professional (M&P) position. She is still at UBC at the time of writing this chapter. Nina is the only one of the thirteen sec-retaries interviewed to have moved from a secretarial position to management.

13 Note Ruth's negative experience with an overwhelmingly female faculty complement. This calls to mind Kersti Krug's experiences reporting to female supervisors (see her chapter in this volume), a theme that merits closer study. As well, Ruth's account of her final years in a department where the faculty "turned" on the staff suggests a hostile workplace, which surely merited investigation and action. The prevalence of bullying and overall incivility at universities is disconcerting. Fratzl and McKay (2013) have explored the impact of bullying on university professional staff. As the "sandwich" between faculty and students, staff are vulnerable to hostility and aggression from both groups.

14 There are similarities between the writing of military history and univer-sity (institutional) history. With few exceptions, both tend to focus on the leadership ranks (generals/officers and presidents/deans, department heads, faculty). As part of a history of the British Army, Ziegler (2001) conducted interviews with nine Chelsea pensioners; his work serves as a model for a possible book on university staff.

15 Eveline (2004, 137–60) argues that staff are the "glue" that holds an insti-tution together, particularly during times of internal reorganization. As units are downsized, merged, or reconstituted, it is often the staff who provide corporate memory and who have the necessary relationships to keep the university's administrative structure afloat.

9

It's Not Just the Glass Ceiling, It's the Caste Ceiling

KERSTI KRUG

INTRODUCTION

Although women in the academy have long been aware of the glass ceiling, which sadly remains for female faculty members after decades of effective struggle, albeit a little higher, a little lighter, and with visible cracks, I argue that it is time to look at how universities might be contributing to the maintenance of another ceiling – what I call here the caste ceiling, the cultural barrier between academics and non-academics. The "non-academics" (in itself a provocative term, and one explored by Isabella Losinger in this volume), or those positioned below the academic layer, are usually well aware of the power imbalance that creates a seemingly impermeable enclave, a tenure-encrusted room that cannot be entered from the floor below. A familiar example of such an impenetrable divide would be the historical one between doctors and nurses. Other professions exhibit similar status and power splits, too often with dysfunctional impacts on the organization.

My exploration of universities suggests that these cultural solitudes are harming not only individual staff careers but also the institution. By surfacing and recognizing their existence, those of us in the academy may be able to effect positive change. However, the organizational structure that supports the caste system is rigid and will not easily be changed without a measured appreciation of its costs, both human and financial, and certainly not without courageous leadership and action. By sharing the stories of those who find themselves wounded by a culture that does not appear to reflect upon itself, we can explore the reality of the structural solitudes at one university, chart some patterns in staff/faculty interactions, determine costs and required changes, and then consider approaches for constructive action.

AN AUTO-ETHNOGRAPHIC APPROACH[1]

My approach to this study draws on the influential arguments of post-modernist, feminist, and other sociocultural scholars who challenge theory-driven, hypothesis-testing research founded in positivist epistemology. Specifically, auto-ethnography encourages subjectivity, stories, and the personal experiences of the author, rather than repressing this voice (Ellingson and Ellis 2008).[2] Furthermore, auto-ethnography can contribute to positive social change and move us to action (Bochner 2000, 271). This is, in essence, the goal of my study.

By drawing on feminist standpoint theory (Harding 1991) to give voice to marginalized groups, we can collectively challenge the status quo. Despite being a member of the "non-academic" staff group that I study, I draw on this theory to give voice to us all. As Betty Friedan (1964) argued many decades ago, sharing stories helps those alone and isolated in their struggles, those who perhaps perceive their problems as their own doing and not shared by others. Most interestingly, Harding suggests that "the perspective from the lives of the less powerful can provide a more objective view than the perspective from the lives of the more powerful" (Harding 1991, 270). Individuals with less power often have a clearer view of what is going on than those in privileged positions. To this, Julia Wood (1993) adds the idea that those in the middle, neither top nor bottom, may bring more objective views because they can look at matters from both sides. The community in this study focuses on my non-academic peers, individuals in the most senior staff positions at the university. They can see clearly those directly above them, and, at the same time, look down the hierarchy, often levels from whence they themselves rose.

SITUATING MYSELF AS RAPPORTEUR

Within these auto-ethnographic and standpoint theory approaches, I situate myself as researcher/writer with some stories of my experience at universities and similar institutions to illustrate what has occasioned this study and what my biases might be. I trust that these short stories will remind us all of organizational life, the high positives and the low negatives.

I call myself an organizational anthropologist, although my scholarly and managerial background in universities and other not-for-profit organizations is varied. Throughout my long career, my fascination with organizations has remained constant, and my focus has been mainly on organizational culture, leadership, change, and women's place in institutions. Recently, a rather unpleasant workplace event occurred to end the more formal part of my long, yet still active, career. This event, which revealed an unequal and unjust balance of power, dramatically focused my attention on some of the disturbing characteristics of the university, including the institutional necessity of power imbalances between faculty and "nons," characteristics that I had not seen clearly before, partly because the positives of university life had clouded my critical consciousness. Prompted by this aha moment, I began to explore whether the revelation extended beyond my own personal experience. My ensuing conversations with other women in senior management and professional staff positions showed that there was, indeed, something to this – even more than I had imagined.

My career began to take form in high school where the counsellor advised me that I could become a nurse, a secretary, a school teacher, or, of course, a housewife. I had wanted to be a medical doctor, but as that was not an option for a girl, and as I tended to defer to authority figures, I wandered elsewhere. In my early years, I worked at a university in an innovative interdisciplinary research setting, earning consistently good performance reviews. In my fourth year, my faculty supervisor told me that although I deserved another merit increase, he could not give it to me because one of my male colleagues, in a lower classified position, was making less money than I was, and, for me, a woman, to make more, was "not right." I was shocked and I quit on the spot. As I was young and as I assumed that I would immediately find another job, I felt that I had done the right thing. Unfortunately, my youthful assumption was somewhat misguided; it took me much longer than I anticipated to find a new job. I learned a painful and expensive lesson.

Still, two decades of moves and several promotions later, I enjoyed high merit evaluations in a senior management role. I happily earned the label "high flyer." But again, I experienced a shock. My boss retired and his incoming replacement was announced – a woman. Before even arriving to meet me, or other staff, she sent me a letter stating that I would be replaced – in this case by a man – but that I could switch to another position in the institution, one several levels lower than my current one and with fewer responsibilities than I had held a decade earlier. Having been thus effectively terminated, I returned to university to pursue an MBA. During my studies, I came to realize that what had happened was not unique. The scholarship involving organizational power and politics now illuminated my experiences in the trenches of organizations.

Upon graduation, I moved into a new job at the university, working for one of the finest leaders I had known. He was a professor and the director of a combined academic/cultural centre. He encouraged me to do a PhD, which helped me to be hired by another faculty as an assistant dean to a dynamic and highly effective female dean. During these years, albeit still in a staff, not faculty, position, I had opportunities to teach, conduct research, and publish, and to enjoy the richness of academic life. However, when the faculty underwent major restructuring, the dean resigned, and I was left to transfer into one part of the now split faculty. The turbulent disruption that ensued and ended painfully – too long a story for this chapter – triggered my awareness of a caste ceiling.

THE GLASS CEILING AND THE CASTE CEILING

Throughout my career, I watched with passion not only the women's movement but also the student, anti-war, civil rights, environmental, and gay rights movements, all working toward social justice. Because I have taken feminism to be about equality, ethics, fairness, respect, and equal opportunity, I have easily called myself a feminist. In my career, I experienced the familiar collection of unmemorable bosses, but I also had three humane and memorable male bosses and one humane and equally memorable female boss. By humane I do not mean that these people were merely nice or kind but they were respectful and demonstrated civility. To my dismay, I also experienced three bosses who were less than ideal and thus "memorable" in a different way. Two were female. Feminism had not prepared me for this, but my feminist ideals kept me from judging these women on the basis of their gender alone.

In the academy, this structural element of the caste ceiling needs further scrutiny. As Elvi Whittaker infers in her introductory remarks to this volume, the university might be described as two solitudes: faculty and non-faculty, academics and non-academics. As Losinger describes in her chapter in this book,[3] universities have been slow to recognize that many kinds of workers contribute to knowledge production, learning, and the running of the institutions, and thus should not be cast off as "non-nons." A term of negation, "non" wipes staff members off the map, out of the community by focusing not on what we *are* but on what we are *not*. Losinger observes that when universities report their activities, staff contributions are undetectable. Faculty members and researchers are mentioned, students and graduates are mentioned, communities and donors are mentioned, staff are not. In fact, the notion of the much-touted "community" does not, and perhaps cannot, exist within university walls. The critical exceptions to the caste ceiling are those genuine, individual working relationships between some faculty and some staff members that span the cultural divide in productive and enriching ways. These relationships involve genuine teamwork, respect for the contributions of the other, and recognition that even more can be accomplished together.

SETTING UP THE STUDY

To discover and illuminate the source and nature of the caste structure that divides faculty and staff at the university, and to uncover the impact not only on staff but also on productivity, effectiveness, and health of the institution, I sought stories from my "non-non" staff colleagues. My auto-ethnographic approach resulted from years of observing universities as an undergraduate and graduate student, a professional, a senior manager, a researcher, and an instructor. What focused my attention was the research undertaken by one of my staff colleagues at the university, Isabella Losinger. As she looked into the relationship between academics and support staff in secretarial, clerical, and lower-level administrative roles at a large university, I chose to focus on staff members at the highest professional and administrative levels at the same university.

To explore the caste structure in the academic side of the university, I restricted interviews to staff working in academic units such as faculties or departments rather than administrative units such as finance or human resources. These staff members not only held significant responsibility themselves but they also worked directly with tenured academics appointed to administrative posts, such as heads of departments, deans of faculties, and vice-presidential offices. Their staff group is part of a collective bargaining unit, not a union.

Further, as the overwhelming majority of senior staff posts are filled by women, I concentrated on a dozen senior female staff members who were willing to share their stories. I focused on all academic, as opposed to administrative, units, such as faculties, and then contacted the most senior staff women who worked there. Participants came from medium to large faculties and had titles such as assistant dean, executive director, director, manager, chief X, or senior Y. (I have left these last two positions untitled to avoid identifying specific individuals.) Because this book was about women in the academy, men in equivalent positions were not approached.

Poking at the Caste Ceiling

Before launching the study, I had formed some tentative notions about the academic caste system. I was aware that academic administrative appointments are essentially temporary; that the person who held a post before a new appointee arrived was often already absent on administrative leave, thereby providing uncertain overlap during a transition period; and that although a training program in management was offered by the university to new appointees, attendance was not required. As a result, an incumbent could begin with little direct experience in management, with marginal mentoring, and with little or no relevant training. Given the complexity of large post-secondary educational institutions, such beginnings are not easy. In his book *Learning to Lead in Higher Education*, which offers practical tools to improve management and leadership of academic institutions, Paul Ramsden (1998) acknowledges that throwing someone with skills in one area into another area without the necessary skills is costly for both the organization and individual.

I also formed a fuzzy, and no doubt simplistic, idea about the kinds of academics who inhabit these administrative posts. It began with my assumption that academics arrive to their roles via an arduous process, requiring major time and financial commitments. The path begins with completing the PhD, attaining postdoctoral appointments, getting hired as an assistant professor, struggling for tenure and promotion, and finally achieving full professorship, the level at which most appointments to headships or deanships occur. During this demanding rite of passage, faculty would have become expert in their special field of study, lauded by those in their field, both across and beyond their university. When appointed to the role of a department head, dean, vice-president, or their associates, these individuals might have to adjust from being a celebrated expert to being a relative novice in the role of leadership and management – disciplines that are themselves researched and taught at universities. With this in mind, I posited three scenarios that I asked the participants in this study to critique.

The first scenario involves those who, by dint of personal characteristics, interests, and values, or through mentorship, training, or earlier experience, fly through their roles, providing exceptional academic leadership, vision, strategic analysis, and courageous decision making. Moreover, they effectively involve staff to achieve their goals. They understand their roles as leaders and delegate appropriate administrative, professional, and managerial duties to experienced staff. A second scenario involves faculty members who assume their posts only to discover that expertise in their disciplinary field does not fully equip them for their new role. They turn to staff to aid their transition, using what experienced staff do well, while learning and eventually increasingly contributing to effective outcomes. The third scenario begins in the same way as the second but, instead of seeking help from existing staff, the new incumbents find their egos bruised by the realization that their brilliance as an academic does not translate to leadership and management. If there is a highly experienced and knowledgeable staff member who might heighten the leader's discomfort by asking difficult or challenging questions, or simply by making informed, substantive offerings, the new incumbent may decide, consciously or unconsciously, that the underlying reason for their discomfort is that this staff member "doesn't fit." An easy solution becomes "restructuring."[4]

Framing the Study: Characteristics of a Healthy Organization

Let me provide a brief framework to define the characteristics of a healthy and productive organizational culture so that the findings of this study can be better assessed and placed in comparative context.

The scholarship on this organizational topic is huge.[5] Common elements usually include that everyone understands their roles in making their unit and/or institution effective; that all are aware of the organization's mission, priorities, and goals; that the policies, structures, and reinforcements ensuring that responsibility, authority, and accountability are aligned; that people work respectfully with each other; that knowledge and experience are balanced with organizational values when making appointments; that communication is open and timely on matters relevant to everyone's work; that broad input is sought and alternatives discussed to ensure best decisions and outcomes; that formal evaluations are conducted along with informal feedback to improve performance and provide career development; that alternative views are accepted, not punished; and that everyone has access to a safe place to expose wrong behaviours, and have wrongs corrected by someone in authority when evidence is clear. It is the rare organization that fully meets all these dictums, though most private and public sector organizations work toward them. One institution that truly exemplifies these standards is the Mayo Clinic (Berry and Seltman 2008). According to Berry and Seltman, the clinic exemplifies the powerful balance of clarity, collegiality, courage, and critique. No one is afraid of criticizing approaches that do not meet the essential principles and values of the institution. This drive for and delivery of excellence are continually reinforced.

THE CONVERSATIONS: REFLECTING ON THE CASTE EXPERIENCE

My conversations with a dozen senior staff members supported the simplistic scenarios I had created. However, and somewhat to my surprise, individuals also added new interpretations and weight to my existing notions of the university's organizational culture and caste structure. I launched the discussions by asking people to tell me what they had done after graduating from high school. These became deep histories, with a wide range, depth, and diversity of experiences, in private corporations, other non-profits, entrepreneurial ventures, and, in one case, overcoming such crushing early tragedies that I was awestruck at the person's courage and ultimate career achievement. I asked them to describe why they chose the university. Some arrived by chance, others with a specific aim. All said they enjoyed working at this or any university. As one put it, "It is the access to ideas, the diversity of ideas, and the quality of discourse that attracted me to the university, and what keeps me here." In essence, all treasured the excitement of research, the energy of students, and the clear sense of contributing to individual potential, to health, to society, to the environment, and to multiple communities around the world. Virtually everyone also acknowledged that they enjoyed inspiring and enriching relationships with *some* faculty members. I could agree with them all. My next questions about their jobs, careers, and experiences at this university led to darker reflection.

As the breadth of the responses could not fit into a single chapter, I have placed sample comments into categories that reflect the most commonly shared views. Quotes, in a few instances, have been slightly rewritten to ensure anonymity and job protection. Also, position titles have not been included because identification would readily be possible. As we are aware, when faculty members lose administrative posts, they return to their regular tenured faculty positions. When staff members lose their jobs, they are gone. Protecting participants, therefore, became a critical priority.

Value of Staff Work

Administrative work is not valued. It's seen as women's work. This is a gendered university. What I mean by gendered is that women are the secretaries. Program managers and other administrative staff are virtually all female. What we as women do would not be done if the jobs were filled by men. People ask me to fill up their soap dispensers. What type of person do they see sitting here? All staff want is a little bit of respect. It doesn't take much.

When talking about their jobs, everyone agreed that the very nature of staff work was considered of lesser value than academic work, that those in positions of academic authority often had little experience with, knowledge of, or even respect for the work that staff members performed, and that staff work was gender-based. As one participant put it, "even at very high levels, you're still stuck in the secretarial role." Others added that it was "incredibly frustrating and insulting to do one's best, yet always be reprimanded" and, therefore, that "the university as 'best employer' is mere hype."

Career Development

Whether or not performance appraisals are done is not consistent, but depends on the manager. I know of circumstances where they're unprofessionally done – too late or concentrating on small things, not on more substantial matters. The outcome of your performance is not really assessed. Students and faculty are treated completely differently from staff regarding performance and career goals.

Most participants spoke about the lack of career development for staff members, including inconsistency and irregularity in performance evaluations. Faculty careers are regularly and systematically assessed; staff careers are not. "No one has ever sat down with me," one noted, "to discuss how I could develop a career here at the university." Another added, "There are definitely two classes [when it comes to career development]."

Fit vs. Competence

In an interview I had in the '90s in a faculty here, it was as if I had returned to the '50s or '60s. I hadn't come across such arrogance. There's an arrogance of academics to non-academics. The dean was like a demigod. They didn't want to know what I knew, but whether I was nice and would fit. They didn't seem to understand that one can have respectful differences.

An unexpected discovery was how many staff perceived that academic administrators principally sought "niceness" and "fit" from staff members when hiring or promoting, rather than experience, knowledge, or competence. One added, "Academics hire women who are not only nice and popular, but also attractive." The difficulty for staff members was trying to "please everyone all the time," which is demoralizing and made more difficult when one is "trained in critical approaches."

Communication Breakdowns

There is no communication with staff about high-level strategies. Consultations happen with faculty members, not with staff. But decisions then go out to the external community without checking the knowledge that we could have contributed to make these projects more effective. It's like we don't exist.

In the broad area of communications, people reflected on the lack of sharing relevant information or seeking timely input, especially when the staff member could have contributed to avoiding mistakes or embarrassments. "They also don't tell us what we need to know, even when it's about the job I'm doing. It means I can't do my best job." Another added, "It's been frustrating to seek clarity regarding the faculty's vision and mission, but every time I asked, I was shut down. It was just 'not important.' One time I was really shut down with, 'You can't use business speak at a university; your HR [human resources] speak is driving us crazy.'"

Communicating Risks

It's not worth it for me to stand out and say something because I'll pay the price. A lot of people getting into senior staff positions have learned not to challenge. It's not safe. It's the "nice" people who know how to suck up. They play well within the system. Anybody who is critical can't make it here. A lot of people are ready to walk. They're that frustrated. It's still very much a male-dominated institution.

Even more disturbing than the lack of effective, timely communications were the risks staff took when voicing views that differed from those in power. As one participant remarked, "Just for having a different opinion, staff can be reprimanded." More disturbing were the revelations of mature staff members who had built extensive knowledge and experience over many years but were now facing negative feedback when they voiced their wisdom; they concluded "it was best to shut up." Interestingly, some of them had discovered creative ways to continue contributing positively to their colleagues, their unit, or the university by smiling politely in public but working actively behind the scenes.

Academics as Administrators

It's typical that when there's a leadership change, they bring in new people from their own background. And as these academic administrators change jobs almost every five years, and there's no overlap with the previous leader, then these massive shifts are crippling for the organization. The most confounding role is for a department head. How can you make hard decisions if you're going back to your colleagues? And deans are judged at re-appointment time by their peers. They enter these roles without any training and even face contempt from some of their colleagues for joining "those" people.

Everyone had a perspective on the nature of academic management, sometimes in apposition to management styles in other organizations or other units within the university. Many felt that management problems arose because "academics don't always feel that they work *for* the university; their allegiance being to their discipline." Most acknowledged that there were different breeds of academic administrators: "Those who leave the dirty work to staff, albeit with little appreciation; others who believe that they know how to manage, but have no concept how to manage people." Another added, "Academics think that if you're smart, you can automatically step into the job. You cannot."

Connecting Competence, Risk, and Academic Administrators

The lack of toughness regarding hiring people is different from the toughness imposed when criticizing different opinions. Some sins are accepted. Others are not. There is the sin of not fitting in, for not getting along, for rocking the boat. These are judged more sternly than doing a poor job. What is seen as teamwork is all about a positive attitude, or not criticizing colleagues. In a normal organization, it's my responsibility to bring up other possibilities, to warn my colleagues of potential poor alternatives. But not here.

In connecting the three overlapping issues of competence, risk, and academic administrators, most agreed that niceness, candour, and styles were entangled in the way summarized here. In other words, the essential nature of universities in critiquing and furthering knowledge apparently did not transfer to wanting or allowing a staff member to critique process or content of work. For some staff members, not questioning but silently smiling seemed to be more helpful for receiving positive performance appraisals.

Tracking Accountability

I've seen some very bad management. For when you're a department head or dean, you learn about the crap happening in your unit. You don't stop bad behaviour because eventually you have to go back to work with them as colleagues. Faculty are never fired. These rotational appointments make imposing corrections very difficult.

Although the word *accountability* did not specifically come up, most participants recognized that faculty members and academic admin- istrators were not always held accountable, either as individuals who committed wrongs or as inattentive or ineffective administra- tors. As one put it, "There is no penalty for non-compliance." A most disturbing story starts with the "wonderful" position that a staff member held for many years in an "exciting" academic unit coming to an end after years of being sexually harassed by one of the faculty members. She found no way to stop the abuse other than move her- self to another job across campus – unfortunately one that was far less appealing. In the meanwhile, the faculty member was promoted to the head of a major program, with no one seeking references.

Discovering Competition

When staff get training (e.g., a PhD) and more experience, academics don't know how to use us. They feel threatened. I find that I have to be careful what I say now. I feel vulnerable. I no longer challenge. And I don't speak up. I'm thinking of leaving, though it would be a very hard adjustment. I want to stay at a university for the intellectual environment and the opportunity to continually learn. So I'm torn.

There were stories about what could be seen as a curious competi- tiveness that faculty members have with staff. Two examples arose. The first example dealt with titles for staff positions, such as assis- tant dean, given that the word *dean* was perceived to belong to fac- ulty appointees only and thus inappropriately used for staff. The second example dealt with staff members who had PhDs and who somehow created a degree of discomfort, perhaps because these PhDs were potentially equal in knowledge but had not earned the right to be equal in that they had not undergone the demanding ritu- als of promotion and tenure. In one faculty, the two senior staff members terminated by the dean's office were the only two with PhDs. One of them had an assistant dean title. She was replaced by someone doing the same job but with a different title.

The Caste Culture

When I got my PhD, I was told to publish in academic journals. I didn't want to. I was offered a faculty appointment, but withdrew my application because my professional career was what I had chosen. Still, I regretted this in part when I discovered the caste ceiling. Under my first professor boss, I was encouraged to teach, do directed studies, sit on graduate student committees. But under my current boss, these special arrangements for me began to erode. I'm no longer involved in departmental meetings. I also lost my opportunity for an academic appointment. As well, I've been removed from a critical internal committee, and in other ways find myself sidelined. As the most senior person, that's disappointing.

Many also spoke about the nature of the caste structure, sharing their experiences of struggling through the divide. All agreed with the existence of the caste structure, the fact that "power is so unbalanced between faculty and staff that trust will never exist at a university, competence maybe, but not trust." A few were even more critical, suggesting that "faculty have no capacity to understand anything other than being an academic." So the tendency to undervalue non-academics is returned in kind.

Counting Terminations

How people get terminated is inhumane. The way the university gets rid of staff, disposes of them. These are people with huge skills. The university's investment in them gets thrown out. We don't treat this resource well. That whole people side needs work. It's cruel. The university has to take more care.

Most participants were aware of the increase in terminations, especially of senior staff, over that past few years that were being tracked by their administrative and professional staff association, virtually all with no recourse to appeal or assistance to find another job on campus. All agreed that in these cases the damage not only to the individual but also the university is significant: both "memory and experience are lost." The previous year apparently "was the worst year for terminations of staff – these are very expensive." And as one respondent creatively put it, "We have more people putting wheels on the car, not designing a better car. In the private sector, we immediately took steps if there was a financial downturn. Here we're still talking, three years out of the gate, how to adjust. In the meanwhile, resources, history, and knowledge go out the door."

Comparing Administrative to Academic Units

When leaving a job in an administrative unit where we all communicated openly and worked positively together in an academic unit, I became aware that the interactions between faculty and staff were more negative. I saw this as stratification as a caste system. When going to another faculty, it was even more so. In fact, in that first job, I had access to more senior academics than I do now that I am in an academic unit. Everyone there knew their roles. It was very transparent and clear what our ultimate goal was. We could therefore all see our own and others' contributions. We would have short but regular meetings. We could bring our ideas to the table for discussion. We could make suggestions. Then when everyone agreed, we had a clearly approved way of proceeding.

This quote from someone who had once worked in an administrative unit captures the difference in culture and productivity working in a non-academic unit relative to an academic one. In other words, in many cases, staff who had worked in administrative units or organizations outside the university suggested that contributing collectively, yet sometimes critically, to departmental decisions was a far more open and collaborative experience than in faculties and other academic units.

Exploring Gender

In considering the glass ceiling and the caste ceiling, it made me wonder whether they aren't in fact related. My guess would be that for a long time the quintessential staff member as far as academics were concerned was the secretary – always female, and perceived as having little schooling, low skill, and being good only for taking dictation and making coffee; whereas the vast majority of faculty were highly educated males. And despite the fact that the gender distribution has changed, and staff positions have exploded. The range of skill and experience is now vast, I don't think the academy ever caught on, and misogyny and arrogance have become perversely intertwined.

Although the matter of gender comes up throughout the categories shared here, a few participants contributed their thoughts on how gender specifically makes a difference. One put it succinctly: "Women faculty members say they wouldn't treat me like this if I were a man. Even feminist academics only talk about fairness with respect to their colleagues or their students. It's hard for them not to be drawn into the culture that exists." Another pointed out that some staff members (always "girls") are sidelined such that "a once outgoing and challenging colleague has turned into a 'good girl,' now always quiet, saying nothing. Although the department is full of women, the power is held by men." A third explained, "The lot for women didn't improve while the university had a woman president." Over the years, this participant explained, she had found herself "not wanting to work for women because good female leaders are rare," to which a fourth added, "The most difficult academics to work with are older women. It's an age thing, not seen among the younger faculty."

Assessing Costs

I'm bored out of my mind with the caste system. Students are suffering, but despite their horrible stories, there's absolutely no support from faculty members. Mental stress at this university is higher than any other university. It's taking its toll. Academic advisors who don't know how to deal with this are making things worse. They have no experience. They haven't lived in the real world. Associate deans are not skilled. They don't study the issues. They don't learn.

Many individuals were aware of the costs of the caste structure on the financial and cultural health of the university. One of these costs clearly involves students. Another is the withdrawal, either productively or physically, of thoughtful, experienced staff. As one participant remarked, "Human fallout on people and its impact on the organization is worse at a university than what we see in corporations." And one concluded, "We have the smartest people at the university, and yet we don't use them. The system isn't working." At one of the interviews, the participants touched on another more material cost; they discussed a rumour that some senior staff members, who apparently had sizeable estates, had once considered donating significant sums to the university but rejected the idea after being mistreated and witnessing colleagues' mistreatment.[6]

Making Positive Change

There should be a prerequisite for all deans and department heads to take one or two of the management courses offered by the university. The problem is that academics are not required to take the program for new heads and associate deans. Deans are not required to take these. Some of the people who really need it are the ones who don't go. It's a shame that it's not mandatory. But if people are not ready to hear, they won't listen.

Toward the end of our conversations, I suggested that contributors imagine themselves in the role of president with ultimate power to make change. What would you do? All struggled, yet everyone offered suggestions for the sorts of changes that could make positive differences at the university. These included "appointing an ombudsman to report to the president or higher"; "creating strong policies to give heads an excuse to make effective, even courageous decisions"; and "separating church and state" – that is, recognizing that "the church [i.e., the academic or spiritual side of a university] could no more run the government [i.e., administrative services and governance] than the government could run the church." Both sides need to understand each other's roles, work together, learn from each other, and become strong at both. One person's perception of the future offered a hopeful, albeit neither certain nor swift, solution: "The new generation of academics is less caste oriented. It is changing."

IS THERE A NEED FOR ACTION?

This chapter provides a preliminary look at the impact of the two solitudes – and the caste structure – at one university. More stories are needed, from men as well as women, faculty members as well as staff, and from other universities. We should aim to understand which structures and leadership styles can be transformative, to bring about a healthy workplace culture and reduce institutional costs.

Although this is not an exhaustive study, it is safe to say that the basic elements of a healthy organizational culture, as described earlier, are not being consistently met. Unlike the excellence in research and teaching in which the university can take pride, leadership and management appear to erode and potentially damage such excellence. Some harm is certainly done to staff and their careers, and significant financial costs are borne by the institution as a result of not using the best people in the smartest ways. Institutional memory and history are lost when extensive experience is too readily silenced.

Broader and deeper studies are needed not only to convince those in power to consider change but to seek examples of where and how such change has already successfully occurred. In all social justice movements, the first step towards change is consciousness raising. Change happens with courageous leadership and spirited activists, followed by changes in policies, practices, and laws. Hopefully, the stories presented in this chapter, albeit from one particular university, raise consciousness and motivate others to take the first steps toward improving the culture of universities for all who work in them.

ACKNOWLEDGMENTS

I wish to express my gratitude to Elvi Whittaker, former member of my PhD committee, not only for inviting me to contribute a chapter but also for helping clarify the approach I was taking. I am grateful for the help offered by Pat Kaufert to make my chapter stronger and more readable. I wish to also express deep appreciation to all those contributing to this study by offering thoughtful and courageous perspectives.

Notes

1 I would also direct the reader to an excellent overview covering the history, process, potentials, issues, and critiques of auto-ethnography (Ellis, Adams, and Bochner 2011).

2 There exist a number of criteria applied by scholars to auto-ethnographic approaches. I list some of them here: (a) *Substantive contribution.* Does the piece contribute to our understanding of social life? (b) *Aesthetic merit.* Is the text artistically shaped, satisfyingly complex, and not boring? (c) *Reflexivity.* How has the author's subjectivity been both a producer and a product of this text? (d) *Impactfulness.* Does it generate new

questions or move me to action? (e) *Expresses a reality*. Does this text embody a fleshed out sense of lived experience? (Richardson 2000, 15–16).

3 It is hard to put into words my gratitude to my colleague Isabella Losinger, who gave me access to one of her PhD research papers, "The Non-Nons: A Snapshot of University Staff," which launched me on my own study. She provided the necessary foundation for understanding the relationship between faculty and staff in universities. Given her extensive study of these institutions, her chapter in this book provides a strong underpinning to both our work.

4 The collective agreement between senior staff members and this university does not require a specific reason for terminating an employee. As long as financial payment is made, legal or other appeals are not successful.

5 See, for example, Drucker 1999; Hesselbein, Goldsmith, and Beckhard 1997; Lundin and Lundin 1998; Newstrom and Davis 2002; Pugh and Hickson 1997. Online, see also Ethix, 2009, "Eight Traits of a Healthy Organizational Culture," online publication of the Center for Integrity in Business in the School of Business and Economics at Seattle Pacific University, 1 October, http://ethix.org/2009/10/01/ eight-traits-of-a-healthy-organizational-culture.

6 Interestingly, a recent news release regarding the United Way campaign at the university reflects the only instance where the word "staff" appears before "faculty." Apparently, staff members contribute more per capita to the campaign than do faculty members.

10

Contractual University Teaching:
The Question of Gender

LINDA COHEN

This chapter begins as a confessional. I chose to work as a contractual university teacher for more than two decades. Contractual teaching is temporary and can be part-time or full-time, so its flexibility was especially attractive to me when raising young children. Contractual teaching felt "right" for me, but I had a nagging sense of capitulating to a gendered assumption that, as a working mother, I could not anticipate the same standard employment relationship traditionally expected by family men. In this better quality work, the worker is full-time, permanent, and relatively unencumbered by family demands (Beck 2000; Vosko 2010).

Contractual teaching, by contrast, is remarkably insecure. As the most flexible of workers, contractuals are easiest to eliminate when financial exigency demands. The flexibility of contractual teaching translates into job insecurity, which eventually circumscribed my personal experience. Waiting to find out whether or not I would teach in the following year was stressful and after the first six years of teaching contractually, I began to show health symptoms related to job insecurity: emotional stress, anxiety, and repetitive strain injuries (Lewchuk, Clarke, and de Wolff 2008). Was I being too sensitive or even obsessive about my work conditions? After all, contractual university teachers do not match the usual description of job insecure workers with low education, low income, and few opportunities. Why, then, did I experience the same symptoms? Was it insecurity or something more – low self-confidence or my gender perhaps – creating these problems? Was I alone in this?

As a sociologist, I know that my private troubles are connected to public issues (Mills 1959). Based on gaps found in the literature on contractual teaching, my doctoral fieldwork explored the experience and occupational health challenges of job insecurity for a small group of contractual university teachers in an Atlantic Canadian university that I call Provincial University. This chapter focuses on one question posed by the data collected: Are there gender differences in the experiences and interpretations of job insecurity and its health outcomes for highly educated workers? Selected narratives reveal what participants in my research did and did not see as gender differentials in contractual teaching work.

THE RESEARCH

The research is based on a mixed methods study conducted in 2008 with thirty-two contractual university teachers who self-selected in response to my advertisement for participants. Twenty women and twelve men agreed to complete the first stage of the research by meeting with me and answering a demographic and a health survey. The twenty-seven who continued in the second stage did one or more task diaries, a second health survey, and a semi-structured interview. Participants were asked to recount their work histories and discuss their daily task diaries in light of their workload. They described one or more critical incidents (see also Kennedy's use of critical incidents in this volume) that happened at work and how they dealt with them. Additional methodologies include my observations and experiences as a long-serving contractual university teacher and the diaries I kept. This was participant observation, which I followed with questionnaires and interviews. My status as a contractual teacher and my interest in the study as a dissertation were made clear to those participants at the initial contact. I also interviewed representatives of unions and checked relevant human resources information.

ACADEMIC CAPITALISM AND THE EXPANSION OF CONTRACTUAL UNIVERSITY TEACHING

Previously considered a risk in lower-income jobs, job insecurity and the "flexibilization [of the standard employment relationship is] ... occurring at the top of the skills hierarchy" (Beck 2000, 82). In 2009 in Canada, 24 per cent of all contract jobs were in the "social sciences, education, and public administration" and 54 per cent of all contract workers were women (Galarneau 2010, 13). In universities, short-term teaching and research contracts were traditionally used as entry-level jobs for academic careers. They now comprise a growing type of teaching employment that is easily segregated from the traditional academic career. The American Association of University Professors estimated that contingent adjunct teachers, defined as either part-time or full-time but always non-tenure-track and temporary, were more than 68 per cent of all faculty in degree-granting American universities in 2005 (Glazer-Raymo 2008). The trend is similar in Canadian universities. Drawing on data gathered by the Canadian Association of University Teachers (CAUT) in 2010, then president Penni Stewart indicated that almost 50 per cent of academic positions at larger Canadian universities are now "off the tenure track" (Stewart 2010, A3).

Critics argue that the growth in the contractual teacher cadre is a goal of academic capitalism (Slaughter and Rhoades 2004), which has been prioritizing market economics, cost-effectiveness, and the overall commodification of education since at least the early 1980s. Under academic capitalism, contractual hiring is strategically used as a cost-effective means to deliver courses by replacing professorial teaching. Essentially, contractual teachers with "lower levels of degree certification" (Slaughter and Rhoades 2004, 18) can be hired at lower pay than tenured and tenure-track faculty to teach larger classes. Because the administration does not have a long-term commitment to them, they can be easily let go when they are no longer needed. For Aronowitz, the tenured professor holds the "last good job in America" (1997, 202, 219). He or she is both supported and undermined by a growing "academic proletariat" of contractually hired teachers and researchers. Many sociologists argue that this constitutes a workplace injustice for all faculty because it undermines the tenure and job security essential to academic freedom (Donoghue 2008; Rhoades 1998; Turk 2008). Fewer study the effects of job insecurity for contractuals themselves.

The job insecurity of contractual teaching is related to status in an academic hierarchy. In most universities, status and sometimes collegiality is determined by appointment to a tenure-track position. Permanently hired faculty at the early, middle, and later stages of their careers are assistant, associate, or full professors. Contractual teaching is rarely counted as a career and long-term contractual work carries a stigma of failure in many academic circles. Contractual teachers are not expected to do research, or publish, or even participate in departmental committees. Teaching is the only reason they are hired, so their credibility as researchers is often devalued or ignored. Contractuals counter that their teaching work is essentially the same as that of tenure-stream faculty but usually at less pay, benefits, and autonomy, and with higher task demands (Glazer-Raymo 2008; Rajagopal 2002). Contractuals are treated as adjunct to tenure-track and tenured faculty in administrative matters no matter how long or in what types of contract or status they have been delivering courses.

Contractual status varies widely in Canadian and North American universities and is frequently misunderstood. Rhoades (1998), for example, labels contractual teaching *part-time*, implying that it involves fewer hours than the work of full-time tenured or tenure-track professors. Indeed, research and administrative service is not usually required of contractuals, but the teaching can become full-time very quickly (Muzzin and Limoges 2008).

Rajagopal (2002) partially addresses this misunderstanding by identifying two types of contractual teachers in Canadian universities. The *classic contractual* is a per-course or sessional instructor who holds a good quality job elsewhere. For the classic contractual, per-course teaching constitutes a small extra income, usually at a set fee per course. Some are tenured faculty who teach extra courses as overload. As Muzzin and Limoges (2008, 119) point out, classic part-time teaching tends to favour men and those women who have more money coming in from other sources like pensions or a day job.

Contemporaries in Rajagopal's categorization rely on temporary, full-time, per-term contracts as their primary source of income. My study focused on both full-time and part-time contractuals, but all depended on contractual teaching for their primary source of income.

ACADEMIC WOMEN

Even though their position is improving, academic women have still not reached parity with men, and men still predominate in the hard sciences. In Canadian universities, women were 35 per cent of full-time teachers in 2005, up from 29 per cent in 1999 and 13 per cent in 1970 (Statistics Canada 2005, 2006a, 2006b). The proportion of women in the soft disciplines is growing at different levels of the hierarchy. CAUT (2004–10) has found proportionately more women than men among the non-tenure-track *Other* teachers of disciplines like sociology.

A note on terminology is in order here. CAUT distinguishes *Other* positions from full, associate, and assistant professorships by virtue of being non-tenure-track positions. These include lecturers whose hiring is contingent on market demand and who are members of affiliated faculty associations. They did not count per-course appointments, which are excluded from the member faculty associations. At Provincial University, those who would be counted as *Others* by CAUT were per-term teachers with contracts of two or more consecutive semesters. The category excluded per-course teachers or per-terms with contracts of only one semester. *Other* was replaced by *Lecturer* in the 2009–10 CAUT almanac. In sociology departments across Canada in the 2007–08 academic year, women comprised 76.9 per cent of the lecturers (non-tenure-track), 75.6 per cent of the assistant professors, 60 per cent of the associate professors, and 36 per cent of the full professors. In the 2005–06 CAUT survey, men were 45.6 per cent of *Other* full-time teachers in all disciplines on the national level.

The imbalance in the gender ratio was more pronounced at Provincial University: women in the *Other* category (all departments) outnumbered men by almost two to one (64.3 per cent: 35.7 per cent) in the 2005–06 academic year (CAUT 2007). The gender distribution in this study's sample was coincidentally proportionate to this, though still not representative because participants self-selected in answer to an advertisement. The gender ratio in contractual teaching would be more balanced if per-course contractuals with better jobs elsewhere were included. More men ostensibly occupy this category. They were not included in this study because their primary source of income was from another job.

Gender differences in academic teaching work are more evident in studies of full-time tenured and tenure-track faculty women who cite gendered expectations for emotional and service labour (Baker 2010; Glazer-Raymo 2008; Hannah, Vethamany-Globus, and Paul 2002; Currie, Thiele, and Harris 2002; see also Abramson, Rippeyoung, and Price, and Moloney in this volume). Metcalfe and Slaughter (2008, 100) note that, in American universities and colleges, "women

have made significant gains in careers associated with the public
good [e.g., teaching] ... but do not fare as well in the resource-rich
academic capitalist knowledge/learning regime." Alemán (2008)
concluded that American tenured and tenure-track faculty women
spend more time on teaching activities than men, likely at the
expense of engaging in publishable research, which is a requirement
for tenure. Most of the tenured and tenure-track academic women in
Currie, Thiele, and Harris's (2002) Australian surveys felt they were
valued for their sociability, supportiveness, collegiality, conscien-
tiousness, and contributions to the university. This working style
was deemed less powerful and less rewarding than "being aggressive
and competitive [for which] ... men are both rewarded and con-
demned" (104).

Auto-ethnographic literature sheds light on such gendered expectations. When they started teaching university classes in Britain,
Barnes-Powell and Letherby (1998, 67) found that students and
some full-time faculty and administrative supervisors expected new
women teachers to do gendered care work and be "interruptible" in
their daily work. Because university administrations were fostering a
consumerist mentality, students were frequently rude and demanding, particularly with young women teachers. Webber (2007) describes
similar pressures for North American contractual women and men
that induce them to act like "Miss Congeniality" and lower their grad-
ing standards to win over students and ensure positive course evaluations. In some universities, course evaluations by students determine
whether or not contractuals are rehired. Add age to this formula and
middle-aged contractuals become "dinosaurs" struggling for academic credibility (Cotterill and Waterhouse 1998, 12, 16).

GENDER DIFFERENTIALS: NARROWING IN THE QUANTITATIVE DATA, PERSISTING IN THE QUALITATIVE

To what extent does gender influence the experience of job insecurity and health among the highly educated contractual university
teachers in this study? I found little evidence of persisting gender
differentials in the quantitative data, but more indications in the
qualitative details.

The results of my quantitative research instruments confirm other
research finding that gender differentials in mental health, stress,

and sense of control are narrowing for men and women in similar occupations and among those who face the threat of job loss (Denton, Prus, and Walters 2004). Briefly, the men's mental health scores in this study's SF-12v2 Health Surveys were very similar to those of women and both were significantly *below* the 1998 norms for their age and gender. The SF-12v2 Health Survey is a clinical tool designed to provide doctors with preliminary and subsequent measures of patients' health. Both individual and group measures can be compared to the age- and gender-adjusted norms of the US population. It is useful in studying small non-representative samples. Men and women in this study likewise had comparable results on physical health in the SF-12v2 Health Survey data and both had scores higher on physical health than the 1998 US norms. No discernible gender differences were evident in the self-rated health of participants, which is in accord with National Population Health Survey data (Denton, Prus, and Walters 2004).

From the quantified survey results of this study, contractual teaching at Provincial University seems gender-neutral. For all of the participants, "[Contractuals] have an inequality of income and of status. They feel invisible, that they really deserve something better" (Janice). Gender was not a pressing concern, but gender differences in the experience of contractual teaching were implicated in the minutiae of their narratives. During the interviews, participants defined health and described how three sources of job insecurity (hiring, status, and money) were linked to health outcomes. They then explained how they coped with these health challenges. The following selections from the data reveal how participants tacitly expressed gender.

Gender differentials were first evident in participants' definitions of health. Men and women placed different emphases on the physical and mental components of health. The majority of men emphasized functionality and the majority of women highlighted emotional balance or calmness. Brad provides a response typical among the men: "Oh boy. I guess [health is] feeling well, as in feeling good about yourself, feeling as if you have energy. Like you're not just tired and *you're not inhibited from what you want to do*" (emphasis mine).

Many women, like Catherine, alluded to problems in work–life balance and social interactions that are typical of North American women (Higgins, Duxbury, and Lyons 2010; Hochschild and

Machung 2003): "Hmm, I think health is *balance in your life*. Really having enough [time to] ... balance your work with ... the things that are important to you like family, friends, spirituality, recreation, exercise. I get none of that at the moment, which is bad" (emphasis mine).

Gender differences also appeared in my categorization of the general level of job insecurity participants expressed in their narratives. Those respondents who explicitly said they had few concerns with insecurity were designated as *low on insecurity*. These were proportionately more men (five of twelve) than women (three of twenty).

Nine respondents – four men, five women – were categorized as having *medium job insecurity* because they qualified their worries about not being rehired with "back-up plans," or hopes that their seniority would be recognized and upheld, or assumptions that they had departmental support that would carry them from year to year. Fifteen of the thirty-two respondents – 55 per cent of the women (11 of 20) and 33 per cent of the men (4 of 12) – were categorized as having *high job insecurity* because remarks in their interview narratives revealed unmitigated anxieties. They related stories of how co-workers were (unfairly) not rehired and how this affected them, of worries that others in their department were lobbying against them, of having no other employment prospects. They repeatedly discussed the uncertainty and lack of "safety" they felt in the hiring process. Stephanie recounted, "One year it was mid-August before I found out [if I was going to get a teaching contract] ... In June, [they offered me a contract], then in July it was 'no, we don't need you now,' and then in August it was 'yeah, we will get you to teach it after all.' That happened to me a couple of times. And there were a few semesters when I didn't have any teaching at all because it was all pulled at the last minute. Like last summer I had nothing. Worst of all were the few semesters when I was knocked back from a [per-term] contract to a per-course at the last minute. That's really hard on the budget!"

Women disclosed the health effects of their job insecurity more often than did men in these narratives, but they were also well aware that admitting to anxiety and stress was a risk. "There's an added dimension when you are both contractual and a woman – you don't want to be seen as one of those unstable women or you may never get hired back. So emotional management is really important on the job, more so than it would be for others who are more secure" (Gerry). A few other women stated that that they did not want to appear "too feminine" or "always emotional." As Spitzer (2005) argues, stress is considered a female complaint in the discourse surrounding gender and precarious work, which is worth exploring in future research.

Are women more job insecure than men or do they perceive more insecurity in contractual teaching? Or are they simply willing to articulate their sense of insecurity while men are not? Women are more risk-aware, according to Lupton (1999), being more socially and economically vulnerable than men. This gender difference was apparent throughout participants' narratives – remember that greater than half of the women compared to a third of the men were highly job insecure in my categorizations. These participants also voiced high anxiety during their narratives but were publicly silenced by the process of contractual hiring. Sarah stated that "People in my department who have worked there for almost twenty years ... still have to reapply, make a case for themselves. And it's true that if someone else younger comes along, they can be tossed. There has been this fear that once people start expecting a lot from their departments, the departments get uncomfortable and want to let them go, to get someone else who doesn't really expect a long-term employment relationship. You don't get a lot of complaint because of that."

While identifying their three top sources of job insecurity, women made fewer references to gender difference in hiring practices and financial concerns, more in the status and marginalization of contractuals in the academic hierarchy. Again, gender differences were apparent in the details. For example, sixteen of the thirty-two sample women and men were active parents at some point in their contractual teaching careers. They appreciated the "choice" of working as a contractual because it was "a good fit" with their responsibilities of child care. All but one indicated how contractual teaching allowed them to "keep a foot in the door" (Naomi) of the academic labour market. The gender difference in combining parenting with contractual teaching was in how they perceived and managed this fit. The six mothers of young children at the time of the interviews shaped their working time around child care: "In terms of my work requirements ... I certainly have some flexibility to care for my family and I certainly make that a priority. It's very important, which is one of the reasons why I'm here and not other places" (Barbara). The three fathers of young children spoke of current scheduling issues but did not indicate that family was their priority over career.

In addition to raising families, the men spoke of combining contractual teaching with career-building activities such as working on degrees or developing other skills.

Another gender difference that appeared in the task diaries (which recorded all activities on a single teaching day) was in the number of "personal hours" respondents allotted themselves for anything that was free of work, family, or community obligations. Personal hours included exercise, watching television, and socializing with friends and ranged from 1 to 9.5 hours per day among the 28 participants who completed the task diaries. Of the 8 participants who recorded 8 to 9.5 personal hours per day, 6 were men. Of the 5 who reported 3 or fewer personal hours, 4 were women. Men in this study either had a better work–life balance or were more apt to employ individual lifestyle solutions to their problems of scheduling work, family, and personal time.

Gender difference was further evident in the descriptions of goodwill in hiring and of how teaching performance was measured. By 2008, academic hiring was moving away from the traditional process based on mentoring and sponsorship by superiors (goodwill), which previously discriminated against women and some men (Hannah, Vethamany-Globus, and Paul 2002). Most participants applauded the new hiring framework of application and administrative selection as more transparent. Nevertheless, goodwill was an implicit issue for the majority of both women and men who did not know if they would get a contract in the following year. Combined with vague performance standards, relying on the goodwill of mentors exacerbated feelings of insecurity for Jessica: "I know there's people who think that I'm doing a good job, and want me back – they asked me to apply! But there's still uncertainty there. What would really irritate me if I don't get that [contract] is that I won't know what I could have done differently. Nobody told me what I was supposed to be doing when I got here – I just did what was thrown at me and I dealt with difficult situations as best I could, for my first year here. But nobody told me I wasn't doing a good job. There is no evaluation *except by the students at the end of term*" (emphasis mine).

Student evaluations of teaching were requested by Provincial University in hiring applications as "evidence of effective teaching." Eleven of the twenty-seven interviewees found this measurement of their performance markedly stressful (Cohen 2011) and there was a slight gender difference in this. Unlike the eight women who found the process stressful, the three men did not blame themselves for the student critiques. In fact, none of the sample men voiced concerns over whether or not they were doing a good job, as did several women. Christine generalized that men "[did] not seem as concerned about whether students like us or not ... I don't know if it's a female thing or whatever." Women, on the other hand, combed through the student evaluations to figure out where they "went wrong" and how they could improve their teaching. Six of the eight women but only one of the three men who mentioned student evaluations were in the high category of job insecurity.

Financial problems were another source of job insecurity cited by almost half of the men and more than half of the women. Contractual teaching is temporary and pays less salary and benefits than does a tenure or tenure-track position. Per-course remuneration was particularly low at Provincial University, with no benefits offered. Qualified per-term contractuals were relatively well paid in 2008 on a scale that was capped just below the starting salary of a tenure-track position. However, the salary and benefits accruing were pro-rated for the length of the contract so the annual salary of a per-term contractual looked about a third higher than the actual income earned by an eight-month contractual. All but one of the per-term contractual women felt the remuneration was excellent, but none of the per-term men said this. Both men and women among the per-course contractuals unanimously stated that the salary was too low and the benefits non-existent. One-third (ten) of the total thirty-two respondents supplemented their teaching income with outside work as tutors, research assistants, writers, musicians, and sundry other occupations. Nine were per-course contractuals, seven were men and seven were single. Clearly the unmarried per-course respondents who rely on contractual teaching as a primary source of income would have to supplement their salaries. The question of why more men than women felt compelled to do so is an issue that could be explored in future research.

Respondents did not relate the symbolism of pay to gender but four women who were primary or sole breadwinners in their households worried about their ability to provide for their families.

Natalie: This is all affecting my family finances as well and that's really stressful. Every year, we're going backwards in terms of

money because I don't work for four months of the year. I get EI
but that's not enough to meet all the bills ... So the pressure's
been building and my anxiety levels are going through the roof.
I've actually had to go and get a prescription for tranquillizers,
which has never happened to me before ... [crying] The stress of
being laid off is always worse in the first month, when there's no
cheque coming in at all. I'm really getting upset, now, dreading
this first month coming up. I find that my anxiety skyrockets
because I'm not providing for my husband and child the way I
should be. I have no control over anything that's going on in that
first month. It gets better as the summer goes on and I get more
relaxed and once EI kicks in, I feel a lot better about the
finances, although we're getting seriously into debt right now. It's
something [for you] to look at – the idea of how debt builds up
over time because of contingent work.

Among the twelve men in the sample, eight were married to working wives and seven earned less income than their spouses. This
raises the issue of a failing breadwinner ideal for these men, but only
Phil mentioned it and then to downplay its significance: "Well ... if I
had that belief that I should be out supporting the family, then maybe
I should be stressed out. There might be contractual men out there
who really feel that 'I'm letting the family down, I'm letting us all
down.' And maybe it's having an effect on them personally, health
wise, and on the family life. I don't look at it like that because for
one thing I could have had tenure in a number of different places. I
chose to stay here because [my wife] had a full-time job so it's a
choice for me."

The most frequent references to gender differences were in participants' narratives of teaching work, student attitudes, and treatment
within their various departments. Several women emphasized the
significance of emotion work in their teaching, particularly when
they worked closely with younger or newer students. They felt this
was a valuable aspect of their job and were happy to comply with
student needs for nurturing and assistance, but it was still exhausting work. Renee states, "Once the fall hits and you get past week
four ... once [the students are] getting ready for the first assessment,
then it starts and it just [constant go] – from week five to thirteen,
and even after week thirteen, week fourteen and fifteen, right? The
demand from students! There's always something, somebody grossly

failing, or some issue that you need to spend a lot more time with outside the classroom. So I do do a lot of tutoring [and counselling]. And I find that you just get exhausted. You feel like you're being picked to death! I find it overwhelming, there's so much! If you do your job well and give your students what you believe you should be able to offer them, you end up paying a price, an exhausting price. Like sometimes I leave feeling pretty bad." Those women like Renee who spoke of their work–life balance were trying to moderate the time and emotional work they were willing to devote to teaching. Only one of the twelve men referred to this problem of balance in "helping students along their way" (Hal).

Student needs turned into distressing (or for two men, positive) situations in fourteen of the twenty-seven narratives that included critical incidents. Students were unhappy with their grades and appealed to a higher authority in the cases of four of the eight women but none of the six men. This mirrors student surveys and anecdotal reports that expectations of men and women are very different. Catherine notes,

I remember being called down to the head's office to discuss a letter that had been written about me by a student who complained that I didn't give her a high enough mark, that I wasn't sympathetic enough to her case. She wanted special consideration. She was registered as a full-time graduate student [so she could get student funding but was also] working full-time at a job and on top of that, she was assigned as my graduate assistant. And it wasn't just a complaint – she was also reporting me for using her as a graduate student to do work for my thesis, as though I didn't have that right. I got her to look up papers for the course I was teaching but that course is also in the area of my research topic ... So she reported me for doing that. And I had to defend myself! The department didn't take my side, so I felt like I was on the hot seat the whole time. At first I couldn't believe that that they were really pursuing this, you know?

Participants told me stories of other women who stopped teaching contractually altogether because of the lack of administrative support in light of such student complaints.

Student disrespect was an issue for one-third of the twenty-seven interviewees – seven women and two men. Six were relatively new to contractual teaching and were developing strategies for dealing with such situations. The other three, experienced per-term contractuals, effectively dispensed with the problems. Some women felt they were targets for student retribution more often than their male colleagues: "They wouldn't be doing that to Dr Tenure who I'm temporarily replacing – it's because I'm contractual and partly my age, because most of the other professors are older." Della did not directly mention gender in her description but other women did. Terry spoke of receiving less support and even basic courtesy than did her male colleagues: "Oh, if I was a man [this student would have treated me differently], most definitely. Do you think she would be going to Dr John Doe and saying I'm getting Dr So-and-So to reread this paper because he's a much fairer grader than you are? I don't think so. He doesn't get that from students. He's been here forever and I've only seen him have one problem with one student … yeah, if I were a man they would never treat me like that. I don't think having a PHD would really affect it as much as [would] being a man."

When discussing student disrespect, all nine complainants stressed the importance of upholding academic standards and "not reneging." One newer contractual man was disturbed by his own reactions to his students' aggressive classroom behaviour when he graded and returned a mid-term exam. Instead of pointing out that the exam was fair and that students paid him little attention during class, he made "promises and concessions that I was really disappointed with after" (Damien). However, only he and two others felt pressured to "mark leniently" because of the aforementioned students' evaluations of their teaching.

Incidents of student disrespect and stress from student critiques are not solely determined by contractual status or gender. Students do occasionally complain and act disrespectful towards tenured faculty. Nevertheless, a few women on contracts echoed tenured women in studies by Currie, Thiele, and Harris (2002) and Hannah, Vethamany-Globus, and Paul (2002) who spoke of tenured male faculty as "more privileged" in a number of ways. These participants pointed out that tenured faculty have a much stronger network of support and can easily deflect the repercussions of student disrespect.

None of the participants in this study considered contractual men to have an easier time than women. More than half of the women and a third of the men expressed a "low level of personal control." But only two of the twelve men compared to ten of the twenty women indicated "little to no departmental support." Like Rachel, these women felt they were treated differently in their departments *because* they were women. Three younger women on contract felt they received less feedback, support, and even basic courtesy than their male counterparts. Rachel notes, "I think that I'm treated [with disrespect] by some people in the department because I'm young and female and it does play a part. I really do believe that. Absolutely. And the reason is you can see the interaction of some people in the department with their male PhD students and it's very different. They would get away with just grumping at me whereas you know, if Joe or John walked down the hall, gosh, it would be a big conversation with them. That stuff is hurtful." For these women, the experience of job insecurity and marginalization as contractual teachers was confounded by gender.

CONCLUSION

To reiterate my initial question, are there gender differences in the experience of job insecurity in contractual university teaching? This was more difficult to answer than anticipated. As in other university workplaces, the gender gaps in hiring and occupational health are narrowing at Provincial University and job insecurity is structurally embedded in contractual teaching for both men and women. Gender differences were more apparent in the qualitative narratives when participants discussed their perceptions and experiences of marginalization. Some women attributed their marginalization as contractuals to the lower value placed on teaching work because it demands emotional and interactive labour, usually associated with "feminine work." They worried that expressing any emotion would elevate their risk of job insecurity. Time prohibited an in-depth consideration of how "gender performativity" (Butler 1990) might mediate the experience of job insecurity. I leave this and the question of how contractuals' insecurity intersects with the "gendered organization" (Acker 1990) of university workplaces to future research. This study also begs the question of whether or not articulating gender differences in a workplace that defines itself as gender-neutral would elevate the risk of job insecurity. I caution researchers to weigh such vulnerabilities in their final analysis of contractual workers' responses.

The findings of my research call for comparisons of contractual teaching in other departments and universities with particular union policies and worker protections to find out which practices create more or less security for women and for men. Finally, this research mandates a closer gender-based examination of what constitutes protection against job insecurity and the practical means for instituting such protection. Without understanding how solutions to the health challenges and workplace injustice of job insecurity might differ by gender, contractuals are left to deal with it individually and as best they can.

ACKNOWLEDGMENTS

I am grateful to so many who were indispensable in my research, especially the thirty-two women and men who volunteered to participate despite any misgivings of risk and vulnerability. Thank you to my dissertation committee – thesis supervisor Linda Cullum and committee members Barbara Neis and Robert Hill – who had the patience to see me through the thesis on which this chapter is based. Finally, a huge thank you goes to Elvi Whittaker for her encouragement and assistance. I am thankful for the insightful comments from the three anonymous reviewers of this chapter.

11

The Missing Link:
Research Nurses and Their
Contribution to the Production
of Research Knowledge

PATRICIA KAUFERT

This chapter originated in a 2005 Canadian Institutes for Health Research–funded joint project between ethicists and social scientists from the University of British Columbia (UBC) and the University of Manitoba called Centring the Human Subject in Health Research: Understanding the Meaning and Experience of Research Participation. The project's objective was to explore research ethics from the bottom up – that is, from the position of participating subjects – rather than from the top down, from the different perspectives of ethicists, researchers, and lawyers. The UBC research team focused on the experiences of those individuals who had been participants in research – namely, scholars, policy makers, researchers, research ethics board (REB) members, and human subjects. At Manitoba, we were particularly interested in the relationships within research, and we concentrated on interviews with researchers, chairs, and members of REBS, interpreters, community-based research workers, and a small group of research nurses. These nurses and their perspectives on research and research ethics are at the centre of this chapter.

Clinical researchers, the funders of research, and the bioethicists are all acquainted with research nurses in one way or another, but research nurses' contributions to research are rarely acknowledged. Not only are they invisible in the formal research; research nurses also feel that no one listens to them. This chapter explores the consequences of this neglect for both the research nurses and the ethics of research.

The meaning of *research nurse* is not always immediately clear. The research nurse is an older and more inclusive title that has subsequently come to include more differentiated roles, such as nurse research coordinator and clinical research associate. They are usually nurses with formal training and credentials (BN, RN) often hired on contract to work as a member of a research team who perform research functions without involvement in clinical care. In recruiting and interviewing human subjects, they often wear identification badges with the title "Research Nurse," thereby engaging the trust of the potential research participant.

But the combination of *research* and *nurse* can be confusing. In a review of the literature on the research nurse, for instance, Ocker and Plank complained that "searches for references to 'research nurse' disclosed almost exclusively articles of nurses conducting self-initiated research" (2000, 288). There was also the problem of other names for research nurses. For example, Hastings, Fisher, and McCabe note, "An internal assessment conducted in 2007 at the NIH Clinical Center found 5 formal and 39 informal titles associated with nurses practicing on the clinical research patient care units or the coordinating of studies on behalf of individual NIH Institute principal investigators" (2012, 151). These changes sometimes reflected an upward shift in the position of nurses in the research hierarchy. Carter, Jester, and Jones (2007), for example, discussed the importance of creating a role for a clinical research manager as distinct from the clinical research coordinator. At a Society of Clinical Research Associates (SOCRA) conference in Vancouver, the list of job openings included clinical coordinators, clinical field specialists, clinical research coordinators, clinical research administrators, clinical research project managers, and clinical trial monitors. Jill Fisher's book *Medical Research For Hire: the Political Economy of Pharmaceutical Clinical Trials* (2009) describes the increasing reliance of physicians in the United States on contracts in which trial participants were recruited by research nurses. Participants were often attracted by offers of "free" diagnostic services and medication. Fisher interviewed clinical research coordinators who recruited and interviewed human subjects. In contrast to Fisher's research, the original interviews for Centring the Human Subject in Health Research focused solely on the relationship of research nurses to other researchers and to the REBS.

It was evident, however, that the research nurses we interviewed had a place as members of a different collectivity within the university, usually hired from within the university and recognized as essential to the process of research. Identified as research "workers" or research "assistants," they were essential to the research, but their working contribution was rarely acknowledged publicly. In the title of their paper, Hobson, Jones, and Deane (2005) describe research assistants as the "Silenced Partner in Australia's Knowledge Production." The title of the present chapter describes research nurses as the "missing link," rarely acknowledged and rarely heard.

These other categories of "missing link" assistance in research include graduate students hired as research assistants by university researchers. Graduate students research assistants serve as apprentices and are thereby given the opportunity to learn research methods and skills by doing and observing (Benton 2004). Some students simply become part of research teams to provide an income while in graduate school. These research assistants are hired based on their experience and skills, the nature of the project, and its budget. Some research assistants are, as Roth calls them, "hired hands" (1966), one part of a casual contracted workforce of universities. Years later, however, Staggenborg writes another account, seeing these students not as "hired hands" but as "research workers" with the need for extended contracts and training about the theoretical grounding and the justification for the research (1988). Among the small number of writings about these research assistants is that of Duncombe and Jessop, who describe their experiences as graduate students hired as contract researchers (2002). They report their discomfort at the inequities of the research process and of the "faking of friendship" to facilitate the "rapport" needed to acquire data. Florez and Kelling (1984) point to a crucial difference between "solo researchers" and "hired hands" where the latter share the observational methodology and work of the research with the former, but have no part in the conceptualizing of the research, how it is conducted, the analysis of the data, or its publication. Their involvement is acknowledged in a footnote. Hobson, Jones, and Deane (2005) note that research assistants are usually hired on contract, and often they are women looking for flexibility in their working conditions. In her chapter on sessional work as "feminine work" in this volume, Linda Cohen also refers to the decision to opt for such contract employment. The research nurses that we interviewed, and who shared their histories with us, also identified the advantage of flexibility as a motive.

The tasks for which research assistants are generally hired include the rather important duty of procuring and supporting research subjects. They may also protect the time and energy of those directing the research, manage quantities of information, code data, specialize in technical tasks, do library or Internet work, act as language interpreters in overseas projects, interview, do fieldwork, coordinate research activities, and take on other perhaps unspecified duties, which, in some cases, might include making coffee for project meetings. While some graduate students negotiate the use of data for dissertations, they do not usually have open access to, or ownership of, the research data, its analysis, and publication. Intellectual property rights are laid down before they are hired. Unlike the majority of university workers, for whom conditions of employment are carefully specified, research assistants work on contracts for limited periods, with salaries measured by their qualifications and a workload decided by the principal research investigators. Thus, they lack many of the privileges afforded to other employees of universities. They are usually not protected by bargaining units as are many teaching assistants. Their job descriptions and salaries vary widely from project to project, and also by the discipline of the research. Nevertheless, their contributions are crucial, yet they remain at the margins of research agendas and protocols. Usually, their names do not appear in the list of authors on articles; they may be relegated to the familiar acknowledgment in footnotes, which makes them essentially invisible in the knowledge-making process (Hobson, Jones, and Deane 2005). With very few exceptions, the research assistant is seldom the subject of academic articles, and they remain the "missing links" in any ethnography of knowledge production.

I turn now to the case of research nurses who stand in an important position in the informed consent and ethical process of the research project for which they are contracted.

THE CASE OF RESEARCH NURSES

Research nurses are well known among medical researchers, funding agencies, and members of research ethics boards (REBs). For example, if a medical project involves humans, principal researchers will include the costs of hiring research nurses within their budgets. If their application is submitted to the Canadian Institutes for Health Research (CIHR), these costs are usually accepted as a routine requirement. REB committee members are not involved in budget decisions, but they are responsible for the ethics of a project and, more often than not, it is the research nurse who carries out the ethical regulations. This places these nurses at the frontlines of acquiring subjects, teaching, and counselling them. In some sense, they constitute the public face of the project itself, at least in its initial and most vulnerable interaction. Even though the guidelines and the answers to possible questions have been laid down by the researchers, the nurses approach the subjects, render the necessary explanations, inform them what they need to know, offer support for their as yet unknown role. They arrange for informed consent, which is central to research viability. This vital step in engaging, recruiting, and informing patients as research subjects is enhanced by the solid reputation of the nurses. (Fisher and Kalbaugh 2012). One of them explained that when she walked into a hospital room, "where they don't know me from Adam," the badge she wore saying "research nurse" helped to engage their trust because it identified her as a nurse.

Clinical researchers, the funders of research, and the bioethicists are all acquainted with research nurses in one way or another, but research nurses' contributions to research are rarely acknowledged. Not only are they invisible in the formal research; research nurses also feel that no one listens to them. This chapter explores the consequences of this neglect for both the research nurses and the ethics of research.

Since the early 2000s, research nurses have been hired in large numbers by contract research organizations (CROs) and pharmaceutical companies (Fisher 2009). Although research nurses work within universities, they are difficult to place within the academic structure, despite the university's long tradition of contract hiring for teaching and research assistants. They are members of the general coterie of women who work for universities in one capacity or another, from lawyers and accountants to security and housekeeping staff. In *Sciences from Below*, Harding refers to this amorphous group as the "the kinds of women who do in fact work in or on behalf of scientific institutions" (2008, 127). However, this is a little misleading as research nurses are rarely engaged in the basic sciences, while they do "work in or on behalf of" the medical sciences.

Faculties of medicine are the primary homes of clinical research-ers, who are supported by a cadre of workers with many different skills. They include research nurses but also statisticians, laboratory technicians, computer programmers, and data analysts. A list of job openings looking for research nurses revealed several slightly differ-ent titles, including nurse coordinator, research coordinator, moni-tors, or clinical research coordinators. However, *research nurse* is an older term and was the title used among the people interviewed. They are trained nurses but not members of the hospital nursing staff. They are not employees of the university, although they work for academics. Rather, they are contract workers, in a sense subcon-tracted by the principal researchers. Some research nurses may be hired for only a few weeks, while others may have contracts lasting for months or even years. The contract also includes the conditions of their work and how they will be paid. One of the differences between student assistants and research nurses is that students may go on to become researchers themselves. Although some research nurses do retrain and take an advanced degree that equips them to become researchers, this is not a general expectation. One research nurse we interviewed expressed regret that she had not taken advan-tage of this opportunity when she was younger.

BACKGROUND

As already mentioned, the material for this chapter comes from a joint collaboration between ethicists and social scientists from UBC and the University of Manitoba.[1] Our initial interest in research nurses arose out of a review of the research ethics literature con-ducted by our colleagues at UBC in 2005. It produced online very few hits for research nurses, which triggered our curiosity as we knew that research nurses played a major role in implementing the many regulations laid down by REB committees, and we decided to include a small group of research nurses among our interviewees. They became "key informants," valuable for their knowledge of the community of research nurses, its history and future. We recruited a small group of research nurses based on the depth of their work experience and their interest in research ethics. The interviews were individually based and in-depth. As the community of research nurses is small, we have been very careful to avoid material that might identify them, and we also decided not to attach names or numbers to quotations. The interviews usually began with a few introductory questions on their training and experiences as nurses and then turned to the reasons why they left nursing to become research nurses, the advantages and disadvantages of contract work, the challenges they faced in recruiting potential participants, and the difficulties of administering informed consent. These topics were left relatively open to allow the research nurses to introduce issues and themes and to speak with their own voice.

The decision to become a research nurse was sometimes based on the need to balance the demands of work as a nurse and care for their families, particularly for young children. Thus, by becoming a research nurse, they were able to remain connected with nursing but avoid demands such as night duty. Another advantage was being able to negotiate favourable contracts so that their working hours fit with the responsibilities of child care. Linda Cohen refers to contract teachers' comparable motivations for staying in their chosen fields.

While many women in the labour force make similar choices when coping with the care of young children, we had not anticipated the importance some research nurses attached to the notion of freedom. One of the research nurses described how contract work had given her the opportunity to organize her own time: "I really was interested in doing work that I could go in and out of, and it was more sort of contract-based where I knew something was going to start and was going to end and wouldn't necessarily be a full-time employment." Another told us how contract work and being a research nurse had helped her escape from the hierarchy of nursing. She particularly valued being "freelance," able to negotiate her pay, the number of hours she would work and, very importantly, for whom she would work: "I have been in the same institution now for twelve years so that when job postings go up, I know that there are certain people I would not work for because it is a constant battle. So there are people I would not work for and job opportunities I've passed over." Others were interested in medical research and became research nurses for that reason.

Yet the freedom gained from working on a contract was counterbalanced by the loss of insurance and the other health benefits. Sometimes, depending on the nature of their contract, research nurses also lost the protection of their union. Contracts varied in length as well as rates of pay and benefits. Furthermore, a contract might not be renewed because a researcher had plans for other research, or did not want to rehire the same research nurse, or because the research proposal had not been funded. In two of the interviews, the research nurses knew that their contracts were running out and they were uncertain whether the researcher would be able to rehire them.

Interviews with older research nurses gave us insight about the conditions of the profession from the 1980s on. For example, we learned that contracts between researchers and research nurses were introduced between twenty and thirty years ago, although clinical researchers may have used their nursing staff as surrogates for research nurses. One research nurse recalled when she first took the initiative to approach researchers and asked to be hired as a research nurse: "When I started doing this, people were just hearing about me or I was hearing about someone's work and I called them up and they'd say 'ok, sure.' It wasn't as formal as going through an application." She was surprised when she learned that she had to bargain with the principal researcher over the conditions of her contract: "Initially I was paid per patient and that was a real conflict of interest because we didn't get paid for the patients we saw, but didn't include in the study." In those earlier days, the transition from nursing to being a research nurse could be difficult. In one interview, we heard about the loneliness of a research nurse who moved into a clinical department. She recalled a deep sense of isolation: "I couldn't exactly say what it was, because we worked in such isolation in those days. We didn't know who the other research nurses were."

Work conditions and ethical frameworks for protection of human subjects changed dramatically between 1990 and 2005. For example, the same research nurse described how she was now paid: "You are hired as per all the usual union rules and you get paid by the hospital, so you just submit your hours. I fill in the pay sheet every week saying how many hours I work and for whom." She attributed many of these changes to the relatively recent creation of an office of clinical research. In her view, "then the world changed here because there were more educational opportunities, an orientation program, there's mentoring and accountability in a much more visible way because they can do audits, they can check up on complaints." In another interview, a research nurse described her experiences when she was hired and treated as a member of a research team. She told us that she was "treated with great respect and I was given responsibility and autonomy." She was also able assume a more meaningful part in the research: "I'm able to make decisions and I'm able to come and go as I please." Despite her enthusiasm, she added, "I don't think it's purposely done, but nurses aren't always seen that way" – that is, as autonomous, responsible, valuable members of the team.

Other recent changes reflect the increasing financial pressures on universities. For example, one of the research nurses decided to attend a meeting held by a visiting nurse for the purpose of recruiting research nurses for a major project. The visitor discussed the money that could be earned from the project, but only if "they were able to recruit the number of people that you are supposed to be recruiting in a given amount of time." As she ended the tale, the research nurse added, "I remember it just crossing my mind that we didn't have those kinds of pressures." The emphasis on money and speed are more generally associated with CROs, but, as this research nurse described, these pressures can be carried into faculties of medicine.

RECRUITING AND OBTAINING CONSENT

The recruitment of potential participants and the administering of consent forms are central to the relationships between researchers, participants in research, research ethics committees, and research nurses. Since the publication of the *Belmont Report* in 1979, consent forms have been a driving force in the construction of a network of REB committees across and within universities.[2] These procedures are also a dominant theme in the research ethics literature. For the research nurses interviewed, they were a challenge. For example, one research nurse told us how she prepared herself when starting to recruit participants: "When I plan I try to think about all the recruitment pieces and the potential pit falls, and looking at ethics and any conflict of interest on my part, and recruitment and where I'm going and those types of things."

There are several ways of recruiting participants, including putting up posters in clinics and use of the telephone or the Internet. These methods put the onus on the potential participant to make the decision to contact the research nurse. Direct contact by a research nurse has also grown more complex over time. One of the older research nurses recalled how it was when she first started: "When I started working, I could go up to the labour and delivery floor and look at the list of patients and just on the board I could see their names and see where they were in their labour and all that and ask questions. Well, now I can't do that." With the new rules she is dependent on a ward nurse to approach patients and ask whether they would be interested in taking part in a research study. The difficulty of this method is that ward nurses are often busy, and telephoning the research nurse is not always a priority. Although she accepted the decision of the REB to require a ward nurse to approach patients, she complained that it had got "much harder to get people to take that extra step to call you as the researcher." Another research nurse told us that "generally, it is the nurse manager who approaches people to see if they are agreeable to talking to a research nurse and then their names are released to myself and we go and approach them that way, but we can't go directly to them." One solution was to devise a way of persuading ward nurses to phone them: "So you spend a lot of time networking with them and going to meetings and explaining the study and why you need their help and why the study is important and there's a lot of staff education that goes along with that." A research nurse could be turned down by an individual patient who is feeling too sick, tired, or angry to participate. One of the research nurses described some of these difficulties: "I've had sick, older people tell me 'just leave me alone. I don't want to be your guinea pig today' kind of thing ... They have this perception of scientific research that what we do is to take advantage of the sick." Other people were too sick or depressed, or their family members did not want them to take part.

Getting consent forms signed can be even more complex, partly because most research nurses have no control over how they are written. In structuring the forms, the researcher must follow guidelines established by the university, which are usually available on the university's website. The individual consent form then becomes a joint product between the formal regulations, the researcher, and the members of an REB. The REB is particularly concerned with the passages that describe the risks and benefits of participation in the study. Once agreed, the consent form is attached to the application for funding and is sent off to CIHR or some other funding agency. Usually, it is not until the project is accepted and the money provided that a research nurse is hired. She will be given the instructions for what type of individual to recruit and the consent form. One research nurse observed that the "consent process itself usually takes about fifteen to twenty minutes to allow somebody to actually read it and ask any questions. If you read it to them, of course it takes longer to read it out loud to someone than for them to read it themselves." Research nurses are expected to ensure that the potential participant meets the criteria required, understands the risks and benefits of the research study, and is willing to sign the consent form and initial each page.

Clearly, research nurses are very committed to the signing of the consent form and to ensuring that it is understood. Not all participants and researchers saw the consent form and process of obtaining informed consent in quite the same way. Researchers, unlike their research assistants, were usually seemingly only concerned with obtaining the signed consent from potential participants. According to one research nurse, the process of consent has many perplexities and nuances: "Some people, you can tell, they're just sort of skim reading and then they're prepared to sign it." Another expressed some anxiety about the "number of people who say 'argh, I'll just sign the consent, don't worry about it,' or 'I'm sure, I would just like to help you out' and without even looking at the consent form. Whatever."

As they were the main negotiators and promoters of informed consent with participants, research nurses advanced explanations as to why individuals were sometimes even reluctant to read the consent forms. One suggested that they "could not read well enough." Another research nurse opined, "People are very proud, and if they can't read it or they don't understand, I'm not always sure that they're going to tell you. They'll say, 'Yeah, yeah, I understand.'" One noted that "They are willing to sign, but they say that you want that to use them as a guinea pig. Well, I just found that terrible. I said, 'No I would never treat you like that. I want you to read the consent form,' but they will still tease you." Another questioned how many people who signed a consent form had understood it: "People are very polite and always wanting to help but that politeness doesn't mean that they truly understand. They say 'sure dear, I'll sign for you,' but that doesn't mean that they understood a word you said."

The question of how the consent form was understood was very critical to the research nurses, as they felt it put participants in jeopardy of one sort or another. However, they tended to blame the researchers and REB committees rather than the participants. One of the research nurses was very articulate on this theme. In her interview with us, she held the researchers and REB committee members responsible for long and complicated consent forms. Speaking about the length of consent forms, she told us, "I have some major issues with the whole process. They are seven pages long sometimes. The readability is probably at a university level ... When I've read consents to people I'm not quite sure if it's fully an *informed* consent." A supporter of "plain language," she talked about the importance of shorter sentences, fewer words, and a layout "formatted differently so that there might be more white space." She also raised other difficulties: "As a frontline person, because you have to go through it all and you are working with different people of different socio-economic stages. It's supposed to be at a grade-six level, but some of the concepts are hard." She declared that she "understood what the research board is trying to do. They want people to be completely informed and that's a good thing, but I don't think it needs to be done with more words."

Other research nurses were equally worried about the consent process: "I really question whether sometimes it's truly informed consent when the language is convoluted, or it sounds more complicated than it needs to be, and then, are the people really, truly informed?" A third research nurse remarked, "the role of the ethics board is crucially important, but I think they need to be careful that sometime ... it's too long. As a frontline worker, you do go paragraph-by-paragraph, the person is almost asleep by the time you get to the end."

DISCUSSION

At the beginning of this chapter, I stated that research nurses feel not only invisible but also unheard. They feel that no one listens to them. We chose to discuss recruitment and consent to illustrate how research nurses are treated and to show that ward nurses, patients, researchers, and the institution itself rarely pay attention to research nurses' experience. Many research nurses do not believe that they can intervene or change things. One research nurse, for instance, criticized the regulations governing consent but then concluded, "I have thought about, how does one influence those committees? How does one influence that process? I really don't think that people like myself can influence them directly. I think the influence has to come from the principal investigators." Another research nurse suggested that researchers and ethicists did not want to know too much about how recruitment and consent are managed: "I think they have a research nurse so that they are trying to put a space between critical care and research. So yes, it might be their patient, but people are free to say 'No' to me because they will never see me again as part of clinical care. I'm only the research nurse, so if they say 'No' to me, that's okay, their clinical care will carry on and I'm gone." In another interview, the research nurse suggested that the relationship between researchers and research nurses was a "hangover from the past when your nursing training told you not to question a physician, you just did what you were told." Finally, the power of the researcher to sack a research nurse who asks too many questions or is too critical is still very real.

Admittedly, there are structural barriers to research nurses' full participation in the research process. It was obvious from the interviews that research nurses were quite capable of drawing on their experience and advising researchers on changes in the length of a consent form, its language, or its appropriateness for the projected population. Yet, unless they were already working with the researcher, they would not see possible recruits or be able to assess the language of the consent form. Under the current funding regime, a researcher has to submit the grant application to the REB committee when applying for research funding from CIHR, for example. The long application includes sections on the study budget and participant information and consent forms. If the researcher's application is successful and CIHR money is forthcoming, then the researcher can put out a contract and hire a research nurse. However, by the time the participant and consent forms are given to the research nurse, it is too late to change them. Making changes to the forms and resubmitting to the REB committee is unlikely. As one nurse told us, "Once you have a randomized control trial for instance, and instruments have been decided beforehand and what they are measuring, and so on, so once you get into the study, it's hard then to say, 'Well this instrument, we're finding it difficult for people to do this' – or whatever. Well, at that point it's a little bit late to think about wording changes and stuff, so you kind of have to think."

Some specific requirements involve the research nurse and appear of questionable intent, such as the rule that participants should initial each page and sign their full name on the consent form. Somewhat rhetorically, a research nurse asked, "Does it really protect the human subject or is it protecting the organization? Yeah, I mean obviously this whole business of the initials and 'I consent to this, this and this.' I mean, somebody's covering their arses." At first reading, this seemed a relatively innocuous matter, made with good intentions, but she may be right that it does seem more legalistic and protective of the institution than the participant.

The research nurses found themselves in an ethical trap. Many participants do read and sign the form as requested. Others are not interested in the detail of the consent form but will sign and initial the form, leaving the research nurse uncertain about how much they have understood. Another group might not want (or might not be able) to read the form, but would say that they would sign it to please the nurse. The dilemma faced by the research nurse is whether she should take these prospective participants out of the study or encourage them to sign the consent form even though she is aware that they do not fully understanding the risks and benefits. Should she tell the researchers, knowing that many of them would prefer a signed consent form rather than an ethical gesture?

Going through some of the other regulations, I raised the ruling that a ward nurse should approach potential participants and ask them whether they would be willing to see the research nurse. Initially, it seemed quite simple, until I started to ask myself questions from the perspective of a social scientist. Were the researchers asked for an opinion about this? More importantly, were the research nurses consulted? Did someone interview potential participants for their responses? Did the ward nurses have a say? Were any measures taken before introducing the change to include the ward nurse? Did anyone check with or obtain feedback about whether changes were actually implemented, effective, or had actual impact on communication or ethical process? If so, did this new regulation make any difference in the number of recruits? Were there changes in the demographic characteristics of participants? For example, did the ward nurse see them as more likely to consent? Did anyone investigate the impact of this regulation on the quality of the data?

Although it was too late to answer these particular questions, I decided to explore what the Canadian Tri-Council Agencies said about the work of research nurses and their contribution to the research process. The Tri-Council Agencies, made up of the Canadian Institutes of Health Research, the Natural Sciences and Engineering Research Council of Canada, and the Social Sciences and Humanities

Research Council of Canada, was initiated in 1996. It took time to establish because it required not only the collaboration of the three councils but also the agreement of seventy Canadian universities (van den Hoonaard 2011). Now the Tri-Council plays a major role in research ethics and its 2010 policy statement, the *Ethical Conduct for Research Involving Humans* (TCPS2), is an important guide for all university researchers.

There is no mention of research nurses in the TCPS2 2010 or in the TCPS2 2014, not even in an early statement that explains that it was written to "assist those who use it – researchers, sponsors, members of research ethics boards (REBs), participants, and the public." There is also no mention of research nurses in the chapters on the consent process and on the governance of research ethics, yet the success of both in the research process depends on the performance of research nurses as pivotal frontline research workers. The connection between the Tri-Council Policy and what is actually happening on the ground seems tenuous at best. While Tri-Council policy makers communicate through policy documents and online tutorials, the Tri-Council Policy does not appear to be listening to researchers, whether research nurses or social scientists.

Miller and Boulton suggest that regulatory bodies, such as the Tri-Council, see "research participants as rational, individual, modernist – and Western – subjects for whom the concept of informed consent and its documentation by a signed form is unproblematic" (2007, 2204). If the Tri-Council listened to the research nurses, they would hear that some of the potential participants were angry, hostile, perhaps suspicious, and possibly irrational. Others might seem to be representative of the general population, but that does not make them "rational, modernist, and Western." To take another example, Flory and Emanuel (2004) reviewed the literature on how to ensure that participants were able to understand the information on consent forms. They concluded that person-to-person contact, rather than forms or multimedia interventions, was the best way to improve understanding. By contrast, the Tri-Council's 2014 policy statement suggests that an expanded use of technology will increase understanding. One of the research nurses shared her strategy of ensuring that everyone understands the consent form: "I don't let them sign it until they've repeated back to me what they understand to be the risks." This strategy would be an effective alternative to expensive and possibly time-consuming technologies.

Not incorporating the views of research nurses who work within universities, the Tri-Council also ignored the research nurses who work for pharmaceutical companies and contract research organizations, despite a rapid expansion in the size and number of clinical trials and CROS since the 2000s.[3] In a 2001 article, nursing professor and sociologist Mary-Rose Mueller reported on nurses and clinical trial coordination in the 1990s. She ended with a vision of the future: "The social organization of clinical trial research is undergoing a significant transformation. It appears that at least among the pharmaceutical company sponsored trials, the decentralized research team based model, wherein physician-investigators hire, orient and counsel nurse trial coordinators, is being supplanted by a more centralized, factory-production model in which the routine aspects of trials are managed by off site personnel in clinical research organizations ... and some of the routine tasks undertaken by nurses will be transferred to less skilled and less expensive workers" (2001, 189). Mueller's vision has indeed proven true. Consequently, the roles of research nurses and the structure and process of ethical protection of human subjects has become more centralized but less mediated by the research nurse as a source of moral oversight and trust relationships.

The final word in this chapter on the roles and responsibilities of research nurses, however, goes to one of the research nurses who took part in our interviews. Reflecting on her position in the dual ethical worlds of nurse and researcher, she remarked, "I have an ethical responsibility not to harm anyone or to cause harm ... and I have to ensure that everything possible is done to make sure that this is safe and secure." As research ethics evolve inside and outside the university, we'd do well to listen closely to research nurses.

ACKNOWLEDGMENTS

Our project, Centring the Human Subject in Health Research: Understanding the Meaning and Experience of Research Participation, was supported by a Canadian Institutes for Health Research Grant (2005–12). The project was directed by Susan Cox (principal investigator), Michael McDonald (co-principal investigator), and Anne Townsend (co-investigator) from the Maurice W. Young Centre for Applied Ethics, University of British Columbia. Co-investigators Patricia Kaufert and Joseph Kaufert are based in the Department of Community Health Sciences at the University of Manitoba. Research team members from U B C include Natasha Damiano-Paeterson, Sara Hancock, Darquise Lafrenière, Christina Preto, Cathy Schuppli, and Kim Taylor. From the University of Manitoba, team members include Dhiwya Attawar, Lisa LaBine, and Toni Morris Oswald.

This chapter could not have been written without the willingness of the research nurses to share their experiences and their knowledge of the research process. I also owe a debt to our two research associates, Lisa Labine and Toni Morris Oswald. Elvi Whittaker has been an extraordinarily supportive editor as well as a wonderful friend. Finally, this chapter could not have been written without Joe Kaufert, his interviewing skills, sensitivity, and tolerance of my slow pace.

Notes

1 A paper on interpreters and community-based workers has been published (Kaufert, Kaufert, and LaBine 2009). Also published by members of the project team on research relationship are: McDonald and Cox (2009) and McDonald et al. (2008, 2009). The present chapter is dedicated to the research nurses and their views on research and research ethics.

2 Produced by the National Commission for the Protection of Human Subjects of Biomedical and Behavioral Research, the *Belmont Report* became something akin to the sacred bible within medical ethics. It is known for laying down the three principles – respect for persons, beneficence, and justice – as well as the foundation for informed consent and recruitment of subjects. See *The Belmont Report: Ethical Principles and Guidelines for the Protection of Human Subjects Research*, April 18, 1979, http://www.hhs.gov/ohrp/humansubjects/guidance/belmont.html.

3 More on such changes can be found in Jill Fisher's book, *Medical Research For Hire: The Political Economy of Pharmaceutical Clinical Trials* (2009).

12

Collective Insecurity:
An Exploration of the Experiences
of Women Faculty in Atlantic Canada

ZELDA ABRAMSON, PHYLLIS L.F. RIPPEYOUNG,
AND E. LISA PRICE

INTRODUCTION

Women's roles in academia have been a topic of debate at least since Aristotle deemed women's intellects inferior to men's. However, since the 1960s, women have been entering all aspects of university life in rising numbers, largely due to the work of the feminist movement in arguing for women's ability to have a place in public life. Even though women have been entering the academy in larger numbers, they continue to be underrepresented as faculty members (Drakich and Stewart 2007) and have reported having experiences distinct from those of men, particularly regarding the tenure process and their ability to attain promotions, to be supported in their work, to achieve pay equity, and to find a satisfying work–life balance (Acker, Webber, and Smyth 2012; Monroe et al. 2008).

Most research on women in academia is from the 1990s, and the few more recent studies on Canadian women in higher education tend to examine statistical trends (Acker and Armenti 2004) with one exception. The collection edited by Wagner, Acker, and Mayuzumi (2008) focuses largely on the non-tenure-track work force in higher education. The chapters on tenure-track faculty present individual narratives of marginalized women faculty and the ways in which they navigate the academy. Although these are important areas of inquiry, there nonetheless remains a gap in the literature. We fill in this gap in the literature by studying women faculty at a small, primarily undergraduate university in Atlantic Canada to assess whether the historical patterns of gender inequity remain today.

According to the Canadian Association of University Teachers (CAUT 2014–15), women made up 57.2 per cent of undergraduate students, 54.6 per cent of master's students, and 47.5 per cent of doctoral students in 2011–12. Yet, in 2013, women comprised 39.5 per cent of full-time permanent university professors in Canada (CAUT 2014–15). In contrast, in 2012–13, 48.2 per cent of full-time university professor positions that are neither tenured nor tenure-track are occupied by women; these are positions that characterize the academy's contingent work force (CAUT 2014–15). Furthermore, in 2011 women comprised 22.8 per cent of full professors, 38 per cent of associate professors, and 46.4 per cent of assistant professors (CAUT 2013–14).

Not only are women faculty more likely to be underrepresented in tenure-track positions in Canada, but research has shown that they also are more likely to have negative experiences than their male counterparts in Australia (Kjeldal, Rindfleish, and Sheridan 2005; Probert 2005), the Netherlands (Benschop and Brouns 2003), New Zealand (Baker 2009), the UK (Blackaby, Booth, and Frank 2005), and the United States (Allison 2007; Geisler, Kaminski, and Berkley 2007; Laube et al. 2007; Misra et al. 2011; Monroe et al. 2008; Stout, Staiger, and Jennings 2007). The literature repeatedly demonstrates that they are paid less than men on average (Ginther and Hayes 2003). They are denied promotion more often than men (Leahey 2006), and when they are promoted, it typically takes longer than men (Ornstein, Stewart, and Drakich 2007). Women are more likely to face sexual harassment than men (Monroe et al. 2008) and endure not having their work taken seriously (Valian 2004).

In their interviews of eighty American female faculty, Monroe et al. (2008) found that women carried a greater burden for service work, which was then not valued for promotion and did not translate into leadership positions. Commonly, the women in their study pointed to family responsibilities as a significant barrier to advancement as the work they were required to do at home limited their ability to carry out research, and the university did not support their familial responsibilities in meaningful ways. These findings have been shown in numerous other studies. Stout, Staiger, and Jennings (2007), in interviewing American female associate professors, found that they confront "an accumulation of disadvantages throughout their academic careers." It was not uncommon for these women "to question seriously whether it is worth their effort to continue as proactive members of the faculty. They perceive the rewards for their hard work to be minimal and unsatisfying" (Stout, Staiger, and Jennings 2007, 137). Bird, Litt, and Wang (2004) refer to this type of service work as "institutional housekeeping" because, similar to women's unpaid work in the home, "institutional housekeeping" is usually performed without resources and recognition (195). Furthermore, women faculty, in addition to their teaching and scholarly work, are generally responsible for monitoring gender equity in their universities. Overall, then, women have been found to be at a distinct disadvantage in faculty positions around the world.

Canada is unique in a number of respects, particularly in comparison to the United States, by offering federally subsidized parental leave linked to employment insurance (Ray, Gornick, and Schmitt 2009). Canadian universities are also more likely to be unionized, and unionized employment sites tend to have smaller gender wage gaps (Kidd and Shannon 1996). Thus, Canadian universities may provide a number of the remedies to gender inequity not found elsewhere. In their study of twenty-seven women faculty members in education, however, Acker and Feuerverger (1996) found many of the same patterns here as previously found in the United States. Nonetheless, their interviews were carried out in 1995, prior to the current parental leave programs that are common across Canada and in a context with even fewer women faculty than there are now. Atlantic Canadian universities, in particular, have many characteristics that are considered solutions for gender inequity; they are small universities with less research intensity, paid parental leaves, strong faculty unions, and some history of the promotion of women. This study examines one such university to assess how much gender inequality there is in an environment that is theoretically more conducive to gender equality.

To uncover the women's experiences in academia, we carried out a series of focus group interviews of faculty in May 2008. The focus groups were semi-structured, meaning that a series of questions and themes were prepared ahead of time but discussions were allowed to progress naturally. Three key questions were identified:

- What key strategies do women faculty members employ in negotiating the academic environment successfully?
- What challenges do women faculty members confront?
- How they balance their work and life inside and outside of the academy?

In 2008, there were 88 female faculty members (35.9 per cent of a total of 245 faculty) at this small university, of which 31 participated in the focus groups (35.2 per cent), and of the focus group participants, 25 completed the questionnaire. We ran 6 focus groups organized by rank and experience – full professor, associate, assistant, instructor, librarians, and one mixed group. We decided to combine "senior" associates with more than 6 years at the associate levels and full professors because we were interested in probing the differing experiences of women who were promoted to full-professor and those who either choose not to apply or had their application denied.

Each focus group lasted one and a half hours and was video recorded. The interviews were transcribed and analyzed using Strauss and Corbin's (1990) grounded theory approach. We also gave a short questionnaire to the focus group participants at the start of each focus group session, asking how much they negotiated for starting salaries, with whom they negotiated, their placement on the salary grid, the faculty start-up funds they received, partner status, and number of children. We also drew on data provided by the university to the faculty union on salary, rank, and date of appointment.

The participants represented each of the faculties of arts, science, and professional studies, as well as the library. There were multiple participants at each rank from contract faculty through to tenured full professors. There was also great diversity in terms of when the women were hired at the university, the earliest being in 1975, the latest in 2007. The women ranged in age from twenty-seven to sixty at the time of the interview, with a median age of forty-four years old.

There was diversity in terms of their family lives. Twenty-four per cent lived alone without a partner or children, 44 per cent lived with a partner/spouse without children, and 28 per cent lived with a

Table 12.1   Percentage of Female Faculty by Rank, Comparing the University
to National Statistics, October 2008

Rank	The University 2007–08	National Average 2007–08
Full professor	16.1	20.9
Associate	31.8	36.4
Assistant	38.2	44.0
Contractually limited term	58.8	n/a
Tenured faculty	27.5	30.2
All full-time female faculty	30.8	34.3

Source: University Human Resource Data October 2008 and CAUT 2010–11
Note: n/a=not available

partner/spouse and with children. Of all of the participants, 60 per
cent were the primary income earner in their household and 40 per
cent shared income and expenses equally.

THE STATUS OF WOMEN

In October 2008, women in this small university constituted 38.2 per
cent of all full-time faculty but only 30.8 per cent were tenured or
held tenure-track appointments (see Table 12.1). They were underrepresented at all ranks with the exception of the contractually limited term (CLT) appointments (referred to as sessional appointments
at some universities, see also Linda Cohen's chapter in this volume).
Not shown in the table is the fact that only 25.6 per cent of all new
tenure-track faculty hires between 2000 and 2007 were women.

We have run numerous regression analyses to assess the extent of
pay equity at this university between 2007 and 2011. Controlling for
gender, year of hire, rank, and faculty, we found that during the 2008–
09 academic year, women in regular faculty positions earn approximately $1,800 less on average than their male counterparts. If we
mapped a male and female faculty member's career path based on this
difference, and giving each a 3 per cent yearly increase, over thirty
years, this amounts to $80,878.21 in lost earnings. This model does
not take into account promotions or grid step increases (progression
through the ranks). Thus, the loss in earnings is likely a conservative
estimate, as research has consistently shown that men progress through
the ranks more quickly than women, especially to full professor.

Although each group addressed specific concerns for their respective rank, common to all ranks were negotiating salaries at hiring, barriers to tenure and promotion, pay inequity, mentoring, administrative/service responsibilities, transition from contractually limited-term appointments to tenure-track appointments, juggling private and public lives, and confidence. These themes are presented in four broader categories.

NEGOTIATING THE HIRING PROCESS

We were particularly interested in learning whether the women negotiated the offers made in the hiring process at the point when first hired into junior positions in the university. Although the women in the assistant professor group did, those in the other groups typically did not. Either the senior faculty members did not know they had a "right" to do so or they were excited at the prospect of a "real job," that they lost sight of the larger picture.

Those who tried to negotiate at the point of hire stated that they had little luck, and many reported, in their words, an overall professed naïveté about the process. Some women negotiated with their department heads, some with their dean, and others with the vice-president academic. In some instances, information was given "that actually wasn't the case," such as having "to make a decision within an hour," or that an offer was made without the authority to do so. Based on promises made by the department head, one faculty member refused offers from other universities to end up "much lower on the grid than [the head] had originally promised, and with much reduced start-up funds."

At this university, CLT positions often lead into tenure-track appointments and the person holding the CLT is seriously considered for the tenure-track position. However, when a CLT appointment is offered, applicants are generally unable to negotiate where they are placed on the grid. Should the position convert to a tenure-track, the faculty member is then told that she is unable to negotiate her salary as she is already on the grid. One assistant professor explains, "I came in as a CLT. So I just got a phone call and they said, 'here's what we're going to offer you.' And it was considerably more than what I'd been making working as a sessional. And I said … 'hey, that sounds brilliant.' And so then I got … interviewed for and was awarded the tenure-track position, and didn't get to negotiate my salary at all. And when I asked about it, I was pretty much told [that I get] a step up from my CLT contract. And I was told that if I had tried to negotiate, I probably wouldn't have gotten the job." Given that proportionately more women than men are CLTs, then proportionately more women than men are placed at a lower grid, making for a long-term salary disadvantage. We understand that this hiring practice is typical at other universities in Canada as well.

THE SERVICE DILEMMA

Service to the university, which involves participating in committees such as hiring, curriculum, and by-laws, to name a few, was reported as a barrier to scholarship among all groups. Although faculty in a small university can be expected to do more service work than those in larger universities because there are fewer people to do the work, there are distinct ways in which female faculty are doubly jeopardized. Further, the discussion of the dilemmas of service work matched nearly word for word the findings of similar studies carried out at a large university in the United States (Misra et al. 2011) and at a variety of Canadian universities in the 1990s (Acker and Feuerverger 1996).

Given the limited number of women in a small university, in order to have women represented on committees, they inevitably end up doing more service work than men: "[Women] got called on disproportionately more often because people like me were saying, 'I want a woman on that committee.'" Furthermore, according to an associate professor group member, there are occasions when the university recognizes that representation by gender and rank is a good idea: "And I still remember the day [Professor x] two years ago phoned me up and said, 'I need to find a [specific rank] professor, a woman in [the Faculty of x].' I said, 'well, there's three. One's on sabbatical, and the other two I named.' And there's a silence on the other end of the phone ... 'That's it?' I said, 'Yeah, that's it. Have a look around. Haven't you noticed?' And he called one, and of course she said, 'I get called for everything' because ... it's kind of desperate at the upper ranks for representation.'"

A common theme that emerged in all the groups was that not only did women faculty do more service work than their male colleagues but there was a qualitative difference in the work they do: "hardly ever [is there] a woman who goes into a service position ... without just working so hard." Another woman added, "So I do-do-do-do-do ... It sucks, it sucks your lifeblood, a lot of that work."

The overall impression is that men tend to shy away from service. For example, an associate professor shared her experience on a committee that evaluates research proposals. In one year, there were over fifty applications: "It was huge. A lot of work. Read them, evaluate them, and score them ... And interestingly enough I received an email from every one of the men on the committee to say the workload was too high and they were trying to get out of it ... It's not talked about. Everybody just goes away."

In another focus group, the gendered nature of service work was described in terms of positions of power. Although women may do more service than men, they do not sit on committees that are identified as high-powered. For example, women faculty have been historically underrepresented on the committee that approves or denies tenure and promotion applications. There were two barriers identified for why this is the case. The first is external or beyond the individual's control: women faculty members have more difficulty being elected to the committee. The second is internal or one of personal decision making: women with children are reluctant to put their names forward to sit on the committee because of the time of day meetings are held. According to a full professor, "they tend to be 7:30 [a.m.] meetings ... it's not family-friendly." The Senate similarly meets at a time that is difficult for families, as was discussed in another group: "I remember ... getting up and leaving Senate at six o'clock ... From eight to six, that was a long day for a kid" (full professor). Thus, to sit on policy bodies that are highly influential such as Senate, she needs either to have no children, or a very supportive partner and a willingness to "take time away from her family" (associate professor).

The frustration around service for the assistant professors was that their service work does not get the recognition it deserves: "I don't think it's going to be recognized when I apply for tenure." Heavy involvement in service means "you can't do as much on your research." Men do less, or the "bare minimum," service work, which leaves them more time for scholarship. Consequently, they have seemingly stronger tenure and/or promotion files. Indeed, when the senior faculty women were asked why there are proportionately fewer female full professors, one answered, "It seems to be the research part of their career that holds them back. It's certainly not the service part. Oh, my Lord, and not the teaching. But, it's hard ... to get what they need to keep their research moving forward."

Furthermore, the senior faculty group noted that some of women's scholarly work such as writing major government policy papers or university reports is confused as service and goes unrecognized as scholarly work: "Take a major project and collect data and write the report, and then actually work in community to set [the project] up; you know, people to benefit from that research. That those things are not credited in the same way. I mean it's just women out dipsy-doodling around." Another group member added that policy reports are not valued in the same way as scholarly work in a peer-refereed journal even though "two thousand people" may read the policy paper compared to "two hundred who might [read it in] a refereed journal" (associate professor). The latter faculty member applied for promotion to full professor, and her application was rejected because of her research record. There was disagreement on her file, "which some would say is really quite adequate." Her publications, however, were not viewed as sufficiently scholarly.

THE "SYNCING" FEELING: PUBLIC AND PRIVATE LIVES

The perceived dilemma for "many of the younger" women faculty was to choose between having a family and having a successful career. It is for this reason that some of the junior faculty are opting not to have families, believing it is impossible to juggle an academic career and a family: "no balance; can't be done." Another member added, "I just don't think, it's possible for me to have children and be [successful]." Those who decided to have children reported they experience regular feelings of stress as they navigate their home and work lives. The difficulty of juggling private and public lives, we were told, begins with maternity leave. One associate professor described the emotional turmoil she experienced when she found out she was pregnant: "I was really frustrated with the whole process, because as soon as I found out [I was pregnant], I felt super-guilty ... Here I am in this new position, and now this is what I've done. And I've agreed to take on an honours student. And what am I going to do with her? And I have all this [research] money. And I have to deal with this research. And of course our department was very supportive, but there was always that, you know, if you're going to get tenure, and you're going to get promotion, you've got to keep it up. You've got to keep it going and whatever. So I ended up working on my maternity leave a lot. Like a lot." Being untenured, she stated, "[my] guilt saying, I will do this." So, the day after she came home with her newborn, "I had him on the bed, and I'm on my computer and I'm emailing marks. And I'm trying to get things in, because like he was three weeks early. I didn't time it quite right ... I was trying to keep up-to-date. I've aged twenty years in five years, let me tell you, physically and mentally, I think."

When asked if the administration offered to stop the tenure clock (one additional year credit towards tenure), she adamantly said, "I didn't want that to happen because financially that's a huge impact, right?" In this university, promotion is linked to higher salary levels and delays in promotion have long-term financial implications. Her department, although in theory supportive of her maternity leave, reinforced her tenure and promotion concerns and consequently made demands that necessitated work throughout her maternity leave.

One associate professor, who did not feel compelled to work throughout her maternity leave, described a very different experience, although she felt horribly guilty when she learned that she was pregnant: "I too didn't understand the timing and shocked myself and ended up with a baby born at the end of March ... the classes were still on." The head of her department adamantly stated, "'that's not your problem. It's in the Collective Agreement. They will bring someone in. You go away. You go away for a year.' And I was completely uninterrupted that whole year."

She too was asked whether the one-year maternity leave affected her tenure and promotion application. She applied for tenure but did not for promotion: "See, I wasn't strategic in those ways. I hadn't really thought about the implications. I just assumed that I would continue to do things, and then I would apply for things as they came up ... I was relying heavily on that head of department to give me advice on these things. Perhaps more than I ought to, I sort of had the courage of my own convictions. But I think his read on it was mat-leave equals minus a year. And I don't think it needed to mean that." However, there was no policy in place that a one-year maternity leave equals a one-year delay in applying for promotion, and in fact in this case the delay was much longer: "The head of department was very conservative in his recommendations about that. And so I was just consistently told, 'don't apply, don't apply, don't apply.'" And so she did not. But her male counterparts did, and they were promoted. Finally, three years after she was eligible for promotion and nine years since her tenure-track appointment began, she applied successfully for promotion.

The two maternity stories above capture two broader experiences: women faculty who work throughout their maternity leave to ensure that they progress through the ranks within the expected time frame, and those who take a "no-work" maternity leave, possibly at a personal cost to their academic career. A member in the assistant professor focus group forewarned that policies on academic women and families could work against her career: "There's been a shift towards so many accommodations that women's careers sometimes do suffer … if you have kids, you have these accommodations made. But, then you end up not going as far, not earning as much money. You're taking longer to get ahead, and that's a significant problem in terms of gender [pay]."

The returning to work full-time after maternity leave added new layers of challenges both in her home and work lives, shared the associate professor: "So I almost died my first year [after the baby was born]. I had felt I had to be in the office all the time that my male colleagues were in the office … I was busy trying to prove being super-mom. And there weren't enough hours in the day. So I just felt guilty and wrenched … guilty because you're not doing the work you think you should be doing. And then you're guilty because you're not parenting the way you think you should."

Even with very supportive partners, many members reported that the burden of child care disproportionately falls on them. In part, this may be due to the hegemonic notions of mothering. The associate professor above explained, "[My partner's] amazing. He does an incredible amount of work. But I'm the mommy. And I don't know if that's innate or the way I've raised them up … but so yes, I do disproportionately more child care. It's mommy, mommy. And [my partner says], 'like I spend all kinds of time with the kids. How come they don't want [me]?'" Or women assume certain responsibilities for the family, such as when the storm comes or children get sick; it is the woman who "rush[es] home to them … figure[s] out child care … or whatever."

COLLECTIVE INSECURITY

Balancing a work environment that was hostile to women with their family responsibilities had taken a toll on the women's confidence, leading to a serious questioning of their scholarly abilities. The surprising turning point in the discussion with the junior associate professor group was when a number of the women said they were not considering promotion to full professor at this time: "I do not feel that I can, I don't want to pressure myself."

This leads to our final theme uncovered from the focus groups, which we have called "collective insecurity." This term refers to the subtle and not so subtle ways that women's confidence in their scholarship and their place in academia are undermined. Although confidence is typically seen as an individual problem, the lack of confidence across all ranks indicates that the problem is actually collectively held.

One of the ways in which confidence is undermined is through watching other women faculty struggle at the institution. A number of senior members recounted how many of the "female stars" had left the institution because of a lack of support or recognition for their research efforts. Furthermore, "it was easier for them to do their research someplace else ... in a friendlier environment" (full professor).

A second way is through perceiving that the men on faculty had been given unfair advantages with regard to grid step placement on the pay scale at time of hire and/or promotion. A number of women faculty reported that they knew of men hired in their departments at a higher grid step. One saw firsthand in her work on the Tenure and Promotion Committee an instance of how male faculty receive preferential treatment: "I'm looking at [the files of] three men who were promoted. And I know their files are probably not as good as [that of the female candidate who has been rejected], so we ... managed to make an allowance for these guys, you know, who are great guys and everybody reveres ... But see, they can't quite do it for the one woman."

The female faculty member who was denied promotion was devastated, and consequently, she refused to reapply for promotion: "That's it, it's my life. It's an identity. So why would I put myself through that? There are many more things in life that are more fun, will have more of an impact. And will put my energies where things are, so I can have impact. And going through that process again isn't part of, isn't in the cards."

A third way confidence is undermined is through scholarly activity. For example, one group member raised concerns about potential bias against women faculty in funding agencies such as the Natural Science and Engineering Research Council (NSERC). She was appalled when a reviewer noted that her strengths lay in "training under-graduate students" and then addressed her as "Ms." even though the reviewer knew she had a PhD. Her equally qualified male colleague had a similar proposal but his received glowing reviews while hers were only mediocre. Although both received funding, these types of messages can influence how women academics see the value of their own work and their confidence in applying for subsequent grants.

The women in the focus groups also spoke of not being heard or of having little influence in decision making on committees, a fourth way confidence is undermined. Some reported that they "relied on the system" to ensure that their opinions were heard and used. One of the senior group members shared a story that had been told to her fifteen years earlier in a study on the status of women faculty: "One of the things we asked was whether or not the women felt that they were being heard on committees. And there was this one woman ... unlike all the other women who said yes; 'I have no problem what-soever.' And we said, 'well that's interesting. Can you tell us more?' And she said, 'Well, do you know this fellow... he's got this lovely deep voice ... I just tell him my idea and he says it.' This was her image of having her voice heard." The other group members chuck-led sardonically, realizing this story could have been told by any one of them in the room to capture the present-day experiences of these senior scholars. In fact, two members in the junior faculty focus group shared similar stories: "I'm in a committee meeting or some-thing, and it might be majority men and me. And, I say something, and the people take little notice of it. And five minutes later, a man says the same thing." A second member added, "Oh, that happens all the time. I just learned to use it. I've been on Senate for three years. Instead of making a straightforward motion to Senate, I just give some hints of an idea, and then one of the senior males will finally make the motion, which I wanted to make. But I'll let him do that. You just use the system."

Such examples tell women faculty that their ideas are less impor-tant than men's ideas, which can have an impact on their confidence and, in turn, their ability to push their careers forward. One associ-ate professor spoke of being advised not to go for promotion because she had been on maternity leave even though she had a book con-tract and numerous publications: "I didn't have that faith. I thought here's someone [the head of her department] who knows these committees and knows how they respond, and he's able to predict the future. And it would be just absurd of me to set myself up psychologically for this horrible defeat ... I say it doesn't really matter, but I think I would find it difficult to be turned down ... Plus, he will be offended if I don't take his advice. I'm sure that was part of what was playing. There's a whole kind of crazy good-girl thing going on."

THEORIZING COLLECTIVE INSECURITY

Although a lack of confidence can be seen as an individual problem, when looking at the extent of how many women "didn't have that faith," one begins to see a pattern of treatment that is far from an individualized insecurity. Participants in the focus groups demonstrated a strength of character and a persistence to carry on fulfilling their duties as teachers and scholars. None of the women appeared to lack confidence in a way that made them seem weak or unable to do their jobs. Nonetheless, the repeated messages about the lower worth of women and the work that they do made many of these impressive scholars share feelings of frustration and inadequacy. This led them in many instances to "choose" *not* to pursue promotions, apply for prestigious research grants, publish in high-ranking journals, or pursue other forms of advancement that would improve their status or financial gain.

An understanding of this "collective insecurity" can come from looking at the expectation states and status characteristics theories found in the social psychology literature (Ridgeway 1993). According to expectation states theory, interactions between people involve negotiations of power and prestige that will determine individual behaviour. Status characteristics theory states that women in our culture have a lower status than do men overall, which becomes both a cause and a consequence of men's greater power within interactions. Within this context, people then expect certain behaviours of people according to their status which "becomes self-fulfilling, shaping the resulting power and prestige order" (Ridgeway 1993, 177).

Thus, gender stereotypes in society at large can influence how one is expected to perform in individual interactions. A woman's hesitancy to speak, or when she speaks in public, can be interpreted, according to Ridgeway (1993), as lacking self-confidence at best and, at worst, an assumption that "you cannot be too certain of your point and quickly dismiss your concerns." In the end, "when the final decision is made, your opinions carry little weight" (Ridgeway 1993, 184). In this way, the social structural order of male domination leads to individual responses within interactional settings, which then reinforces a social structure based on male domination. The example of women asking men to speak on their behalf discussed earlier illustrates this pattern.

There are times in which women will have a higher status than men, but only if the task of the interaction involves a stereotypically female task. For example, women have more authority in groups discussing parenting matters, but less in groups discussing political economy. Additionally, individuals have many statuses that together form expectations of others and of themselves. For instance, a surgeon carries more status than a mail carrier, but a female surgeon will carry less status than a male surgeon. When someone combines multiple lower statuses, they are more likely to experience more difficulty. This was true of the women faculty in the focus groups. They reported the most difficulty at the time of appointment, when transitioning to motherhood, when going up for promotion, and in their disproportionate amount of service work, all of which are moments when one's lower status becomes salient.

Ridgeway (1993) further points out that this pattern of lower social statuses leading to lowered expectations during interactions is then reinforced by the various reward levels and external feedback that people receive. Not only are those of a lower status less likely to be positively rewarded, but also the lack of a reward will further reinforce and justify the member's lower status. These processes were clearly observed in the focus groups. Generally, the women experienced men being more likely to shirk the service work, leaving women to do it, but, at the same time, the service work was discounted as grounds for promotion. Thus, a vicious circle is created where the lower-status faculty (women) are left to do the lower-status work (service) and have less time to do the scholarly work, which reinforces feelings of lower status, which then leads to a collective insecurity.

The examples of collective insecurity from the focus group are many. Women reported feeling unheard in meetings and resorted to using men to put forth their ideas in meetings to get their ideas considered. Based on being seen as having good ideas and speaking with authority, men were more likely to be given the benefit of the doubt by the university's tenure and promotion committees. This has meant that men have moved through the ranks more quickly and earned higher salaries. The greater number of better-paid men at higher ranks then justifies and legitimates the notion that men have been more productive and do more important work, and why the lower-status service work can be left to the women. Thus, although women faculty members experience a collective insecurity, the root of that insecurity lies in a complex gendered structure of the university and society, and not in individual pathologies.

CONCLUSION

This study provides a comprehensive understanding of the experiences of women faculty at a small university. Although it might be expected that working at a small, teaching-intensive university provides women academics with a more equitable work environment, the results of this study show that inequity continues to be manifested in a variety of ways, including negotiating the hiring process, managing the burden of service work, balancing private and work lives, and coping with a collective insecurity about their scholarship and place in academia. Overall, there is clear evidence that even at a potentially equitable university, there remain significant gendered inequalities. The experiences described above in many ways are no different than those reported in the literature at earlier time periods (Acker and Feuerverger 1996; Misra et al. 2011). What is perplexing is how and why so little has changed since the 1980s. Thus, this research underscores the need for universities to look beyond the bare minimum of policies and begin to assess how their cultures are working to create gendered divisions in pay, hiring, promotion, service responsibilities, and work and family stress.

Change can begin with a transparent process of assessing equity within universities. For example, annual reports of the status of women faculty on campus, which would detail the number of faculty hired by gender, the number at each rank and pay salaries offered, is one way to achieve transparency. Such a process, at worst, publicly identifies and raises awareness of the extent of inequity, which helps people realize that what on the surface may appear as an individual problem is, in fact, experienced collectively. At best, it results in action taken to remedy the inequities. This may mean the implementation of programs such as equity training for all faculty members and senior administrations in terms of hiring and tenure and promotion, and then followed by a systems review to ensure that equitable practices have occurred. Without such recourses, it is all too easy to justify pay differences between men and women in hiring practices, the awarding of tenure and promotion, and scholarships by claiming they are based on merit or some other quantitative formulation. Many of these criteria are faulty and discriminate against women scholars.

There is a literature that illustrates the ways in which women are disadvantaged in the academy from the time they enter graduate school (Dua 2007). Briefly, whereas male students tend to be mentored by senior faculty members by being included in large-scale research projects, female students typically are not. Such opportunities for male students translate into publications, presentations at conferences, and networking. Male students, therefore, are better situated for funding from such agencies as SSHRC and NSERC (Bornmann, Rüdiger, and Hans-Dieter 2007). In turn, young PhD male graduates are immediately better-positioned to compete in the academic job market. They are able to negotiate better salaries because their CVs are "more" impressive; they have a funding record, which begets more funding. So, the opportunity gap widens quickly and continuously, and women play catch-up throughout their academic careers.

At the same time, strategies must be adopted within the university to support women in their scholarly work (Expert Panel on Women in University Research 2012). Faculty unions might consider providing women candidates with a faculty mentor to help with their integration to the academy. An Australian study has indicated that female faculty who were mentored were more likely to remain at the university, be promoted, receive grant money, and feel better about their place in academia (Gardiner et al. 2007). Thus, mentorship should be a priority at universities.

To strive for a university that is not only more equitable in its hiring practices but also committed to an environment where women and other disadvantaged faculty members have equitable scholarly opportunities, policies need to be set in place that are rooted in a fundamental belief that inequities are structural and systemic. Without such policies, thirty-five years from now, the next generation of women scholars will share stories of collective insecurity similar to those voiced above.

ACKNOWLEDGMENTS

We would like to thank the inspiring and wonderful scholars and teachers who participated in our focus groups and openly shared their stories. We would also like to acknowledge the research fund of the university studied for supporting this project.

Afterthoughts

ELVI WHITTAKER

Most books, I believe, aim to convey meanings and messages beyond what are explicitly presented by the text. Each author presents her case and sets it parameters, yet there is the lingering hope that their words will do more than merely inform. Authors hope that their words will inspire new insights, fresh interpretations, and perhaps even lead to needed change. The narratives gathered here are not mere chants about troubles. Rather, they are first steps, texts of resistance, messages of optimism, harbingers of change. Most chapters were written with the belief that the basic entitlements they raise would be easily recognizable beyond their own borders, that they need merely to state the details of their case. The challenge for each narrative is to sensitize the reader and reach the conscience of the university workplace. Can they promote the critical rethinking to which they aspire? Can their ideas jostle and interact, not only with each other but with the ideas of those in power, who create missions and manage change? Each author is in search of the supportive sentiments of the readers and the wisdom of mediators.

The foregoing chapters aimed to provide experience-laden perspectives of unexplored spaces in institutional life. They constitute a counter-ethnography of the university, one that highlights "the native's point of view" – a phrase owed to Malinowski who could not understand the Trobriand Islanders without knowing their point of view, transforming "savages" into people he could understand. They fill empty spaces of knowledge. The narratives about solitude present not only personal vignettes but also sociocultural ones about life across the university. They constitute a very different version of the university and provide valuable data to supplement that of their quantitative cousins.

The essays serve as basic contributions to ethnographies of morals, a consideration of some importance for the future of social science. They reverberate with a sense of entitlement, of rectitude, the rubric under which the familiar rallying cry "social justice" is positioned. From each narrative, which is at once specific to one person as well as universal to many, a moral culture can be discerned. With an increasing awareness of moral cultures, lives become understandable and disjunctures emerge more clearly. Without the recognition of these hidden factors, the contributions in the volume would be denied the gravitas they deserve. Thus, these moral avowals, which were once much more mysterious, now await ethnographic and theoretical description.

The book is also about identities and categories – perhaps most notably that of "woman," which seems to continue to effect most identities. It remains in the formal lexicon, in most classifications systems that are basic to the university's operations. Most importantly perhaps, "woman" is strongly present in its traditional trappings. Even as the multiplicity of gender is championed by universities, even recognized in the renaming of some of its institutes, it does not appear to be as fully embraced in documentary knowledge as it is in formal knowledge, and even in everyday knowledge. The designation thus remains legitimate and "normal" and, moreover, is imbued with the authority of being one with ancient tenure. Hence, diversity, even when recognized, remains in search of effective governance – in policy and in the everyday. "Woman" is the gloss that appears to have a lasting stability, and is enshrined in all workplaces – including the university workplace. What does the gloss reveal about the hidden epistemes of university cultures? Quick observations would assert that it permits the continued existence of a large underclass, which in its turn perpetuates a characterization of less power and less intellectual worth. Ultimately, this allows for certain rites of denigration. However minimal its degraded status may be, an underclass, or several such, are usually deemed workplace necessities. Others will point to tradition as an important part of all universities, and that the category "woman" is a display of the expected reverence for tradition. An alternate suggestion is that gender be re-theorized and perhaps dissolved into bureaucratic irrelevancy. How long will gender, mainly of the binary sort, endure? Is the ethos emerging too quickly and the social structure changing too slowly? The obvious question is, what would universities look like if gender disappeared from its policies as it eventually might from passports? That would make for many differences throughout the workplace. Not a new idea, of course, but one worthy of discussion.

The boundaries dividing categories, and therefore identities, seem to be at issue in the narratives. The essays query the rigidity of these lines of separation and seem to ask for a minimization of demarcations and a blurring of formal borders. In favouring a crossing of workplace boundaries and in seeking a laxity in the delineation of duties, they ask for a keen examination of the ongoing classifications and how to avoid the danger of being captured within units with impenetrable limitations. Not surprisingly, the recognition of individual merit and accomplishments is strongly advocated. This goes along with every expectation that an organization fulfills its mandate, even as it accepts modern notions of equity and non-authoritarianism.

What of the destabilization of the idea of the university itself? Many narratives in this book call for a disruption of the status quo. None envisions a complete dismantling. They seem to ask why these important proponents of equal opportunity and champions of merit are not living up to their full promise. Some well-placed pieces of scholarship and journalism, and the internal efforts of universities themselves, have already kept troublesome issues in sight. The idea of the university invites a penetrating theoretical scrutiny. The question asked is how and why the various categories within the university have maintained certain traditional structures and the existing moral order. Along with ideas like "power" and "woman," which have become subject to deconstruction, the idea of "university" awaits its turn. These questions summon inquiry and an invitation to indulge in epistemological questioning.

While the solitudes and the workplaces in this volume are those of universities, they aspire to a wider representation of organizations and work environments. Categories may be differently construed, but they create similar hives of solitude. The burdens of insecurity, the issues about the status of gender, and the moral indignation about denied entitlements would still be there. Not often enough, however, have these issues in workplaces met the researchers' gaze. And when they have been the subject of research, seldom has the worker's versions of affairs been the focus of attention. Should the workplaces of the future continue to allow so many uncertainties and ambiguities? Or, perhaps alternately and even perversely, should solitudes be encouraged in the belief that they lead to reflection and change? Either way, as reflection or burden, every solitude affords a glimpse into a future.

Universities have been devoted to recognizing merit. All organizations claim the right to define merit as they see fit, to diagnose, and measure it. The solitudes give notice that merit, in both its broadest and narrowest implications, has been administered in a fashion long deemed biased, short-sighted, and political, and as a common enigma in need of re-theorizing.

This volume is about hope, the ever-present companion of solitude. Since the early 2000s, hopefulness has emerged as a worthy topic, often seen as embedded in the writings of those living on the margins. Hopefulness is no longer the lightweight concern of former years. It appears in the work of many, including Richard Rorty, Mary Zournazi, Julia Kristeva, Gayatri Spivak, and Michael Taussing. When readers ask for concluding remarks, as they did for this volume, they do not mean a summary of the narratives collected here. Rather, they expect a reconsideration of the constructed landscape into which the whole endeavour fits. This could mean an examination of our productions – the hidden issues, the moral bases from which analyses emerge, the moral bases to which they speak. Such deliberations, ethnographies of ethnography, call for serious attention. This enterprise seems vital the more attention and authority is given social science as a resource, and to the world as a social science construct. Informing the essays in this collection is the analytic reliance on debunking, deconstruction, destabilization, and critical negativity. What are the harms in this? Perhaps, as Bruno Latour suggests, critique has run out of steam, out of its expected power to influence. Yet these theoretical and analytical modes have been the messengers, continuing to produce useful knowledge. Writings in this volume have relied on these envoys, seen by some as dark harbingers, laced with strong opinions, anger, and calls for change. In contrast, I see these same writings as epistles of hope. They embrace a cultural belief in human perfectibility and optimism, in future-orientation and anticipation. Hopefulness as an analytic concept has a promising future.

References

Acker, Joan. 1990. "Hierarchies, Jobs, Bodies: A Theory of Gendered Organizations." *Gender & Society* 4 (2): 139–58.

Acker, Sandra, and Carmen Armenti. 2004. "Sleepless in Academia." *Gender and Education* 16 (1): 3–24.

Acker, Sandra, and Grace Feuerverger. 1996. "Doing Good and Feeling Bad: The Work of Women University Teachers." *Cambridge Journal of Education* 26 (3): 401–22.

Acker, Sandra, Michelle Webber, and Elizabeth Smyth. 2012. "Tenure Troubles and Equity Matters in Canadian Academe." *British Journal of Sociology of Education* 33 (5): 743–61.

Ahmed, Sara. 2004. *The Cultural Politics of Emotion.* London: Routledge.

Alcoff, Linda Martin. 2006. *Visible Identities: Race, Gender, and the Self.* New York: Oxford University Press.

Alemán, Ana Martinez. 2008. "Faculty Productivity and the Gender Question." In *Unfinished Agendas: New and Continuing Gender Challenges in Higher Education*, edited by Judith Glazer Raymo, 142–61. Baltimore: Johns Hopkins University Press.

Allen, Judith A. 1997. "Strengthening Women's Studies in Hard Times: Feminism and Challenges of Institutional Adaptation." *Women's Studies Quarterly* 25 (1/2): 358–87.

Allison, Juliann E. 2007. "Composing a Life in Twenty-First Century Academe: Reflections on a Mother's Challenge." *National Women's Studies Association Journal* 19: 23–46.

Allman, Paula. 1988. "New Perspectives on the Adult: An Argument for Lifelong Learning." *International Journal of Lifelong Education* 1 (1): 41–51.

Altamirano-Jiménez, Isabel. 2010. "Indigenous Women, Nationalism, and Feminism." In *States of Race: Critical Race Feminism for the 21st*

Century, edited by. S. Razack, M. Smith, and S. Thobani, 111–25. Toronto: Between the Lines.

Ames, Michael, E. Hopkins, T. Popoff, J. Grandville, D. Schweitzer, and W.E. Willmott. 1972. "Anthropology and Sociology in the Canadian Context." *Canadian Sociology and Anthropology Association Bulletin* 26 (January): 1–15.

Anderson, Joan M. 2004. "The Conundrums of Binary Categories: Critical Inquiry through the Lens of Postcolonial Feminist Humanism." *Canadian Journal of Nursing Research* 36 (4): 11–16.

Anderson, J.M., J. Reimer, K.B. Khan, L. Simich, A. Neufeld, M. Stewart, and E. Makwarimba. 2010. "Narratives of 'Dissonance' and 'Repositioning' through the Lens of Critical Humanism: Exploring the Influences of Immigrants and Refugees Health and Well-Being." *Advances in Nursing Science* 33 (2): 101–12.

Andreae J., and M.A. Coffey. 1997. "The Lesbian Presence: Ghost at the Banquet, Party Pooper at the Potluck, or Spirit at the Dinner Party?" In *Equity and Justice/Équité et Justice*, edited by D. Hearne and M.L. Lefebvre, 58–63. Montreal: John Abbott College.

Andrews, Jo. 1995. "Effective Communication." In *Human Resource Management in Higher and Further Education*, edited by David Warner and Elaine Crosthwaite, 56–69. Buckingham: Society for Research into Higher Education/Open University Press.

Aronowitz, Stanley. 1997. "The Last Good Job in America." *Social Text* 51:93–108.

Atkinson, Paul, and Amanda Coffey. 2004. "Analysing Documentary Realities." In *Qualitative Research: Theory, Method and Practice*, 2nd ed., edited by David Silverman, 56–75. Thousand Oaks, CA: Sage.

Aubrecht, Katie. 2012. "Surviving Success, Reconciling Resilience: A Critical Analysis of the Appearance of Student 'Mental Life' at One Canadian University." PhD diss., University of Toronto.

Austen, Jane. (1813) 1985. *Pride and Prejudice*. London: T. Egerton. Reprint, New York: Penguin Classics.

Badenhorst, C. 2007. *Research Writing: Breaking the Barriers*. Pretoria: Van Schaik.

– 2010. *Productive Writing: Becoming a Prolific Academic Writer*. Pretoria: Van Schaik.

Badenhorst, C., C. Moloney, J. Rosales, and J. Dyer. 2012. "Graduate Research Writing: A Pedagogy of Possibility." In "Creativity: Insights, Directions and Possibilities," special issue, *LEARNing Landscapes* 6 (1): 63–80.

Baker, Maureen. 2009. "Gender, Academia and the Managerial University." *New Zealand Sociology* 24:24–48.

– 2010. "Career Confidence and Gendered Expectations of Academic Promotion." *Journal of Sociology* 46(3): 317–34.

– 2012. *Academic Careers and the Gender Gap.* Vancouver: University of British Columbia Press.

Bannerji, Himani. 1987. "Introducing Racism: Notes towards an Anti-Racist Feminism." *Resources for Feminist Research* 16 (1): 10–12.

– 1993. *Returning the Gaze: Essays on Racism, Feminism and Politics.* Toronto: Sister Vision Press.

– 2000. *The Dark Side of the Nation: Essays on Multiculturalism, Nationalism and Gender.* Toronto: Canadian Scholars' Press.

Barnes-Powell, Tina, and Gayle Letherby. 1998. "'All in a Day's Work': Gendered Care Work in Higher Education." In *Surviving the Academy: Feminist Perspectives,* edited by Danusia Malina and Sian Maslin-Prothero, 69–77. London: Falmer Press.

Barone, Chuck. 1999. "Bringing Classism into the Race and Gender Picture." *Race, Gender & Class* 6 (3): 5–14.

Bate, David. 1994. "The Mise en Scène of Desire." In *Mise en scène: Claude Cahun, Tacita Dean, Virginia Nimarkoh.* London: Institute of Contemporary Arts. Exhibition catalogue.

Becher, Tony, and Paul R. Trowler. (1989) 2001. *Academic Tribes and Territories: Intellectual Enquiry and the Culture of Disciplines.* Buckingham: Society for Research into Higher Education and Open University Press.

Beck, Ulrich. 2000. *The Brave New World of Work.* Malden, MA: Polity Press.

Belenky, M.F., B.M. Clinchy, N.R. Goldberger, and J.M. Tarule. 1986. *Women's Ways of Knowing: The Development of Self, Voice, and Mind.* New York: Basic Books.

Benhabib, Seyla, Judith Butler, Drucilla Cornell, and Nancy Fraser. 1995. *Feminist Contentions: A Philosophical Exchange.* New York: Routledge.

Benschop, Yvonne, and Margo Brouns. 2003. "Crumbling Ivory Towers: Academic Organizing and Its Gender Effects." *Gender, Work and Organization* 10: 194–212.

Benton, Thomas H. 2004. "Tireless Research Assistants." *Chronicle of Higher Education* 51 (14), November 26, C1–C4.

Benwell, Bethan, and Elizabeth Stokoe. 2006. *Discourse and Identity.* Edinburgh: Edinburgh University Press.

Berry, Leonard L., and Kent D. Seltman. 2008. *Management Lessons from Mayo Clinic: Inside One of the World's Most Admired Service Organizations*. New York: McGraw Hill.

Bhabha, Homi. 1994. *The Location of Culture*. New York: Routledge.

Birchard, Karen. 2005. "Canadian Women Face a Glass Ceiling in University Administration, Survey Finds." *Chronicle of Higher Education* 51 (37), May 20, A34. http://chronicle.com/article/Canadian-Women-Face-a-Glass/17553/.

Bird, Sharon, Jacquelyn Litt, and Yong Wang. 2004. "Creating Status of Women Reports: Institutional Housekeeping as 'Women's Work.'" *NWSA Journal* 16 (1): 194–206.

Blackaby, David, Alison L. Booth, and Jeff Frank. 2005. "Outside Offers and the Gender Pay Gap: Empirical Evidence from the UK Academic Labour Market." *Economics Journal* 115: F81–F107.

Bochner, Arthur P. 2000. "Criteria against Ourselves." *Qualitative Inquiry* 6 (2): 266–72.

Bornmann, Lutz, Mutz Rüdiger, and Daniel Hans-Dieter. 2007. "Gender Differences in Grant Peer Review: A Meta-Analysis." *Journal of Informetrics* 1:226–38.

Bourdieu, Pierre. 1977. *Outline of a Theory of Practice*. Cambridge: Cambridge University Press.

– 1990. *In Other Words: Essays Towards a Reflexive Sociology*. Palo Alto, CA: Stanford University Press.

– 2003. "Participant Objectivation." *Journal of the Royal Anthropological Institute* (NS) 9:281–94.

– 2005. "Habitus." In *Habitus: A Sense of Place*, edited by J. Hillier and E. Rooksby, 43–52. London: Ashgate.

Bowles, G. 1983. "Is Women's Studies an Academic Discipline?" In *Theories of Women's Studies*, edited by G. Bowles and R. Duelli Klein, 32–45. London: Routledge and Kegan Paul.

Bowles, G., and R. Duelli Klein. 1983. "Introduction: Theories of Women's Studies and the Autonomy/Integration Debate." In *Theories of Women's Studies*, edited by G. Bowles and R. Duelli Klein, 1–26. London: Routledge and Kegan Paul.

Boyd, Monica. 2008. "Variations in Socioeconomic Outcomes of Second-Generation Young Adults." *Canadian Diversity* 6 (2): 20–4.

Brah, Avtar, and Ann Phoenix. 2004. "Ain't I A Woman? Revisiting Intersectionality." *Journal of International Women's Studies* 5 (3): 75–86.

Braithwaite, Ann. 2004. "'Where We've Been' and 'Where We're Going': Reflecting on Reflections of Women's Studies and 'The Women's

Movement.'" In *Troubling Women's Studies: Pasts, Presents and Possibilities*, edited by A. Braithwaite, S. Heald, S. Luhmann, and S. Rosenberg, 93–146. Toronto: Sumach.

– 2012. "Discipline." In *Rethinking Women's and Gender Studies*, edited by C.M. Orr, A. Braithwaite, and D. Lichtenstein, 209–24. New York: Routledge.

Brant, B. 1994. *Writing as Witness: Essay and Talk*. Toronto: Women's Press.

Bridgman, Rae, Sally Cole, and Heather Howard-Bobiwash, eds. 1999. *Feminist Fields: Ethnographic Insights*. Toronto: University of Toronto Press.

Bristow, P., D. Brand, L. Carty, A.P. Cooper, S. Hamilton, and A. Shadd. 1994. *We're Rooted Here and They Can't Pull Us Up: Essays in African Canadian Women's History*. Toronto: University of Toronto Press.

Brown, Judith K. 2010. "'You've Come a Long Way, Baby ... or Have You?'" Paper presented at the Women and Universities: Sessions in Honour of the Twenty-Fifth Anniversary of the Women's Network. Annual Meetings of Canadian Anthropology Society / Société canadienne d'anthropologie, Montreal, June 1.

Brown, Wendy. 2005. "The Impossibility of Women's Studies." In *Edgework: Critical Essays on Knowledge and Politics*, 116–35. Princeton: Princeton University Press.

Brubaker, Rogers. 1985. "Rethinking Classical Theory." *Theory and Society* 14: 745–75.

Butler, Judith. 1990. *Gender Trouble: Feminism and the Subversion of Identity*. New York: Routledge.

Butterfield, Lee D., William A. Borgen, Norman E. Amundson, and Asa-Sophia T. Maglio. 2005. "Fifty Years of the Critical Incident Technique: 1954–2004 and Beyond." *Qualitative Research* 5:475–97.

Cahill, Jane. 2003. "A Memoir Only Sometimes Funny." In *The Madwoman in the Academy: 43 Women Boldly Take on the Ivory Tower*, edited by Deborah Keahy and Deborah Schnitzer, 193–8. Calgary, AB: University of Calgary Press.

Canadian Association of University Teachers (CAUT). 2004–15. *CAUT Almanac of Post-Secondary Education in Canada*. http://www.caut.ca/resources/almanac.

– 2014–15. *CAUT Almanac of Post-Secondary Education in Canada*. http://www.caut.ca/docs/default-source/almanac/almanac-2014-2015. pdf?sfvrsn=4.

Canadian Institutes of Health Research, Natural Sciences and Engineering Research Council of Canada, and Social Sciences and Humanities

Research Council of Canada. 2010. *Tri-Council Policy Statement: The Ethical Conduct for Research Involving Humans (TCPS2)*. December. http://www.ethics.gc.ca/pdf/eng/tcps2/TCPS_2_FINAL_Web.pdf.

– 2014. *Tri-Council Policy Statement: The Ethical Conduct for Research Involving Humans (TCPS2)*. December. http://www.pre.ethics.gc.ca/pdf/eng/tcps2-2014/TCPS_2_FINAL_Web.pdf.

Carter, Sheree C., Penelope M. Jester, and Carolynn Thomas Jones. 2007. "Issues in Clinical Research: Manager Education and Training." *Research Practitioner* 8 (2): 48–60.

Carty, Linda. 1991. "Women's Studies in Canada: A Discourse and Praxis of Exclusion." *Resources for Feminist Research* 20 (3–4): 12–18.

Cesara, Manda (pseudonym for Karla Poewe). 1982. *Reflections of a Woman Anthropologist: No Hiding Place*. London: Academic Press.

Chapman, Chris. 2012. "Colonialism, Disability, and Possible Lives: The Residential Treatment of Children whose Parents Survived Indian Residential Schools." *Journal of Progressive Human Services* 23:127–58.

Charon, Rita. 2006. *Narrative Medicine: Honoring the Stories of Illness*. New York: Oxford University Press.

Cixous, Hélène, and Mireille Calle-Gruber. 1997. *Hélène Cixous, Rootprints: Memory and Life Writing*. Translated by Eric Prenowitz. New York: Routledge.

Cixous, Hélène, and Catherine Clément. 1986. *The Newly Born Woman*. Translated by Betsy Wing. Minneapolis: University of Minnesota Press.

Coffman, James R. 2005. *Work and Peace in Academe: Leveraging Time, Money, and Intellectual Energy through Managing Conflict*. Bolton: Anker Publishing Company.

Cohen, Linda. 2011. "Who's the Best Professor? Reflections on Student Evaluations of Teachers." *Sociology on the Rock: MUN Sociology Department's Newsletter* 7. http://sociologyontherock.wordpress.com/category/issue-7/.

Cohen, Marjorie Griffin. 2012. "Federal Budget Bill and Employment Equity." *Policy Note* (The Canadian Centre for Policy Alternatives, BC Office, blog), June 1. http://www.policynote.ca/federal-budget-bill-and-employment-equity.

Cole, Sally. 2000. "Reflections on Anthropology in Canada." In "Reflections on Anthropology in Canada/Réflexions sur l'anthropologie au Canada," edited by Sally Cole, special issue of *Anthropologica* 42 (2): 123–6.

– 2003. *Ruth Landes: A Life in Anthropology*. Lincoln: University of Nebraska Press.

Cole, Sally Cooper, and Lynne Phillips, eds. 1995. *Ethnographic Feminisms: Essays in Anthropology.* Ottawa: Carleton University Press.

Collins, Patricia Hill. 1990. *Black Feminist Thought: Knowledge, Consciousness, and the Politics of Empowerment.* Boston: Unwin Hyman.

– 1992. "Transforming the Inner Circle: Dorothy Smith's Challenge to Sociological Theory." *Sociological Theory* 10 (1): 73–80.

Corson, J.J. 1975. *The Governance of Colleges and Universities: Modernizing Structure and Processes.* New York: McGraw-Hill.

Costa, Lucy, Danielle Voronka, Jenna Reid Landry, Becky McFarlane, David Reville, and Kathryn Church. 2012. "Recovering Our Stories: A Small Act of Resistance." *Studies in Social Justice* 6 (1): 85–101. http://brock.scholarsportal.info/journals/index.php/SSJ/article/view/1070.

Cotterill, Pamela, and Ruth L. Waterhouse. 1998. "Women in Higher Education: The Gap Between Corporate Rhetoric and the Reality of Experience." In *Surviving the Academy: Feminist Perspectives*, edited by Danusia Malina and Sian Maslin-Prothero, 8–17. London: Falmer Press.

Coyner, Sandra. 1983. "Women's Studies as an Academic Discipline: Why and How to Do It." In *Theories of Women's Studies*, edited by G. Bowles and R. Duelli Klein, 46–71. London: Routledge and Kegan Paul.

Crawford, Patricia, and Myrna Tonkinson. 1988. *The Missing Chapters: Women Staff at the University of Western Australia 1963–1987.* Nedlands, Western Australia: University of Western Australia, Centre for Western Australian History.

Crawford, Tiffany. 2013. "This Day in History: September 4, 1974." *Vancouver Sun*, September 4, A2.

Csikszentmihalyi, Mihaly. 1997. *Creativity: Flow and the Psychology of Discovery and Invention.* New York: Harper Perennial.

Currie, Jan, and Bev Thiele. 2001. "Globalization and Gendered Work Cultures in Universities." In *Gender and the Restructured University: Changing Management and Culture in Higher Education*, edited by Ann Brooks and Alison Mackinnon, 90–115. Buckingham: The Society for Research into Higher Education and Open University Press.

Currie, Jan, Bev Thiele, and Patricia Harris. 2002. *Gendered Universities in Globalized Economies: Power, Careers, and Sacrifices.* Lanham, MD: Lexington Books.

Darnell, Regna. 1998. *And along Came Boas: Continuity and Revolution in Americanist Anthropology.* Philadelphia: John Benjamins.

de Beauvoir, Simone. 1973. "The Second Sex." In *The Feminist Papers: From Adams to de Beauvoir*, edited by Alice S. Rossi, 674–706. Lebanon, NH: Northeastern University Press

Dehaas, Josh. 2010. "Ms. President: Why Aren't There More of You at Canadian Universities?" *Maclean's*, November 18. http://www2.macleans.ca/2010/11/18/ms-president/#more-157656.

Dei, George Sefa, and Alireza Asgharzadeh. 2001. "The Power of Social Theory: The Anti-Colonial Discursive Framework." *Journal of Educational Thought* 35 (3): 297–323.

Denton, M., S. Prus, and V. Walters. 2004. "Gender Differences in Health: A Canadian Study of the Psychosocial, Structural and Behavioural Determinants of Health." *Social Science and Medicine* 58 (12): 2585–600.

Dexter, Emma, and Kate Bush. 1994. Foreword to *Mise en scène: Claude Cahun, Tacita Dean, Virginia Nimarkoh*. London: Institute of Contemporary Arts. Exhibition catalogue.

Dhruvarajan, V. 1997. "My Year as Ruth Wynn Woodward Chair: Addressing Systematic Racism and Sexism in the Academy." In *Equity and Justice/Équité et Justice*, edited by D. Hearne and M.L. Lefebvre, 21–34. Montreal: John Abbott College.

Di Leonardo, Micaela, ed. 1991. *Gender at the Crossroads of Knowledge: Feminist Anthropology in the Postmodern Era*. Berkeley: University of California Press.

Donoghue, Frank. 2008. *The Last Professors: The Corporate University and the Fate of the Humanities*. New York: Fordham University Press.

Drakich, Janice, and Penni Stewart. 2007. "After 40 Years of Feminism: How Are University Women Doing?" *Academic Matters: The Journal of Higher Education*, February 6–9. http://www.academicmatters.ca/AcademicMatters/docs/AM%20Feb%202007%20Issue.pdf.

Dressler, Jacqueline Faith. 1995. "Factors which Influence Employee Participation in Training and Development: A Study of Clerical Staff at McGill University (Quebec)." MA thesis, McGill University.

Drucker, Peter F. 1999. *Management Challenges for the 21st Century*. New York: Harper Business.

Dua, E., and A. Robertson, eds. 1999. *Scratching the Surface: Canadian Anti-Racist Feminist Thought*. Toronto: Women's Press.

Dua, E., and A. Trotz. 2002. "Transnational Pedagogy: Doing Political Work in Women's Studies: An Interview with Chandra Talpade Mohanty." *Atlantis* 26 (2): 66–77.

Dua, Priya. 2007. "Feminist Mentoring and Female Graduate Student Success: Challenging Gender Inequality in Higher Education." *Sociology Compass* 1/2: 594–612.

Duncombe, Jean, and Julie Jessop. 2002. "Doing Rapport and the Ethics of 'Faking Friendship.'" In *Ethics in Qualitative Research*, edited by Melanie Mauther, Maxine Birch, Julie Jessop, and Tina Miller, 107–22. London: Sage Publications.

Dunk, Thomas. 2000. "National Culture, Political Economy and Socio-Cultural Anthropology." *Anthropologica* 42 (2): 131–45.

– 2002. "Bicentrism, Culture and the Political Economy of Social-Cultural Anthropology in Canada." In *Culture, Economy, Power: Anthropology as Critique, Anthropology as Praxis*, edited by Winnie Lem and Belinda Leach, 19–23. Albany: State University of New York Press.

Edwards, Rosalind. 1993. *Mature Women Students: Separating of Connecting Family and Education*. Abingdon, Oxon: Taylor and Francis.

Eichler, M. 1992. "Not Always an Easy Alliance: The Relationship between Women's Studies and the Women's Movement in Canada." In *Challenging Times: The Women's Movement in Canada and the United States*, edited by C. Backhouse and D.H. Flaherty, 120–35. Montreal and Kingston: McGill-Queen's University Press.

Eichler, M., and M. Luxton. 2006. "Women's Studies in Focus: Feminist Challenges to Knowledge." *Atlantis* 31 (1): 76–83.

Eichler, M., and R. Tite. 1990. "Women's Studies Professors in Canada: A Collective Self-Portrait." *Atlantis* 16 (1): 6–24.

Ellingson, L.L., and C. Ellis. 2008. "Autoethnography as Constructionist Project." In *Handbook of Constructionist Research*, edited by J.A. Holstein and J.F. Gubrium, 445–65. New York: Guilford.

Ellis, Carolyn S. 2004. *The Ethnographic I: A Methodological Novel about Autoethnography*. Walnut Creek, CA: AltaMira Press.

Ellis, Carolyn, Tony E. Adams, and Arthur P. Bochner. "Autoethnography: An Overview." *Forum Qualitative Sozialforschung/Forum: Qualitative Social Research* 12 (1). Accessed November 26, 2011. http://www.qualitative-research.net/index.php/fqs/article/view/1589/3095.

Ellis, G.W., B. Mikic, and A.N. Rudnitsky. 2003. "Getting the 'Big Picture' in Engineering: Using Narratives and Conceptual Maps." Presentation at the American Society for Engineering Education Annual Conference and Symposium, Nashville, TN, June 22–25.

Etienne, Mona, and Eleanor Leacock, eds. 1980. *Women and Colonization: Anthropological Perspectives*. New York: Praeger.

Evans, Mary. 2004. *Killing Thinking: The Death of the Universities*. London: Continuum.

Eveline, Joan. 2004. *Ivory Basement Leadership: Power and Invisibility in the Changing University.* Crawley: University of Western Australia.

The Expert Panel on Women in University Research. 2012. *Strengthening Canada's Research Capacity: The Gender Dimension.* Ottawa: The Council of Canadian Academies. http://www.scienceadvice.ca/uploads/eng/assessments%20and%20publications%20and%20news%20releases/women_university_research/wur_fullreporten.pdf.pdf.

Fantham, E., H.P. Foley, N.B. Kampen, S.B. Pomeroy, and H.A. Shapiro. 1994. *Women in the Classical World: Image and Text.* New York: Oxford University Press.

Fassin, Didier. 2008. "Beyond Good and Evil?: Questioning the Anthropological Discomfort with Morals." *Anthropological Theory* 8(4): 333–44.

– 2012. Introduction to *A Companion to Moral Anthropology*, edited by Didier Fassin, 1–17. Malden, MA: Wiley-Blackwell.

Fassin, Didier, ed. 2012. *A Companion to Moral Anthropology.* Malden, MA: Wiley-Blackwell.

Feynman, R.P. 1989. *"Surely You're Joking, Mr. Feynman!": Adventures of a Curious Character.* Edited by Edward Hutchings. Toronto: Bantam Books.

Fisher, Jill. 2009. *Medical Research for Hire: the Political Economy of Pharmaceutical Clinical Trials.* London: Rutgers University Press.

Fisher, Jill, and Corey A. Kalbaugh. 2012. "Altruism in Clinical Research: Coordinators' Orientation to Their Professional Roles." *Nursing Outlook* 60 (3): 143–8.

Flanagan, J.C. 1954. "The Critical Incident Technique." *Psychological Bulletin* 51 (4): 327–55.

Florez, Carl P., and George L. Kelling. 1984. "The Hired Hand and the Lone Wolf: Issues in the Use of Observers in Large-Scale Program Evaluation." *Journal of Contemporary Ethnography* 12:423–43.

Flory, James, and Ezekiel Emanuel. 2004. "Interventions to Improve Research Participants Understanding in Informed Consent for Research." *Journal of the American Medical Association* 292 (13): 1593–601.

Fodor, Iris G., and Violet Franks. 1990. "Women in Midlife and Beyond: The New Prime of Life?" *Psychology of Women Quarterly* 14 (4): 445–9.

Forsyth, Louise H. 2011. "Desperately Seeking Equity: Systemic Discrimination and the Canada Research Chairs Program." In *Not Drowning But Waving: Women, Feminism and the Liberal Arts,* edited by Susan Brown, Jeanne Perreault, Jo-Ann Wallace, and Heather Zwicker, 173–93. Edmonton: University of Alberta Press.

Foucault, Michel. 1977. *Discipline and Punish: The Birthplace of the Prison*. New York: Vintage Books.

— 1980. *Power/Knowledge: Selected Interviews & Other Writings 1972–1977*. Edited by Colin Gordon. New York: Pantheon.

Fox, Richard G., ed. 1991. *Recapturing Anthropology: Working in the Present*. Santa Fe, NM: School of American Research.

Franklin, Ursula M. (1990) 1999. *The Real World of Technology*. Rev. ed. Toronto: House of Anansi Press.

Fratzl, Jae, and Ruth McKay. 2013. "Professional Staff in Academia: Academic Culture and the Role of Aggression." In *Workplace Bullying in Higher Education*, edited by Jaime Lester, 60–73. New York: Routledge.

Freedman, Jim, ed. 1976. *The History of Canadian Anthropology*. Canadian Ethnology Society Proceedings no. 3. Ottawa: National Museum of Man.

— 1977. *Applied Anthropology in Canada*. Canadian Ethnology Society Proceedings no. 4, Mercury Series. Ottawa: National Museum of Man.

Freeman, Pamela W., and Robert K. Roney. 1978. "The Neglected Majority: Non-Faculty Employees in Higher Education." *Journal of the College & University Personnel Association* 29 (3): 21–9.

Freeman, S.J.M., and S.C. Bourque. 2001. "Leadership and Power: New Conceptions." In *Women on Power: Leadership Redefined*, edited by S.J.M. Freeman, S.C. Bourque, and C.M. Shelton, 3–24. Boston: Northeastern University Press.

Frenette, Marc, and Klarka Zeman. 2007. "Why Are Most University Students Women? Evidence Based on Academic Performances, Study Habits and Parental Influences." Analytical Studies Branch Research Paper Series, Statistics Canada. Accessed September 12, 2011. http://www.statcan.gc.ca/pub/11f0019m/11f0019m2007303-eng.htm.

Frick, Stephen. 1993. "The Future of the Elite, Tax-Supported University." Unpublished manuscript. Halifax, NS: Dalhousie University.

Friedan, Betty. 1964. *The Feminine Mystique*. New York: Dell.

Frost, Stanley Brice. 1984. *McGill University: For the Advancement of Learning*. Vol. 2, 1895–1971. Montreal and Kingston: McGill-Queen's University Press.

Frye, Marilyn. 1983. "Oppression." *The Politics of Reality*. Trumansburg, NY: The Crossing Press.

Galarneau, Diane. 2010. "Temporary Employment in the Downturn." *Perspectives*, November. Statistics Canada. Catalogue no. 75-001–X: 5–17. http://www.statcan.gc.ca/pub/75-001-x/2010111/pdf/11371-eng.pdf.

Gardiner, Maria, Marika Tiggemann, Hugh Kearns, and Kelly Marshall. 2007. "Show Me the Money! An Empirical Analysis of Mentoring Outcomes for Women in Academia." *Higher Education Research & Development* 26: 425–42.

Gardiner, Michael E. 2006. "Everyday Knowledge." *Theory, Culture & Society* 23 (2–3): 205–7.

Garner, Richard. 2009. "It's Academic: University Women Are Beating Men at Almost Everything." *The Independent*, May 31. http://www.independent.co.uk/news/education/education-news/its-academic-university-women-are-beating-men-at-almost=everything-1693493.html.

Geisler, Cheryl, Debbie Kaminski, and Robyn A. Berkley. 2007. "The 13+ Club: An Index for Understanding, Documenting, and Resisting Patterns of Non-Promotion to Full Professor." *National Women's Studies Association Journal* 19: 145–6.

Genz, Stéphanie, and Benjamin A. Brabon. 2009. *Postfeminism: Cultural Texts and Theories*. Edinburgh: Edinburgh University Press.

Germain, Sylvie. 1992. *La pleurante des rues de Prague*. Paris: Éditions Gallimard.

– 1993. *The Weeping Woman on the Streets of Prague*. Translated by Judith Landry. Sawtry, UK: Daedalus.

Giddens, Anthony. 1991. *Modernity and Self-Identity: Self and Society in the Late Modern Age*. Cambridge: Polity Press.

Gilbert, Sandra M., and Susan Gubar. 1979. *The Madwoman in the Attic: The Woman Writer and the Nineteenth-Century Literary Imagination*. New Haven: Yale University Press.

Gillett, Margaret. 1981. *We Walked Very Warily: A History of Women at McGill*. Montreal: Eden Press.

Gilligan, C. 1982. *In a Different Voice: Psychological Theory and Women's Development*. Cambridge, MA: Harvard University Press.

Ginther, Donna K., and Kathy J. Hayes. 2003. "Gender Differences in Salary and Promotion for Faculty in the Humanities 1977–95." *Journal of Human Resources* 38:34–73.

Glazer-Raymo, Judith. 2008. *Unfinished Agendas: New and Continuing Gender Challenges in Higher Education*. Baltimore: Johns Hopkins University Press.

Glenn, C. 2004. *Unspoken: A Rhetoric of Silence*. Cardondale: Southern Illinois University Press.

Goldin, Claudia. 2004. "The Long Race to the Fast Track: Career and Family." *Annals of the American Academy of Political and Social Science* 596 (November): 20–35.

Gorham, Deborah. 1996. "In Defense of Discipline-Based Feminist Scholarship." In *Graduate Women's Studies: Visions and Realities*, edited by A.B. Shteir, 59–68. Toronto: Inanna.

Gouthro, Patricia A. 2009. "Understanding Women's Learning Trajectories: Examining Life Histories of Women Learners in Canada." In *Learning to Change: The Role of Identity and Learning Careers in Adult Education*, edited by Barbara Merrill, 97–111. Frankfurt: Peter Lang.

Grant, Tavia, and Jennifer Yang. 2009. "The Recovery Gap." *Globe and Mail*, Saturday, July 25, A1, A8.

Greaves, Lorraine. 1992. "What Is the Interrelationship between Academic and Activist Feminism?" In *Challenging Times: The Women's Movement in Canada and the United States*, edited by C. Backhouse and D.H. Flaherty, 150–5. Montreal and Kingston: McGill-Queen's University Press.

Gunn, Barbara, and Lois J. Parker. 1987. "Encouraging Enrollment of Older University Students: A Recruitment Success Story." *Educational Gerontology* 89 (2): 171–8.

Habermas, Jürgen. 1990. *Moral Consciousness and Communicative Action*. Cambridge, MA: MIT Press.

Halpern, Greg. 2003. *Harvard Works Because We Do*. New York: Quantuck Lane Press.

Hannah, Elena, Swani Vethamany-Globus, and Linda Paul, eds. 2002. *Women in the Canadian Academic Tundra: Challenging the Chill*. Montreal and Kingston: McGill-Queen's University Press.

Harding, Sandra. 1991. *Whose Science? Whose Knowledge: Thinking from Women's Lives*. Ithaca, NY: Cornell University Press.

– 2008. *Sciences from Below: Feminism, Postcolonialities and Modernities*. Durham, NC: Duke University Press.

Harrison, Julia, and Regna Darnell. 2006a. "Historical Traditions in Canadian Anthropology." In *Historicizing Canadian Anthropology*, edited by Julia Harrison and Regna Darnell, 2–18. Vancouver: University of British Columbia Press.

– 2006b. *Historicizing Canadian Anthropology*. Vancouver: University of British Columbia Press.

Hastings, Clare E., Cheryl A. Fisher, and Margaret A. McCabe. 2012. "Clinical Research Nursing: A Critical Resource in the National Research Enterprise." *Nursing Outlook* 60 (3): 149–56.

Haug, Frigga. 1999. *Female Sexualization*. Translated by Erica Carter. London: Verso.

Hawkesworth, Mary. 2004. "The Semiotics of Premature Burial: Feminism in a Postfeminist Age." *Signs: Journal of Women in Culture and Society* 29 (4): 961–85.

Hegel, Georg Wilhelm Friedrich. (1807) 1977. *Phenomenology of Spirit*. Oxford: Clarendon Press.

Hesselbein, Frances, Marshall Goldsmith, and Richard Beckhard, eds. 1997. *The Organization of the Future*. San Francisco: Jossey-Bass Publishers.

Higgins, Chris A., Linda E. Duxbury, and Sean T. Lyons. 2010. "Coping with Overload and Stress: Men and Women in Dual-Earner Families." *Journal of Marriage and Family* 72 (4): 847–59.

Hillier, Jean, and Emma Rooksby, eds. 2005. *Habitus: A Sense of Place*. London: Ashgate.

Hitlin, Steven, and Stephen Vaisey. 2013. "The New Sociology of Morality." *Annual Review of Sociology* 39: 51–68.

Hobson, Jane, Gar Jones, and Elizabeth Deane. 2005. "The Research Assistant: Silenced Partner in Australia's Knowledge Production." *Journal of Higher Education Policy and Management* 27 (3): 357–66.

Hochschild, Arlie Russell, and Anne Machung. 2003. *The Second Shift*. Toronto: Penguin Books.

Hohenstein, Walter V., and Bernard Jay Williams. 1974. "The Forgotten Man: The Non-Faculty Non-Classified University Employee." *Journal of the College & University Personnel Association* 25 (4): 25–33.

Holton, G. 2005. "Different Perceptions of 'Good Science' and Their Effects on Careers of Women Scientists." In *Victory and Vexation in Science: Einstein, Bohr, Heisenberg, and Others*, edited by G. Holton, 181–93. Cambridge, MA: Harvard University Press.

The Holy Bible: New Revised Standard Version. 1989. Division of Christian Education of the National Council of Churches in the United States of America.

hooks, bell. 1981. *Ain't I a Woman: Black Women and Feminism*. Boston: South End.

– 2009. *Belonging: A Culture of Place*. New York: Routledge.

Horn, John L., and Gary Donaldson. 1976. "On the Myth of Intellectual Decline in Adulthood." *American Psychologist* 31 (10): 701–19.

Houck, James P. 1990. "The Feudal Society in Today's University." Bayshore Institute Paper 90–1A. Accessed March 21, 2008. http://ageconsearch.umn.edu/handle/123456789/28342.

Howes, David. 1992. "What Is Good for Anthropology in Canada?" In
    *Fragile Truths: Twenty-Five Years of Sociology and Anthropology in
    Canada*, edited by William K. Carroll, Linda Christiansen-Ruffman,
    Raymond F. Currie, and Deborah Harrison, 155–69. Ottawa: Carleton
    University Press.
– 2006. "Constituting Canadian Anthropology." In *Historicizing
    Canadian Anthropology*, edited by Julia Harrison and Regna Darnell,
    200–11. Vancouver: University of British Columbia Press.
Human Resources and Skills Development Canada (HRSDC). 2011.
    "Federal Contractors Program." Accessed December 6. http://www
    .hrsdc.gc.ca/eng/labour/equality/fcp/employer_tool/intro/page01.shtml.
Ingram, J. 2011. Foreword to *Science, She Loves Me*, edited by M.A.
    Moser, 9–10. Banff, AB: The Banff Centre Press.
Jacobson, Joan M. 1991. "Midlife 'Baby Boom' Women Compared to
    Their Older Counterparts in Midlife." Paper presented at the Annual
    Meeting of the American Public Health Association, 119th, Atlanta, GA,
    November 10–14. *ERIC*, ED350499.
    http://files.eric.ed.gov/fulltext/ED350499.pdf.
Johal, Gurpreet Singh. 2005. "Order in K.O.S. On Race, Rage and
    Method." In *Critical Issues in Anti-Racist Research Methodologies*,
    edited by George Sefa Dei and Gurpreet Singh Johal, 269–89. New
    York: Peter Lang.
Joyce, James. (1916) 1976. *A Portrait of the Artist as a Young Man*.
    Reprint, New York: Penguin.
June, Audrey W. 2007. "Presidents: Same Look, Different Decade."
    Chronicle of Higher Education 53 (24), February 16, A33. http://chron-
    icle.com/article/Presidents-Same-Look/19958/.
Kaufert, Patricia, Joseph M. Kaufert, and Lisa LaBine. 2009. "Research
    Ethics, Interpreters and Biomedical Research." In *The Critical Link 5:
    Quality in Interpreting – A Shared Responsibility*, edited by Sandra
    Beatriz Hale, Uldis Ozolins, and Ludmila Stern, 235–50. Amsterdam:
    John Benjamins.
Keller, E.F. 1985. *Reflections on Gender and Science*. New Haven: Yale
    University Press.
Kennedy, Rebecca J.M., and Courtney Vaughn. 2004. "Exceeding
    Expectations." *College & University* 79 (4): 23–6.
Kidd, Michael P., and Michael Shannon. 1996. "The Gender Wage Gap:
    A Comparison of Australia and Canada." *Industrial and Labor
    Relations Review* 49:729–46.

Kjeldal, Sue-Ellen, Jennifer Rindfleish, and Alison Sheridan. 2005. "Deal-Making and Rule-Breaking: Behind the Façade of Equity in Academia." *Gender and Education* 17:431–47.

Koch, Philip. 1994. *Solitude: A Philosophical Encounter*. Chicago: Open Court Publishing.

Kymlicka, Will. 2003. "Being Canadian." *Government and Opposition* 38:357–85.

Laliberte, Verna. 2006. *BC Baccalaureate Graduate Study, 2006, Report of Findings, Class of 2004, Two Years after Graduation*. Prepared for the University President's Council of BC. N.p: Ministry of Advanced Education, Training and Technology, Ministry of Advanced Education, and Centre for Education/Information, Standards and Services. http://www.rucbc.ca/pdfs/data/bgs/bgs2006report.pdf.

Lane, Jeremy F. 2000. *Pierre Bourdieu: A Critical Introduction*. London: Pluto.

Laube, Heather, Kelly Massoni, Joey Sprague, and Abby L. Ferber. 2007. "The Impact of Gender on the Evaluation of Teaching: What We Know and What We Can Do." *National Women's Studies Association Journal* 19:87–104.

Lavell, Eunice Marie Fisher. 1998. "On the Road to Find Out: Everyday Advice for Working-Class Mothers Returning to School." In *The Illusion of Inclusion: Women in Post-Secondary Education*, edited by Jacqueline Stalker and Susan Prentice, 194–208. Halifax, NS: Fernwood Publishing.

Lay, Isabel Mackenzie. 2011. "Ravenous Cow." Unpublished manuscript.

Leahey, Erin. 2006. "Gender Differences in Productivity: Research Specialization as a Missing Link." *Gender & Society* 20:754–80.

Lenton, R. L. 1990. "Academic Feminists and the Women's Movement in Canada: Continuity Or Discontinuity." *Atlantis* 16 (1): 57–68.

Lester, Jaime. 2011. "Acting on the Collegiate Stage: Managing Impressions in the Workplace." *Feminist Formations* 23 (1): 155–81.

Lewchuk, Wayne, Marlea Clarke, and Alice de Wolff. 2008. "Working without Commitments: Precarious Employment and Health." *Work, Employment and Society* 22 (3): 387–406. doi:10.1177/0950017008093477.

Lewis, Paul, Marc Tsurumaki, and David J. Lewis. 2008. *Opportunistic Architecture*. New York: Princeton Architectural Press.

Lichtenstein, Diane. 2012. "Interdisciplinarity." In *Rethinking Women's and Gender Studies*, edited by C.M. Orr, A. Braithwaite, and D. Lichtenstein, 34–50. New York: Routledge.

Liebmann, Jeffrey D. 1986. "Non-Academic Employees in Higher Education: A Historical Overview." Paper presented at the 26th Annual Forum of the Association for Institutional Research, Orlando, FL, June 22–26. ERIC, ED280397. http://files.eric.ed.gov/fulltext/ED280397.pdf.

Littlemore, Richard. 2006. "Martha Piper: Random Thoughts on a Retiring President." UBC Reports 52 (6), June 1. http://www.publicaffairs.ubc.ca/ubcreports/2006/06juno1/interviews.html.

Lizotte, Melanie Anne. 1997. "Visible Minority Support Staff and Their Perceptions of the Employment Environment at the University of Alberta." MA thesis, University of Alberta.

Lloyd, G.E.R. 1966. Polarity and Analogy: Two Types of Argumentation in Early Greek Thought. Cambridge: Cambridge University Press.

Looker, E. Dianne. 1998. "Gender Issues in University: The University as Employer of Academic and Nonacademic Women and Men." In Gender Equity in Canadian Postsecondary Educational Institutions, edited by Rodney A. Clifton, Lance W. Roberts, and Raymond P. Perry, 21–43. CHERD/CSSHE Reader Series no. 3. Winnipeg, MB: University of Manitoba/Centre for Higher Education Research and Development.

Lorde, Audre. 1997. "The Uses of Anger." Women's Studies Quarterly 25 (1&2): 278–85.

– 2000. "The Master's Tools Will Never Dismantle the Master's House." Gender Space Architecture: An Interdisciplinary Introduction, edited by Jane Rendell, Barbara Penner, and Iian Borden, 53–5. London: Routledge.

Lubrano, Alfred. 2004. Limbo: Blue-Collar Roots, White-Collar Dream. Hoboken, NJ: John Wiley & Sons.

Luhmann, Susanne. 2005. "Questions of the Field: Women's Studies as Textual Contestation." In Open Boundaries: A Canadian Women's Studies Reader, 2nd ed., edited by B.A. Crowe and L. Gotell, 8–38. Toronto: Pearson Education Canada.

Lundin, William, and Kathleen Lundin. 1998. When Smart People Work for Dumb Bosses: How to Survive in a Crazy and Dysfunctional Workplace. New York: McGraw-Hill.

Lupton, Deborah. 1999. Risk. New York: Routledge.

MacDonald, M. 2006. "Mini Paper on Feminist Scholarship." Atlantis 31 (1): 87–8.

MacFadgen, Lynne. 2008. Mature Students in the Persistence Puzzle: An Exploration of the Factors that Contribute to Mature Students' Health, Learning and Retention of Post-Secondary Education. Ottawa: Canadian Council on Learning.

MacLennan, Hugh. 1960. *McGill: The Story of a University*. London: George Allen and Unwin.

Magill, Dennis. 1981. "Sociology and Anthropology in the 1975 Symons Report: Re-examination of the Canadianization Issue." *Society/Société* 5 (1): 4–9.

Mahoney, M. 2001. "The Problem of Silence in Feminist Psychology." In *Women on Power: Leadership Redefined*, edited by S.J.M. Freeman, S.C. Bourque, and C.M. Shelton, 61–81. Boston: Northeastern University Press.

Maracle, Lee. 1996. *I Am Woman: A Native Perspective on Sociology and Feminism*. Vancouver: Press Gang.

Marcus, George E. 1991. "A Broad(er)side to the Canon." *Cultural Anthropology* 6 (3): 395–405.

– 1998. *Ethnography through Thick and Thin*. Princeton: Princeton University Press.

Massey, Jennifer, Meghan Brooks, and Cheryl Sutherland. 2010. *Mature Women Students and the Pursuit of Higher Education: An Examination of the Role of the Ban Righ Centre at Queen's University*. Kingston: Queen's University http://www.queensu.ca/studentaffairs/assessment/completed/mature/FINAL.pdf.

Mattson, Kevin. 2003. "How I Became a Worker." In *Steal This University: The Rise of the Corporate University and the Academic Labor Movement*, edited by Benjamin Johnson, Patrick Kavanagh, and Kevin Mattson, 87–96. New York: Routledge.

May, V.M. 2012. "Intersectionality." In *Rethinking Women's and Gender Studies*, edited by C.M. Orr, A. Braithwaite, and D. Lichtenstein, 155–72. New York: Routledge.

McCaughey, Martha. 2012. "Community." In *Rethinking Women's and Gender Studies*, edited by C.M. Orr, A. Braithwaite, and D. Lichtenstein, 135–51. New York: Routledge.

McClintock, Anne. 1995. *Imperial Leather: Race, Gender and Sexuality in the Colonial Contest*. New York: Routledge.

McCormack, Thelma. 1985. "Becoming a Women's Studies Scholar: From Stardust to Section Fifteen." *Canadian Woman Studies* 6 (3): 5–9.

McDonald, Michael, and Susan M. Cox. 2009. "Moving towards Evidence-Based Human Participation Protection." *Journal of Academic Ethics* 7 (1): 1–16.

McDonald, Michael, Susan M. Cox, Pat Kaufert, and Nino Preto. 2009. "Listening to Human Subjects: Reflections on Ethics in Clinical Research." *SOCRA Source*, August 13–19.

McDonald, Michael, Anne Townsend, Susan M. Cox, Darquise Lafrenière, and Natasha Damiano Paterson. 2008. "Trust in Health Research Relationships: Accounts of Human Subjects." *Journal of Empirical Research on Human Research Ethics* 3 (4): 35–47.

McGettigan, Andrew. 2013. *The Great University Gamble: Money, Markets and the Future of Higher Education.* London: Pluto.

McGrath, Earl J. 1936. "The Evolution of Administrative Offices in Institutions of Higher Education from 1860 to 1933." PhD diss., University of Chicago.

McKillop, A.B. 1994. *Matters of the Mind: The University in Ontario 1791–1951.* Toronto: University of Toronto Press.

McMurray, Dorothy. 1974. *Four Principals of McGill: A Memoir 1929–1963.* Montreal: The Graduates' Society of McGill University.

Merleau-Ponty, Maurice. (1960) 1964. *Signs.* Translated by Richard C. McCleary. Evanston, IL: Northwestern University Press.

Merrill, Barbara. 2009. "Introduction: Moving Beyond Access to Learning Careers and Identity." In *Learning to Change: The Role of Identity and Learning Careers in Adult Education,* edited by Barbara Merrill, 8–17. Frankfurt: Peter Lang.

Metcalfe, Amy Scott, and Sheila Slaughter. 2008. "The Differential Effects of Academic Capitalism on Women in the Academy." In *Unfinished Agendas: New and Continuing Gender Challenges in Higher Education,* edited by Judith Glazer-Raymo, 80–111. Baltimore: Johns Hopkins University Press.

Michalko, Rod. 2009. "The Excessive Appearance of Disability." *International Journal of Qualitative Studies in Education* 22 (1): 65–74.

Miller, Barbara D., Penny Van Esterik, and John Van Esterik. 2010. *Cultural Anthropology.* 4th Cdn. ed. Toronto: Pearson.

Miller, Gale, and David Silverman. 1995. "Troubles Talk and Counseling Discourse." *Sociological Quarterly* 36 (4): 725–47.

Miller, Leslie A. 1992/1993. "Alone in the Temple: A Personal Essay on Solitude and the Woman Poet." *Kansas Quarterly* 24/25 (4/1): 200–14.

Miller, Tina, and Mary Boulton. 2007. "Changing Construction of Informed Consent: Qualitative Research and Complex Social Worlds." *Social Sciences and Medicine* 65:2194–211.

Mills, C. Wright. 1959. *The Sociological Imagination.* New York: Oxford University Press.

Misra, Joya, Jennifer Hickes Lundquist, Elissa Holmes, and Stephanie Agiomavritis. 2011. "The Ivory Ceiling of Service Work." *Academe* 97 (1). http://www.aaup.org/article/ivory-ceiling-service-work#.UcIIcvllm9I.

Mohanty, Chandra Talpade. 1984. "Under Western Eyes: Feminist Scholarship and Colonial Discourses." *Boundary 2* 12 (3): 333–58.

Mohanty, Chandra Talpade, Ann Russo, and Lourdes Torres, eds. 1991. *Third World and the Politics of Feminism*. Bloomington: Indiana University Press.

Mojab, S. 2006. "Mini Paper on Feminist Scholarship." *Atlantis* 31 (1): 88–90.

Moloney, C. 2007. "Thinking Yourself into a Scientist or Engineer." Presentation at the Royal Society of Canada Conference, Rooms of Their Own: Women in the Knowledge Economy, Edmonton, May 2–4.

Monroe, Kristen, Saba Ozyurt, Ted Wrigley, and Amy Alexander. 2008. "Gender Equality in Academia: Bad News from the Trenches, and Some Possible Solutions." *Perspectives on Politics* 6:215–33.

Montgomery, S.L. 1996. *The Scientific Voice*. New York: Guildford Press.

Monture, Patricia. 2010. "Race, Gender, and the University: Strategies for Survival." In *States of Race: Critical Race Feminism for the 21st Century*, edited by S. Razack, M. Smith, and S. Thobani, 23–35. Toronto: Between the Lines.

Moraga, C., and G. Anzaldúa, eds. 1981. *This Bridge Called My Back: Writings by Radical Women of Color*. Watertown, MA: Persephone.

Morawski, Cynthia, and Patricia Palulis. 2009. "Auto/ethno/graphies as Teaching Lives: An Aesthetics of Difference." *JCT: Journal of Curriculum Theorizing* 25 (2): 6–24.

Morris, Marla. 2009. *On Not Being Able to Play: Scholars, Musicians and the Crisis of Psyche*. Rotterdam: Sense Publishers.

Morris, M., and B. Bunjun. 2007. *Using Intersectional Feminist Frameworks in Research*. Ottawa: CRIAW/ICREF.

Morton, William L. (1968) 1973. *The Canadian Identity*. Madison: University of Wisconsin Press.

Moser, M.A., ed. 2011. *Science, She Loves Me*. Banff, AB: The Banff Centre Press.

Moss-Racusin, C.A., J.F. Dovidio, V.L. Brescoll, M.J. Graham, and J. Handelsman. 2012. "Science Faculty's Subtle Gender Biases Favor Male Students." *Proceedings of the National Academy of Sciences* 109 (41): 16474–9. doi:10.1073/pnas.1211286109.

Mueller, Mary Rose. 2001. "From Delegation to Specialization: Nurses and Clinical Trial Co-ordination." *Nursing Inquiry* 8 (3): 182–90.

Mukherjee, A. 1992. "A House Divided: Women of Colour and American Feminist Theory." In *Challenging Times: The Women's Movement in*

Canada and the United States, edited by C. Backhouse and D.H. Flaherty, 165–74. Montreal and Kingston: McGill-Queen's University Press.

Murray, D.A. 2008. "Bridging the Gap: I Will Not Remain SILENCED." In *Whose University Is It, Anyway? Power and Privilege on Gendered Terrain*, edited by Anne Wagner, Sandra Acker, and Kimine Mayuzumi, 104–14. Toronto: Sumach Press.

Muzzin, Linda, and Jacqueline Limoges. 2008. "'A Pretty Incredible Structural Injustice': Contingent Faculty in Canadian University Nursing." In *Whose University Is It, Anyway? Power and Privilege on Gendered Terrain*, edited by Anne Wagner, Sandra Acker, and Kimine Mayuzumi, 157–72. Toronto: Sumach Press.

Myers, Margaret. 2000. "Qualitative Research and the Generalizability Question: Standing Firm with Proteus." *The Qualitative Report* 4 (3/4). Accessed September 12, 2011. http://www.nova.edu/ssss/QR/QR4-3/myers.html.

Nelson, J.K., M.A. Hjalmarson, K.E. Wage, and J.R. Buck. 2010. "Students' Interpretation of the Importance and Difficulty of Concepts in Signals and Systems." In *Proceedings of the 40th ASEE/IEEE Frontiers in Education Conference, Washington, DC, October 27–30*. T3G1-6. Piscataway, NJ: IEEE.

Nemiroff, Greta Hofmann. 1978. "Rationale for an Interdisciplinary Approach to Women's Studies." *Canadian Women's Studies* 1 (1): 60–8.

– 1985. "Reflections on Recent Women's Studies Conferences; Or, Watch Out We Don't Sell the Farm!" *Canadian Woman Studies* 6 (3): 45–8.

Newstrom, John W., and Keith Davis. 2002. *Organizational Behavior: Human Behavior at Work*. New York: McGraw-Hill.

Newton, Esther. 2000. *Margaret Mead Made Me Gay: Personal Essays, Public Ideas*. Durham, NC: Duke University Press.

– 2002. *Ivory Bridges: Connecting Science and Society*. Cambridge, MA: MIT Press.

Noble, Bobby. 2012. "Trans-." In *Rethinking Women's and Gender Studies*, edited by C.M. Orr, A. Braithwaite, and D. Lichtenstein, 277–92. New York: Routledge.

Noble, J.B. 2004. "Sons of the Movement: Feminism, Female Masculinity and Female to Male (FTM) Transsexual Men." *Atlantis* 29 (1): 21–8.

Ocker, Bridget M., and Darlene M. Pawlik Plank. 2000. "The Research Nurse Role in a Clinic-Based Oncology Research Setting." *Cancer Nursing* 23 (4): 286–92.

Ornstein, Michael, Penni Stewart, and Janice Drakich. 2007. "Promotion at Canadian Universities: The Intersection of Gender, Discipline, and Institution." *Canadian Journal of Higher Education* 37:1–25.

Orr, C.M. 2012. "Activism." In *Rethinking Women's and Gender Studies*, edited by C.M. Orr, A. Braithwaite, and D. Lichtenstein, 85–101. New York: Routledge.

Palmer, Bryan D. 2009. *Canada's 1960s: The Ironies of Identity in a Rebellious Era.* Toronto: University of Toronto Press.

Palulis, Patricia. 2009. "Geo-Literacies in a Strange Land: Academic Vagabonds Provoking *à Pied*." *Educational Insights* 13 (4): 1–12.

– 2012. "Eavesdropping as Seductive Conversation." In *A Heart of Wisdom: Life Writing as Empathetic Inquiry*, edited by C. Chambers, E. Hasebe-Ludt, C. Leggo, and A. Sinner, 293–301. New York: Peter Lang.

Palulis, Patricia, and Marylin Low. 2005. "The (Im)possibilities of Collecting Conversation(s): A Material Event that Refuses Closure." *Journal of the American Association for the Advancement of Curriculum Studies* 1 (1): 1–20.

Pearson, Ann Kristine. 2008. "Disrespectin' Administrative Staff Work: Can We Talk?" In *Whose University Is It, Anyway? Power and Privilege on Gendered Terrain*, edited by Anne Wagner, Sandra Acker, and Kimine Mayuzumi, 127–39. Toronto: Sumach Press.

Perkins, James A., ed. 1973. *The University as an Organization.* New York: McGraw Hill.

Piper, Martha C. 2002. "Building a Civil Society: A New Role for the Human Sciences." Killam Annual Lecture, University of British Columbia, Vancouver.

Poulos, Christopher. 2010. "Transgressions." *International Review of Qualitative Research* 3 (1): 67–88.

Prentice, Alison. 1991. "Bluestockings, Feminists, or Women Workers? A Preliminary Look at Women's Early Employment at the University of Toronto." *Journal of the Canadian Historical Association/Revue de la S.H.C.* New Series 2: 231–61.

Pringle, Rosemary. 1988. *Secretaries Talk: Sexuality, Power and Work.* London: Verso.

Probert, Belinda. 2005. "'I Just Couldn't Fit It In': Gender and Unequal Outcomes in Academic Careers." *Gender, Work, and Organization* 12: 50–72.

Pugh, Derek S., and David J. Hickson. 1997. *Writers on Organizations.* 5th ed. Thousand Oaks, CA: Sage Publications.

Rajagopal, Indhu. 2002. *Hidden Academics: Contract Faculty in Canadian Universities.* Toronto: University of Toronto Press.

Ramsden, Paul. 1998. *Learning to Lead in Higher Education*. London: Routledge.

Rapaport, Irene. 1997. "Women's Informal Learning Experiences at Work: Perspectives of Support Staff in an Educational Institution." MA thesis, McGill University.

Ray, Rebecca, Janet C. Gornick, and John Schmitt. 2009. *Parental Leave Policies in 21 Countries: Assessing Generosity and Gender Equality*. Washington, DC: Center for Economic and Policy Research. http://www.cite.gov.pt/asstscite/images/grafs11/Parent_Leave_Policies_21.pdf.

Razack, Sherene, Malinda Smith, and Sunera Thobani, eds. 2010. *States of Race: Critical Race Feminism for the 21st Century*. Toronto: Between the Lines.

Readings, Bill. 1996. *The University in Ruins*. Cambridge, MA: Harvard University Press.

Reimer, Marilee. 2004. "Will Women's Studies Programs Survive the Corporate University?" In *Inside Corporate U: Women in the Academy Speak Out*, edited by M. Reimer, 118–37. Toronto: Sumach Press.

Reimer, Marilee, ed. 2004. *Inside Corporate U: Women in the Academy Speak Out*. Toronto: Sumach Press.

Reiter, Rayna, ed. 1975. *Toward an Anthropology of Women*. New York: Monthly Review.

Reyes, Pedro, and G. Smith. 1987. "Faculty and Academic Staff Participation in Academic Governance: The Social Contract Model." Paper presented at the Conference of the Association for the Study of Higher Education, San Diego, CA, February 13–17. ERIC, ED 281446, https://archive.org/details/ERIC_ED281446.

Rhoades, Gary. 1998. *Managed Professionals: Unionized Faculty and Restructuring Academic Labor*. Albany: State University of New York Press.

Rhode, Deborah. 2001. *The Unfinished Agenda: Women and the Legal Profession*. Chicago: American Bar Association, Commission on Women in the Profession.

Rich, Adrienne. 1995. *On Lies, Secrets, and Silence: Selected Prose 1966–1978*. New York: W.W. Norton & Company.

Richardson, Laurel. 1997. *Fields of Play: Constructing an Academic Life*. New Brunswick, NJ: Rutgers University Press.

– 2000. "Writing: A Method of Inquiry." In *Handbook of Qualitative Research*, edited by Norman K. Denzin and Yvonna S. Lincoln, 923–48. Thousand Oaks, CA: Sage.

Ridgeway, Cecilia, L. 1993. "Gender, Status, and the Social Psychology of Expectations." In *Theory on Gender/Feminism on Theory*, edited by P. England, 175–97. New York: Aldine De Gruyter.

Robbins, W., M. Luxton, M. Eichler, and F. Descarries. 2008. *Minds of Our Own: Inventing Feminist Scholarship and Women's Studies in Canada and Québec, 1966–76*. Waterloo, ON: Wilfrid Laurier University Press.

Robertson, Jennifer. 2002. "Reflexivity Rédux: A Pithy Polemic on 'Positionality.'" *Anthropological Quarterly* 75 (4): 785–92.

Ronell, Avital. 2008. "In Interview with Diane Davis" In *ÜberReader: Selected Works of Avital Ronell*, edited by Diane Davis, 98–9. Urbana: University of Illinois Press.

– 2010. *Fighting Theory: In Conversation with Anne Dufourmantelle*. Urbana: University of Illinois Press.

Rosaldo, Michelle, and Louise Lamphere, eds. 1974. *Women, Culture and Society*. Palo Alto: Stanford University Press.

Rosales, J., C. Moloney, C. Badenhorst, J. Dyer, and M. Murray. 2012. "Breaking the Barriers of Research Writing: Rethinking Pedagogy for Engineering Graduate Research." In *Proceedings of the Canadian Engineering Education Association Conference (CEEA 2012), Winnipeg, Manitoba, 17–20 June*. Winnipeg: CEEA, University of Manitoba.

Rose, Gillian. 1997. "Situating Knowledges: Positionality, Reflexivity and Other Tactics." *Progress in Human Geography* 21 (3): 305–20.

Roth, Julius A. 1966. "Hired Hand Research." *American Sociologist* 1 (4): 190–6.

Ruchkall, Barbara Lynne. 1997. "The Campus Climate: A Chilly One for Support Staff at the University of Manitoba." MA thesis, University of Manitoba.

Salamon, G. 2008. "Transfeminism and the Future of Gender." In *Women's Studies on the Edge*, edited by J.W. Scott, 115–36. Durham, NC: Duke University Press.

Samson, F., and C. Moloney. 2008. "Sharing Stories of Our Personal/Professional Lives: Imagining and Working towards New Narratives for Individuals and Professions." Presentation at Narrative Matters, Toronto, May 7–10.

Schaie, K. Warner, and Faika A.K. Zanjani. 2006. "Intellectual Development across Adulthood." In *Handbook of Adult Development and Learning*, edited by Carol Hoare, 99–122. Oxford: Oxford University Press.

Schutz, Alfred. 1967. "On Multiple Realities." In *Alfred Schutz: Collected Papers I: The Problem of Social Reality*, edited by Maurice Natanson, 207–59. The Hague: Martinus Nijhoff.

Scott, Joan. 1999. "A Statistical Representation of Work/La Statistique de l'Industrie à Paris." In *Gender and the Politics of History*. Rev. ed., 113–38. New York: Columbia University Press.

Scott, R.L. 1972. "Rhetoric and Silence." *Western Speech* 36 (3): 146–58.

Seydegart, K., and G. Spears. 1985. *Beyond Dialogue: Immigrant Women in Canada, 1985–1990: A Plan for Action Arising from a National Consultation Commissioned by Multiculturalism Canada*. Erin, ON: Erin Research Inc.

Shohat, Ella. 1975. "The Struggle over Representation: Casting, Coalitions, and the Politics of Identification." In *Late Imperial Culture*, edited by Román de la Campa, E. Ann Kaplan, and Michael Sprinker, 166–78. London: Verso.

Shteir, A.B. 1996. "Making the Vision a Reality: York University's Graduate Programme in Women's Studies." In *Graduate Women's Studies: Visions and Realities*, edited by A.B. Shteir, 59–68. Toronto: Inanna.

Shurmer-Smith, Pam. 2000. "Hélène Cixous." In *Thinking Space*, edited by Michael Crang and Nigel Thrift, 154–66. London: Routledge.

Side, K. 2001. "Rethinking the Women's Studies PHD in Canadian Universities." *Journal of International Women's Studies* 2 (2): 67–88.

Silverman, Marilyn. 1991. "Amongst 'Our Selves': A Colonial Encounter in Canadian Academia." *Critique of Anthropology* 11 (4): 381–94.

Slaughter, Sheila, and Gary Rhoades. 2004. *Academic Capitalism and the New Economy: Markets, State, and Higher Education*. Baltimore: Johns Hopkins University Press.

Skeggs, Beverley. 1997. *Formations of Class and Gender: Becoming Respectable*. Thousand Oaks, CA: Sage.

Smith, Andrea. 2005. *Conquest: Sexual Violence and American Indian Genocide*. Cambridge, MA: South End Press.

Smith, Dorothy E. 1987. *The Everyday World as Problematic: A Feminist Sociology*. Toronto: University of Toronto Press.

– 1990. *Texts, Facts, and Femininity: Exploring the Relations of Ruling*. London: Routledge.

Smith, Gavin. 2008. "Canadian Anthropology Is a Labour Process Like Any Other." Paper presented at CASCA 2008 panel organized by Jim Waldram titled "Canadian Anthropology Is …"

– 2014. *Intellectuals and (Counter-) Politics: Essays in Historical Realism*. London: Berghahn Books.

Smith, Gavin A., and David H. Turner, eds. 1979. *Challenging Anthropology: A Critical Introduction to Social and Cultural Anthropology*. Toronto: McGraw-Hill Ryerson.

Sonnert, G., and G. Holton. 1995a. *Gender Differences in Science Careers: The Project Access Study*. New Brunswick, NJ: Rutgers University Press.

– 1995b. *Who Succeeds in Science?: The Gender Dimension*. New Brunswick, NJ: Rutgers University Press.

– 2002. *Ivory Bridges: Connecting Science and Society*. Cambridge, MA: MIT Press.

Spitzer, Denise L. 2005. "Engendering Health Disparities." *Canadian Journal of Public Health* 96 (2): S78–S96.

Spivak, Gayatri Chakravorty. 2003. *The Death of a Discipline*. New York: Columbia University Press.

Staggenborg, Suzanne. 1988. "Hired Hand Research Revisited." *The American Sociologist* 19 (3): 260–9.

Stalker, Jacqueline, and Susan Prentice. 1998. Introduction to *The Illusion of Inclusion: Women in Post-Secondary Education*, edited by Jacqueline Stalker and Susan Prentice, 12–34. Halifax, NS: Fernwood Publishing.

Stalker, Jacqueline, and Susan Prentice, eds. 1998. *The Illusion of Inclusion: Women in Post-Secondary Education*. Halifax, NS: Fernwood Publishing.

Statistics Canada. 1978–79. *Advance Statistics of Education*. Ottawa: Queen's Printer.

– 2005. *Study: The Rising Profile of Women Academics*. Ottawa: Statistics Canada. http://www.statcan.gc.ca/daily-quotidien/050224/dq050224c–eng.htm.

– 2006a. "Study: Trends in the Teaching Profession, 1999 to 2005." *The Daily*, December 1. http://www.statcan.ca/Daily/English/061201/d061201b.htm.

– 2006b. "Study: Wage Differences between Male and Female University Professors, 1970 to 2001." *The Daily*, December 8. http://www.statcan.ca/Daily/English/061208/d061208c.htm.

– 2008. "Income and Earnings Highlight Tables, 2006 Census." Catalogue no. 97-563-xwe2006002, May 1. http://www12.statcan.ca/census-recensement/2006/dp-pd/hlt/97-563/Index-eng.cfm.

Steans, Jill. 2007. "Negotiating the Politics of Difference in the Project of Feminist Solidarity." *Review of International Studies* 33:729–43.

Stewart, Lee Jean. 1990. *It's Up to You: Women at UBC in the Early Years*. Vancouver: Academic Women's Association, UBC Press.

Stewart, Penni. 2010. "Nothing Casual about Academic Work." *Canadian Association of University Teachers Bulletin* 57 (4): A3. https://www.cautbulletin.ca/en_article.asp?articleid=3071.

Stout, Patricia A., Janet Staiger, and Nancy A. Jennings. 2007. "Affective Stories: Understanding the Lack of Progress of Women Faculty." *National Women's Studies Association Journal* 19:124–44.

Strauss, Anselm, and Juliet Corbin. 1990. *Basics of Qualitative Research: Grounded Theory Procedures and Techniques*. Thousand Oaks, CA: Sage.

Szekeres, Judy. 2004. "The Invisible Workers." *Journal of Higher Education Policy and Management* 26 (1): 7–22.

Takacs, David. 2003. "How Does Your Positionality Bias Your Epistemology?" *Thought and Action* 19 (1): 27–38.

Tancred, P. 1994. "Into the Third Decade of Canadian Women's Studies: A Glass Half Empty or Half-Full?" *Women's Studies Quarterly* 22 (3/4): 12–25.

Taylor, Charles. 1992. *Multiculturalism and the Politics of Recognition*. Princeton: Princeton University Press.

Taylor, Mark C. 2009. "End the University As We Know It." *New York Times*, April 26, A23.

Tedder, Michael, and Gert Biesta. 2009. "What Does It Take to Learn from One's Life? Exploring Opportunities for Biographical Learning in the Life Course." In *Learning to Change: The Role Of Identity and Learning Careers in Adult Education*, edited by Barbara Merrill, 33–49. Frankfurt: Peter Lang.

Thorne, Sally E., Angela D. Henderson, Gladys I. McPherson, and Barbara K. Pesut. 2004. "The Problematic Allure of the Binary in Nursing Theoretical Discourse." *Nursing Philosophy* 5:208–15.

Thornton, Margaret. 2013. "The Mirage of Merit: Reconstituting the 'Ideal Academic.'" *Australian Feminist Studies* 28 (76): 127–43.

Tite, R., and M. Malone. 1990. "Our Universities' Best-Kept Secret: Women's Studies in Canada." *Atlantis* 16 (1): 25–39.

Trinh, Minh-ha T. 1989. *Woman, Native, Other: Writing Postcoloniality and Feminism*. Bloomington: Indiana University Press.

– 1992. *Framer/Framed*. New York: Routledge.

– 2005. *The Digital Film Event*. New York: Routledge.

– 2011. *Elsewhere, Within Here: Immigration, Refugeeism and the Boundary Event*. New York: Routledge.

Trinh, Minha-ha T., ed. 1986–87. "She, the Inappropriated Other." Special Third World Women issue. *Discourse: Journal for Theoretical Studies in Media and Culture* 8 (Winter).

Tulino, A.M., and S. Verdú. 2006. "Monotonic Decrease of the Non-Gaussianness of the Sum of Independent Random Variables: A Simple Proof." *IEEE Transactions on Information Theory* 52:4295–7.

Turcotte, Martin. 2013. "Percentage of Women among University Graduates, by Field of Study, Canada, 1992 to 2008." Table 9 in *Women and Education*. Statistics Canada. Last modified May 13. http://www.statcan.gc.ca/pub/89-503-x/2010001/article/11542-eng.htm#a10.

Turk, James. 2008. *Universities at Risk: How Politics, Special Interests and Corporatization Threaten Academic Integrity*. Toronto: J. Lorimer & Co.

Turkle, S., ed. 2011. *Falling for Science: Objects in Mind*. Cambridge, MA: MIT Press.

University of British Columbia (UBC) Equity Office. 2009. *Employment Equity Report 2009*. Vancouver: UBC Equity Office. http://equity.ubc.ca/files/2010/11/EE-Report/2009-Final.pdf.

– *Employment Equity Report 2010*. 2010. Vancouver: UBC Equity Office. http://equity.ubc.ca/files/2011/07/employment_equity_report-2010.pdf.

University of London, Birkbeck. 2012. "Birkbeck Tops Poll Again for Student Satisfaction." *Birkbeck University of London News*, September 26. http://www.bbk.ac.uk/news/birkbeck-tops-poll-again-for-student-satisfaction-and-teaching-in-london.

University of Sussex. 2014. "National Student Survey." Sussex Internal Report. Survey conducted by Ipsos MORI for the Higher Education Funding Council of England. http://www.sussex.ac.uk/nss/results/previousyears.

Valian, Virginia. 1998. *Why So Slow? The Advancement of Women*. Cambridge, MA: MIT Press.

– 2004. "Beyond Gender Schemas: Improving the Advancement of Women in Academia." *National Women's Studies Association Journal* 16:207–20.

van den Hoonaard, Will. 2011. *The Seduction of Ethics: Transforming the Social Sciences*. Toronto: University of Toronto Press.

Vinnicombe, Susan. 1980. *Secretaries, Management and Organizations*. London: Heinemann Educational Books.

Visweswaran, Kamela. 1994. *Fictions of Feminist Ethnography*. Minneapolis: University of Minnesota Press.

Vosko, Leah F. 2010. *Managing the Margins: Gender, Citizenship, and the International Regulation of Precarious Employment*. Toronto: Oxford University Press.

Wagener, Silke. 1996. *Pedelle, Mägde und Lakaien. Göttinger Universitätsschriften*: Serie A: Schriften. Göttingen, GE: Vandenhoeck & Ruprecht.

Wagner, Anne, Sandra Acker, and Kimine Mayuzumi, eds. 2008. *Whose University Is It, Anyway? Power and Privilege on Gendered Terrain.* Toronto: Sumach Press.

Wang, K., S.E. Stachel, B. Timmerman, M. van Montagu, and P.C. Zambryski. 1987. "Site-Specific Nick in the T-DNA Border Sequence as a Result of *Agrobacterium vir* Gene Expression." *Science* 235 (January 30): 587–91.

Webber, M. 2005. "'Don't Be So Feminist:' Exploring Student Resistance to Feminist Approaches in a Canadian University." *Women's Studies International Forum* 28:181–94.

– 2007. "Cultivating 'Miss Congeniality.'" *Academic Matters: The Journal of Higher Education*, February 6. http://www.ocufa.on.ca/Academic_Matters_February2007/index.htm.

Wechsler, David. 1939. *The Measurement of Adult Intelligence.* Baltimore: Williams & Wilkins.

Wernick, Andrew. 2006. "University." *Theory, Culture & Society* 23 (2–3): 557–63.

Whittaker, Elvi, and Michael M. Ames. 2006. "Anthropology and Sociology at the University of British Columbia from 1947 to the 1980s." In *Historicizing Canadian Anthropology*, edited by Julia Harrison and Regna Darnell, 157–72. Vancouver: University of British Columbia Press.

Wiegman, R. 2005. "The Possibility of Women's Studies." In *Women's Studies for the Future: Foundations, Interrogations, Politics*, edited by E. Lapovsky Kennedy and A. Beins, 40–60. New Brunswick, NJ: Rutgers University Press.

Wolfreys, Julian. 1997. *The Rhetoric of Affirmative Resistance: Dissonant Identities from Carroll to Derrida.* New York: St. Martin's Press.

Women's and Gender Studies et Recherches Féministes (WGSRF). 2012. "Canadian Gender and Women's Studies Programs – Coordinator's List." June. http://www.wgsrf.com/uploads/9/2/7/1/9271669/wsincana-dachartjune2012.pdf.

Wood, Julia T. 1993. "Gender and Moral Voice: Moving from Women's Nature to Standpoint Epistemology." *Women's Studies in Communication* 14 (1): 1–24.

Woodfield, Ruth. 2011. "Age and First Destination Employment from UK Universities: Are Mature Students Disadvantaged?" *Studies in Higher Education* 36 (4): 409–25.

Woodley, Alan. 1991. "Access to What? A Study of Mature Graduate Outcomes." *Higher Education Quarterly* 46 (2): 91–108.

Wright, Handel. 2000. "Nailing Jell-O to the Wall: Pinpointing Aspects of State-of-the-Art Curriculum Theorizing." *Educational Researcher* 29 (5): 4–13.

Wriston, Henry M. 1959. *Academic Procession: Reflections of a College President*. New York: Columbia University.

Ylijoki, Oili-Helena. 2000. "Disciplinary Cultures and the Moral Order of Studying." *Higher Education* 39 (3): 329–62.

Young, Iris Marion. 1989. "Polity and Group Difference: A Critique of the Ideal of Universal Citizenship." *Ethics* 99:250–74.

– 2001. "Equality of Whom? Social Groups and Judgments of Injustice." *Journal of Political Philosophy* 9 (1): 1–18.

– 2011. *Responsibility for Justice*. New York: Oxford University Press.

Young, Kate, Carol Walkowitz, and Roslyn McCullagh. 1980. *Of Marriage and the Market*. London: CSE Books.

Ziegler, Philip. 2001. *Soldiers: Fighting Men's Lives, 1901–2001*. New York: Alfred A. Knopf.

Contributors

ZELDA ABRAMSON is associate professor of sociology at Acadia University. Her research and teaching are in the areas of health, gender, and methodology.

JOAN ANDERSON is professor emerita of nursing at the University of British Columbia. She is a nurse and sociologist. Among her interests are the social production of knowledge, and knowledge exchange in the academy, practice, and policy settings. Her research has examined the complex sociocultural, economic, and political contexts of health, illness, and suffering through different genres of critical theorizing.

KATIE AUBRECHT is a Canadian Institutes of Health Research post-doctoral fellow with the Department of Family Studies and Gerontology at Mount Saint Vincent University. Her research uses phenomenological and interpretive sociological theories and methods to understand the relations between institutional organization and subject formation and focuses on happiness, the family, aging, and disability.

LINDA COHEN is visiting assistant professor (per-term appointment) in the Department of Sociology at Memorial University. Her research interests are in precarious work, health and occupational health, post-secondary education, family studies, and qualitative sociology.

PATRICIA KAUFERT is senior scholar, formerly a professor in the Department of Community Health Sciences in the Faculty of Medicine at the University of Manitoba. As a sociologist her research has been in women's health, the politics of women's bodies, and women in midlife. More recently, she has been part of a study of research ethics as seen from the perspective of research participants and frontline workers.

LELIA KENNEDY retired as the first head of the social science division at Malaspina College and is a registered psychologist. She played a part in the establishment of Malaspina, which eventually became Vancouver Island University. Her research interests stretch from children in hospitals, mature students, to development in middle age.

KERSTI KRUG is retired assistant principal in the College for Interdisciplinary Studies at the University of British Columbia, formerly assistant dean in the Faculty of Graduate Studies, and manager of research and evaluation and director of communication in UBC's Museum of Anthropology. She has taught as a sessional instructor in the Faculty of Commerce and Business Administration and in anthropology. Among her research interests are the organizational culture of universities, the history of interdisciplinarity and strategic decision-making tools for not-for-profit organizations.

ISABEL MACKENZIE LAY is a provincial youth outreach worker at the Griffin Mental Health Services in North York, Ontario and project coordinator of Compass – a program for LGBTQ youth and adults labelled with intellectual disabilities – and member of the disability artists' collective, Project Creative Users. Her work explores sacred hidden relations between madness, spirituality, and the healing arts.

WINNIE LEM is an anthropologist and professor of international development studies and women's studies at Trent University. She has been editor-in-chief and editor of manuscripts in English for *Anthropologica*. Her research interests are on migration between China and France, in transnationalism, citizenship, marginal economies, migrant livelihoods, women and small enterprises, diasporas, ethnicity, women and nationalism, gender and household economies, agrarian change, women and rural politics, racism, culture, and class.

ANNALEE LEPP is associate professor and chair of the Department of Women's Studies (soon to be Department of Gender Studies) at the University of Victoria. She is a senior editor of *Atlantis: Critical Studies in Gender, Culture and Social Justice* and past president of Women's and Gender Studies et Recherches Féministes. Her research focuses on Canadian legal and family history, contemporary labour migration, trafficking in persons, and human rights in the Canadian and international context.

ISABELLA LOSINGER is manager in the Faculty of Medicine at the University of British Columbia. She is the president of the Association of Administrative and Professional Staff (AAPS) at UBC, chair of the AAPS Advocacy Committee, and chair of the Management and Professional Disability Governance Committee. As an amateur historian, her research interests lie in military history, academic leadership, and the university as a workplace.

CECILIA MOLONEY is professor of electrical and computer engineering at Memorial University. From 2004 to 2009, she held the NSERC/Petro-Canada Chair for Women in Science and Engineering, Atlantic Region. Her research interests include nonlinear signal and image processing methods, radar signal processing and applications, transformative pedagogy for science and engineering, and gender and science studies.

PATRICIA PALULIS is associate professor in the Faculty of Education at the University of Ottawa. Her research interests involve language, literacy, culture, spatiality, postcolonialism, poststructuralism, and psychoanalytic theory. Currently, she is pursuing eco-literacies and geo-literacies in Iceland, Greenland, and Nunavut.

E. LISA PRICE is professor of psychology at Acadia University and registered clinical psychologist. Her interests are human sexuality, violence in intimate relationships, risky and coercive sexual behaviour, interpersonal relationships, and psychological well-being.

PHYLLIS RIPPEYOUNG is associate professor of sociology at the University of Ottawa and former coordinator of Women's and Gender Studies at Acadia University. Her research is in the area of social stratification, with a primary focus on gender inequality, on the role breastfeeding plays in patterns of inequality in paid and unpaid work.

SALLY THORNE is professor and former director of the School of Nursing, now associate dean, Faculty of Applied Science, University of British Columbia. She serves as the editor-in-chief of *Nursing Inquiry*. Her research and writing interests are in the social context of health and health care, psychosocial cancer experience, philosophy of science, and applied research methodologies.

ELVI WHITTAKER is professor emerita of anthropology at the University of British Columbia. She has been president of the Canadian Anthropology Society, president of the Social Science Federation of Canada, and chair of the Scientific Screening Committee of the Management of Social Transformations at UNESCO. Among her research interests are Indigenous tourism and intellectual property rights, the self, social science and philosophy, ethnographic/qualitative methods, and research ethics.

Index

Aboriginal peoples, 48–9; and Federal Contractors Program, 53–4, 57–9, 62–3

Abramson, Zelda, 74, 79, 112, 117n4, 195

Acker, Joan, 205

Acker, Sandra, ix, 74, 80, 83, 121, 224, 226, 230, 239

academic: capitalism, 73, 192, 193; feminism and, 26, 31; hierarchy, 156, 193–4, 199; normalizing 83; pathologies, 80; tribalism, 14, 41; versus non-academic units, 184, 186, 187

activism, 8, 24–6; education as 123, 125; hierarchy, 125–6; misguided, 127; texts of resistance, xii, 18, 25–7, 83, 242

Adams, Tony E., 189n1

administration: cultures of, xxviii, 5, 196; equity training for, 239–40; caste in, 4, 78, 172, 175–7, 179, 185–8; glass ceiling in, xxviii, 172, 175, 186; non-academic, 78; recognition of programs, 65; short-term commitments of, 193

administration, academic: accountability of, 184; arrogance of, 181, 182, 183, 187; careers of, 177–8; limited understandings of, 185, 188; "never fired," 184; and secretaries, 186–7; and turnover, 182–3

administration, non-academic, 172, 173, 174, 175; career histories, 179–80; and challenges, 182, 183, 184; collective agreement, 190n4; contributions of; 176; hiring practices 181; lack of career development, 181; lack of consultation, 181–2; lack of respect, 180; negation of, 176, 185; professional association and, 185; silencing of, 183; sucking up, 182; suggestion for change, 188–9; terminations of, 185–6; with PhDs, 184–5; work titles, 177

administrative assistants, 158–9; as corporate memory, 160, 162, 169, 171n15; harassment of, 184; invisibility of, 157; lack of autonomy, 165–6; promotion of,